Introduction to Computer Science

Bassim Hamadeh, CEO and Publisher

John Remington, Senior Field Acquisitions Editor

Gem Rabanera, Project Editor

Alia Bales, Production Editor

Jess Estrella, Senior Graphic Designer

Trey Soto, Licensing Coordinator

Don Kesner, Interior Designer

Natalie Piccotti, Director of Marketing

Kassie Graves, Vice President of Editorial

Jamie Giganti, Director of Academic Publishing

Introduction to Computer Science

FIRST EDITION

Perry Donham

Boston University

cognella® | ACADEMIC PUBLISHING

For Colleen, en amour et amitié.

CONTENTS

Preface xi

Chapter 1 A Short History of Computation 1

Early Calculation 1

Calculators versus Computers 4

Jacquard and Punched Cards 4

Charles Babbage 5

The 1930s and Electromechanical Relays 6

The Second World War 7

The Space Race 9

Oh, IC 10

The Personal Computer 11

What's Next? 12

Bottom Line 12

Figure Credits 13

Chapter 2 Numbers and Bases 15

What a Number Is 15

Symbols, Numbers, and Bases 16

Binary Numbers 17

Bits and Bytes 19

Converting Decimal Numbers to Binary 20

Octal Numbers 21

Hexadecimal Numbers 23

Bottom Line 25

Figure Credit 25

Chapter 3 Data Representation 27

Storing Characters 27

Storing Colors 31

Bottom Line 36

Figure Credits 36

Chapter 4 Data Conversion and Compression 39

Audio: Some Definitions 39

Analog to Digital Conversion 40

Digital to Analog Conversion 41

Sampling Levels 41

Data Compression 43

Compressing Images 46

Bottom Line 48

Figure Credits 48

Chapter 5 Binary Logic and Hardware 49

Electricity and Switches 49

Transistors 50

Gates 51

Binary Logic 52

De Morgan's Law 54

Expressing Logical Equations with Gates 56

From Gates to Circuits 57

Adding Binary Numbers 58

Bottom Line 60

Chapter 6 Networking: An Introduction 61

Protocols 61

Wired Networks 62

Encoding Data 63

Fiber-Optic Cable 65

Encoding with Audio Tones..............66
Connecting Devices 67
Addressing 67
Local Area Networks 67
Framing the Bits 70
Connecting Devices Together 72
Bluetooth 74
Other Protocols 75
Leaving the LAN 75
Bottom Line 75
Figure Credits 76

Chapter 7 Networking: The Internet..........77
Three Ways to Connect 77
Packet Switching..............79
Internet Addresses..............81
Routers 82
Internet Names..............86
Bottom Line 88
Figure Credits 89

Chapter 8 Networking: Services and the Cloud..............91
Bottom Line 101
Figure Credits 101

Chapter 9 FOSS and Web Servers..............103
Richard Stallman and the Open-Source Movement..............103
The Open-Source Community 107
Open-Source and Security..............108
The Apache Web Server 108
Server Operations 109
The Universal Resource Locator (URL)..........110
What Is in the Returned File?..............111
Bottom Line 112
Figure Credits 112
A Brief History of HTML..............113

Chapter 10 Introduction to HTML..............113
HTML and Structure..............117
HTML Tags..............117
Simple HTML Tags..............119
Bottom Line..............120
Figure Credits..............120

Chapter 11 Programming Languages......121
Living Switches..............121
The Language of Ones and Zeros..............123
BASIC..............123
The First Computer Program..............125
Two Approaches to Programming..............125
Libraries..............127
Hello, World..............127
Common Language Features..............128
Loops..............132
Input and Output (I/O)..............132
Math..............133
Bottom Line..............133
Figure Credits..............133

Chapter 12 An Introduction to JavaScript..............135
Some History..............136
Front End versus Back End JavaScript..............137
Running Programs from the Command Line with Node.js..............137
Variables..............139
Comments..............143
Printing Out Values..............144
Reading in Values..............146
The Semicolon Controversy..............146
Math Operators..............146
JavaScript Libraries..............149
Boolean Values and Conditional Statements..............150
Loops..............153
Strings..............157

Arrays 161

Functions 163

Bottom Line 166

Figure Credit 166

Chapter 13 JavaScript and HTML 167

Event-Driven Programming 167

The Document Object Model (DOM) 172

Input Boxes 177

Bottom Line 181

Figure Credit 182

Chapter 14 JavaScript Objects 183

Styles of Programming 183

Parts of an Object 184

Object Constructors 189

Solving a Problem with Objects 191

Bottom Line 199

Chapter 15 Security and Privacy on the Internet 201

On the Internet, Security Is Not Job One 202

Attacks on Privacy and Freedom 207

What Can You Do? 211

Bottom Line 213

Figure Credits 213

Chapter 16 Making Money on the Internet 215

Selling Bits 216

Selling Atoms 217

Selling Services 219

Selling Space 219

Selling Access 221

Bottom Line 222

Chapter 17 Operating Systems 223

What It Isn't 224

Window Managers 224

A Brief History of the Operating System 224

What the Operating System Does 227

Files and Directories 232

Which Operating System? 233

Bottom Line 233

Figure Credits 234

Chapter 18 Computer Components 235

General-Purpose Computers 235

Three Things to Look For 236

Do-It-Yourself 243

Bottom Line 244

Figure Credits 245

PREFACE

Welcome to *Lectures in Computer Science*, a series of discussions on a wide-ranging series of topics in the field of computing. The book is a companion text to CS101: An Introduction to Computer Science as taught at Boston University.

As an introductory course, we try to give students a taste of what it's like to work in the technology sector by covering just enough material in each topic to whet the appetite, but not to overwhelm. In particular there are quite a few simplifications and generalizations made that I'm sure would make a CS professor's hair stand on end, but these are meant to provide a general knowledge of a topic, not an in-depth understanding. Most of the students who take CS101 are not computer science majors, but many find that there's a strong tie-in between tools and techniques covered in the course and their own field of interest. It isn't unusual for non-CS majors to add a CS minor after taking CS101.

About one quarter of the course is dedicated to learning a little about the art of programming. To keep the material interesting to a non-CS audience, I've focused on applying JavaScript programming to HTML pages, including manipulating CSS. It's fun to see your programs come to life on the web page, and many students come out of the section eager to learn more on their own.

I'm always looking for ways to improve the course and the text; if you have an idea, please share it with me at perryd@bu.edu. I hope that you enjoy the course!

A Short History of Computation

The history of computation is really the story of human civilization and its development over thousands of years. We often think of computing as a recent endeavor, but in fact we as a species have been figuring things out with the aid of mechanical devices since we started walking around on two feet. That's not to say that *Homo erectus* roamed grasslands with slide rules, but even primitive man made use of the tools at hand—stones, notched sticks, lengths of knotted grass—to solve the simple mathematical problems of everyday life.

Many of those problems related to the rhythms of the natural world, and so we see early attempts at tools to predict the seasons. The megalithic structures of Great Britain, such as Stonehenge, were constructed such that the sun, moon, and prominent stars would line up in predictable patterns marking transitions from growing season to harvest, from flood time to planting time, from new moon to full. Today we rely on sophisticated electronic devices to make these calculations, but primitive man did seemingly just fine.

An interesting thread runs through this history, which is that computation hasn't changed all that much. Basic mathematical truths laid down millennia ago still hold, as do the methods for transforming numbers based on them; adding two numbers together is the same now as it was in Roman times. What has changed is the speed and precision of our calculations; the computing devices that we use in our daily lives are capable of executing billions of calculations every *second*, a rate that, even just 50 years ago, would have seemed utterly impossible. When we think about the current state of computing, it seems that we have fulfilled Clarke's Third Law: "Any sufficiently advanced technology is indistinguishable from magic."

Early Calculation

Primitive humans didn't need a lot of complex calculations. One can imagine that most of their communication around numbers were focused on how many of something there were: "How many antelope are over that hill?" Holding up a few fingers or waving an arm

FIGURE 1-1   An ancient calculator

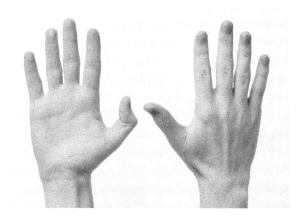

in the air probably sufficed to get the message across (Figure 1-1). It isn't surprising, then, that early calculations were done on our fingers. In fact, even the word *digit*, which we use to represent a number, is the same word that we use for a finger.

Another word that you might be familiar with that relates to mathematics is *calculus*. The English word *calculate* comes from the Latin *calculus*, for pebble, and is derived from methods of early calculations done with systematic arrangements of stones. At first, the stones were placed into piles, with stones being moved around to perform simple mathematical operations like addition and subtraction. In Babylonian times calculating boards (Figure 1-2) were developed with shallow depressions to hold stones in a defined pattern, and these allowed individuals to perform slightly more complex calculations.

For thousands of years, this kind of simple arithmetic was sufficient, and it wasn't until the widespread development of trade and accounting that more complex operations became necessary. Four thousand to five thousand years ago, Chinese mathematicians developed the abacus (Figure 1-3), which was a representation of the earlier simple stone mechanisms

FIGURE 1-2   A counting board

codified into a standard device. The abacus is still in use, and a skilled user can perform calculations as quickly as they can think them.

FIGURE 1-3 A modern abacus made in Poland

In some cases it wasn't a calculation per se that was important, but a prediction, or perhaps a marking of seasonal events. When we look at neolithic installations such as Stonehenge, from about 4,500 years ago (Figure 1-4), what we see today is an enigmatic collection of stones arranged in a very specific pattern. A lot of conjecture over the centuries has tried to identify exactly what these installations were used for, but recent research has shown that at least part of their function was to serve as a calendar of important events, such as solstices and equinoxes, floods and eclipses, and the start and end of seasons.

A sophisticated and fascinating Greek device from around 100 BC was discovered in the remains of an ancient shipwreck in 1901 off of the Greek island of Antikythera. The device, shown in Figure 1-5, was heavily corroded and nearly impenetrable for 100 years after its discovery, but studies have shown that the device is a type of orrery, a complex calculator that demonstrates the positions of the planets, the stars, the passage of time, and was possibly used as a teaching aid. It also tracked the dates of Olympic events, held every four years. A recent study showed that the back of the device had the equivalent of an instruction manual, although it doesn't specify *how* to use the device, but rather all of the features that the device has, an example of some very early computer marketing material.

FIGURE 1-4 Stonehenge, a neolithic mega-calculator

FIGURE 1-5   A modern reproduction of the Antikythera device

FIGURE 1-6   A Pascaline built in 1652

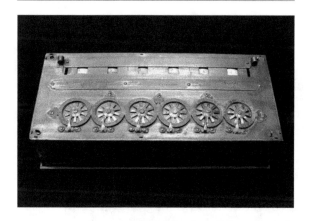

Calculators versus Computers

Early devices were intended for calculation, performing mathematical operations such as addition and subtraction. By modern definition these were not truly computers; they didn't have a way to store and execute instructions or to store intermediate and final results.

We might consider the start of modern computation to be the 17th century. In the early to mid-1600s, mechanical devices started to appear that operated by means of a series of gears, cranks, and springs, designed to do specific calculations. For example, in 1642 Blaise Pascal built a mechanical calculating machine known as the Pascaline (Figure 1-6), which was designed to add, subtract, multiply, and divide. The Pascaline was produced in modest quantities and was the basis for many other calculating machines in that time period. The calculator used a series of rotary dials, not all that different from the ones used in old-style telephone handsets, and numbered discs behind small windows that indicated input and output values. Although there were earlier machines, Pascal's innovation of a carry mechanism that allowed numbers to be carried from one column to another was revolutionary.

The Pascaline was used for rather mundane purposes for such a revolutionary instrument. The device was installed in Pascal's father's office to compute the tax on sales and inventory. About 20 of these were made, and it was the first calculator to receive a royal patent.

Jacquard and Punched Cards

Another innovation that led to what we know as modern computing was developed in the very early 1800s by Joseph Jacquard. The problem he was trying to solve was that textile mills at the time could create beautiful cloth with elaborate patterns, but through a highly labor-intensive process. Workers had to manually feed colored threads and yarns into a weaving machine following a written pattern, and the more complex patterns required that the machine be stopped frequently as new threads or new colors were introduced into the pattern. Jacquard automated this process by creating a system that read patterns off of punched cards; multiple spools of thread or yarn were set up on the loom and as a wheel turned, threads were lifted or retracted depending on whether or not a hole was present on a punched card. The cards, each representing a row of weaving, could be chained together. This allowed extremely complex patterns to be produced with very little manual labor (Figure 1-7).

Although it wasn't a general-purpose solution, the notion of storing information on punched cards to be read later by a machine led to early techniques in computing of storing programs on punch cards. The loom could be "reprogrammed" simply by loading new cards into it. Charles Babbage was inspired by Jacquard's work to use punched cards in the design of his analytical machine.

Charles Babbage

Around the same time that Jacquard was perfecting his card mechanism, mathematician Charles Babbage was working on the designs for a series of what we now would call computers. The first, called the *difference engine*, was designed to calculate polynomial functions mechanically. The problem that Babbage was trying to solve was that these kinds of calculations were done by human computers, compiled into tables, and then bound into books, and it wasn't unusual for these dense books of mathematical formulas and results to be riddled with errors, and of course just the amount of labor required to produce them was vast.

The difference engine was entirely mechanical, and though it was backed by the British government, the metalworking and machining techniques of the day were not sufficient to realize Babbage's designs in metal. After several years of attempting to build a working difference engine, the British government pulled out of the project, and the device was never completed.

The difference engine was built to solve a very specific problem, that of evaluating polynomials. A second device designed by Babbage, called the *analytical engine*, was the precursor to our modern computer (Figure 1-8). It included an arithmetic unit that did calculations such as addition, subtraction, division, and multiplication, temporary storage in the form of a register that could hold dozens of intermediate results, and, more importantly for the history of computing, it was programmable in that instructions could be input to the device using punched cards, similar to those being used by Jacquard in his automated loom.

Unfortunately, funding and the limitations of metalworking of the day doomed the machine in the same way that the difference engine had been. Work was never completed on the analytical engine. Babbage died in 1871, perhaps not realizing the incredible legacy that would lead to computers as we know them today. It wasn't until 100 years later, in the mid-1940s, that his ideas and designs were realized in the first modern electrical computers.

FIGURE 1-7 Punched cards in a Jacquard loom

FIGURE 1-8 A portion of Babbage's analytical engine, built as a test (London Museum)

FIGURE 1-9   Components of a relay: A coil of wire (1) acts as an electromagnet; when energized, it pulls down an armature (2), opening an electrical contact (3)

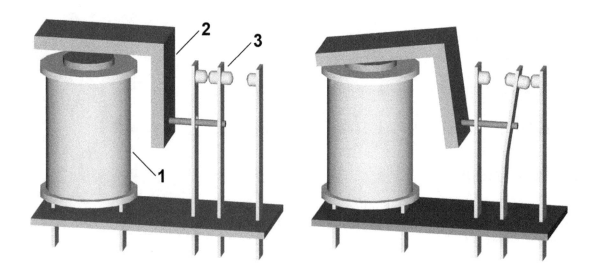

The 1930s and Electromechanical Relays

Prior to the 1900s, "computers" were entirely mechanical devices; although some were powered by steam engines, they essentially relied on complex interactions of gears, springs, levers, and dials to do their work, often driven by a hand crank. In the early 1900s, however, computer architecture was revolutionized by a small electrical component called a *relay*. You can see one in Figure 1-9. The relay is an electromagnetic device that opens and closes a switch based on an input voltage. When voltage is applied to the relay, the switch closes, and when voltage is released, the switch opens.

You might wonder why this was such an important event in computing history. A relay that has two states, open or closed, is ideal to represent a binary number, which is either a one or a zero. By combining relays together into patterns, it now was possible to design electrical circuits that implemented binary logic. Such logic could be applied to any arbitrary computing problem. For example, to add two numbers together required just a handful of relays arranged in a specific pattern; you can see this sort of arrangement in Chapter 5, where we examine a binary adding circuit.

During the 1930s researchers began to build digital computers using relays, such as Zuse (Figure 1-10) in Germany, Iowa State, and Bell Labs, whose team built the Mark 1 computer based on designs by Charles Babbage. The room-sized Mark 1 has fewer capabilities than a five-dollar calculator of today: you could store only 72 numbers; it required a tenth of a second to add two numbers together and over six

FIGURE 1-10   A replica of the Zuse Z3 computer; banks of relays can be seen in each cabinet

seconds to multiply two numbers together. Still, compared to earlier attempts, these early machines were astoundingly fast.

The Second World War

It is a sad commentary on our species that our best innovation comes in finding better ways of killing each other. Such it was with computing. In the early 1940s a device called a *vacuum tube* became economically feasible to manufacture in large quantities. The vacuum tube (Figure 1-11) had been invented at the turn of the century and was essentially an electromechanical relay redesigned to use only electricity.

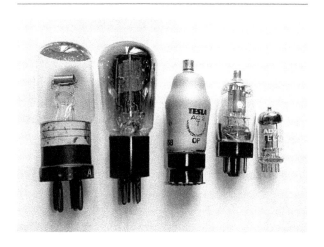

The relay's switch was replaced by two terminals, separated by a vacuum, sitting inside a sealed glass cylinder. Electrons would flow across the vacuum from one terminal to the other when electricity was applied to a control grid placed between the two. The tubes operated very similarly to the mechanical relay, but because electrons were used instead of mechanical switches, they were vastly superior in terms of speed.

As the hostilities that led up to World War II ramped up, governments around the world searched for more efficient ways to perform the calculations required for war. One major application for this kind of computing was the compilation of ballistic tables. Imagine that you are a field commander on the battlefield, and you want to shoot your cannon at an enemy located on a distant hill. You might make an educated guess about the elevation of your cannon; that is, how high up in the air you will aim, based on the distance to the target and your relative elevation to it. That first shot is probably going to miss, and so a spotter will call out a correction: "Two degrees to the left! And one degree up!" The second shot is likely to miss, also. Eventually, though, you'll home in on the target and drop your shells right on the enemy's location.

The problem is that only an exceptionally stupid enemy would just sit there while you dial in the correct parameters for your cannon. By the time you home in on their location, the enemy has moved well away.

The difficulty is that there are many factors in play that affect the flight of your projectile. The temperature, wind direction and velocity, relative humidity, and other factors all combine to make each engagement unique. To solve this problem, war departments would employ human calculators, primarily women, who would sit in rooms all day long calculating all of the variables that need to be taken into account when firing artillery. The result would be thick books full of tables that a field commander could consult, plugging in the current conditions and reading off the correct settings to aim their cannon.

Automating this sort of calculation was a huge boon for the military, as it allowed for the rapid production and dissemination of this specialized information, and the numbers produced by computers tended to be more accurate than those produced by hand. And so, many of the early computers, especially in the early 1940s, were tasked with this sort of military application. One of the first modern computers, ENIAC (Figure 1-12)

FIGURE 1-12   Glen Beck (left) and Betty Snyder (right) program ENIAC (US Army photo)

was built at the University of Pennsylvania in 1946. It contained just under 20,000 vacuum tubes and over 1,000 relays, weighed 30 tons, and consumed 140,000 watts of power. It was the size of a large room, and workers circulated behind the cabinets nonstop replacing tubes that had burned out, or relays that had corroded. It was primarily used to calculate ballistic tables, but was also used to study the effects of thermonuclear weapons.

Other wartime applications included breaking enemy codes, such as was done by the Colossus computer built in 1943 by the British government based on designs by Alan Turing.

The Von Neumann Architecture

All of these early machines designed and built in the 1940s were single-purpose computers. The program of interest would be loaded in to the computer, data input, and the computer essentially worked as a giant automated calculator outputting results, albeit much faster than calculators could, and probably more accurately. If you wanted to run a different program, the current program had to be stopped, unloaded, and the new program loaded in, often by configuring jumper cables on the front of the computer console, similar to the way that a telephone switchboard worked at the time.

John von Neumann, a Hungarian mathematician working in the United States at the University of Pennsylvania, coauthored a paper in 1945 describing an architecture that allowed the computer to store a logical program for sequence of operations in internal memory, along with the data that was being operated on. This design had a logical unit, a control unit, input and output devices, and memory to store the program in data. In practice, the computer would fetch instruction from memory, fetch data, process it, and place the results back in memory. It became known as the Von Neumann architecture, shown in Figure 1-13.

You might recognize the Von Neumann architecture as being similar to Babbage's analytical engine, and you would be correct. It took 100 years of thought and development to realize Babbage's dream of a universal computer. Nearly all general-purpose computers built in the 1950s onward employ the fundamental architecture, and it's the same architecture that you'll find in your laptop or desktop computer. That's not to say that the architecture was a cure-all and that immediately following publication of the team's paper the face of computing changed forever; programming these machines was still extremely tedious, and even though the analog method of inputting a program using patch cables was eliminated, programming still involved putting instructions in binary code, ones and zeros, which was an arduous process and

FIGURE 1-13   The basic Von Neumann architecture

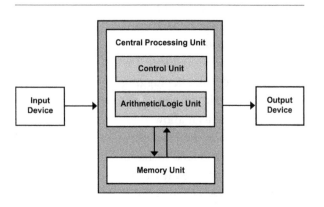

prone to error. It wasn't until the 1950s and later that higher-level programming languages were developed that used human readable keywords to implement programming logic.

The Space Race

The introduction of digital computers in the 1930s and 1940s, powered by electromechanical relays, and then later on by vacuum tubes, set the stage for the next large revolution in computing. In the 1940s the team of Bardeen, Brattain, and Shockley developed a new device called a *transistor*. The transistor operates in essentially the same way as a vacuum tube or relay in that it can turn on or off, depending on the application of a control signal. The major diffrence is that transistors are solid-state devices and have no moving parts; they are manufactured out of silicon, which is derived from sand, and even the earliest transistors were orders of magnitude smaller than any relay or vacuum tube that had been produced up until that time. Further, they were smaller, faster, more reliable since there are many parts, and much cheaper to mass-produce than either relays or vacuum tubes. They also consumed significantly less power than earlier devices.

Since the transistor was essentially an improvement on the electromechanical relay and the vacuum tube, the architecture of computers designed around those two devices could be extended by using transistors in their place. As the 1950s moved into the 1960s and the space race began to heat up, transistors moved to the forefront of electronic development. Imagine that you were sending men into space on top of a massive rocket. Electronic devices on that rocket can't really be made of vacuum tubes, which are made of glass and easily break, nor can they be made of relays, which are mechanical devices and prone to jamming, bending, and corruption of their contacts. Neither of those devices could really withstand the enormous forces generated by launching a rocket. Transistors, however, have no moving parts and are tiny, which means that they are light, and they require far less power than either tubes or relays. They were ideal for designing electronics meant to be launched into space.

This was the age of the transistor radio and other consumer devices that fell out of the enormous engineering development effort undertaken by space agencies around the world. As consumer electronics became more popular, the cost of manufacturing individual devices fell significantly, which meant that computers in general became less expensive to manufacture. We started to see large computers being deployed not just for military purposes but also in businesses to do all sorts of tasks; accounting, human resources, documentation, design, and just about anything else that a business needed.

Along with the spread of these new computers into environments such as business and education came a need for new and more efficient ways to program them. This was the golden age of programming languages, with new languages such as Fortran in 1957 and COBOL in 1960 being developed to serve specific populations. Fortran, which stands for FORmula TRANslation, was designed for academic and research purposes, while COBOL, which stands for COmmon Business Oriented Language, was developed for generating reports and doing the kinds of accounting that businesses required. Other languages from this time included the Beginners All-purpose Symbolic Instruction Code, or BASIC, developed in 1959, and LISP (LISt Processor), also developed in 1959 at MIT.

FIGURE 1-14   Katherine Johnson

This era also saw the rise of strictly computer-oriented companies, such as Digital Equipment Corporation, founded in 1957, and International Business Machines, IBM, which had in fact been in the business of computing for a very long time, but now saw new markets open up as the demand for computing resources ramped up.

This was a massive shift; in the 1950s a calculator literally was a person sitting at a desk with a slide rule or table of logarithms doing complex calculations by hand. For example, Katherine Johnson, shown in Figure 1-14, worked at the agency that would become NASA as a mathematician, designing airfoils, calculating trajectories of rockets, and other highly computationally intensive tasks. John Glenn, the first American to orbit the earth in his Mercury aircraft, distrusted the numbers that had been generated by NASA's computers, and asked Katherine Johnson to verify the calculations by hand. Johnson went on to work with the Apollo moon missions and the space shuttle program.

Oh, IC

There was one more enormous innovation to come. The transistor was revolutionary in that it miniaturized the hardware required to build computers, but the designs were not all that different than the tube- and relay-based computers of the earlier era; the transistor essentially just replaced the tube or the relay. The electric circuit boards that made up these transistor-based computers were still quite complex, and the logic circuits built from the individual transistors required quite a bit of physical space to implement. In the mid-1960s multiple teams in academia and industry were working on a way to package transistors more efficiently. Jack Kilby at Texas Instruments and Bob Noyce at Fairchild Semiconductor independently developed ways to package transistors together on a single substrate, or chip, and this led the way for further miniaturization as several transistors could be packaged together onto a single piece of silicon. This *integrated circuit* (IC), as it became known, further reduced manufacturing costs, reduced the size required for electronic circuits related

FIGURE 1-15   The Intel 4004 4-bit CPU chip (1971)

to computing, and allowed for mass production of common building blocks for computers. For example, the NE555 timer chip, a simple circuit that provides precise clock signals on a signal chip, first appeared in 1972 and continues to be manufactured today, with over 1 billion of the devices sold each year.

Around the same time, in 1971, Intel marketed the first microprocessor, the 4004 chip (Figure 1-15), that included all the circuitry necessary for general-purpose calculations, implemented with just over 2,000 transistors. This was the birth of what we now consider the modern era of computing.

Even those advances pale in comparison to what has been done since. Early Intel calculator chips comprised

FIGURE 1-16   Moore's Law fitted to devices from 1971 to 2011

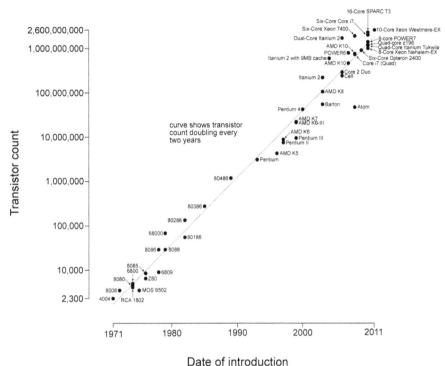

just a few hundred individual transistors packed together onto a single integrated circuit chip, but by the late 1970s that number was approaching 50,000 transistors. In the 1980s Intel continued to push the boundaries of how many transistors could be packed onto a single chip such that by 1989, the 80486 CPU chip broke the 1-million-transistor boundary. In 2000 the Pentium 4 reached 42 million transistors, and in 2016 Intel's Core i7 Broadwell CPU chips packed 3.4 *billion* transistors onto a chip about half an inch on a side. Large-scale integration (LSI) and very large-scale integration (VLSI) have been on a pace for the past 40 years of doubling the number of transistors packed into integrated circuits while at the same time reducing the price of the circuits (Figure 1-16). Gordon Moore, cofounder of Intel, made this observation (soon after dubbed "Moore's Law") in 1965; so far it is held up for nearly 50 years.

The questioning in circuit design these days is whether Moore's Law will continue to hold up—we are starting to reach the physical boundaries of shrinking circuits. The individual "wires" on an integrated circuit, typically made of aluminum, are approaching the width of just a few atoms, and it's unclear whether new technologies under development now will be able to push this boundary even further to the subatomic realm.

The Personal Computer

As the integrated circuits making up computers became more powerful and less expensive in the 1970s, we started to see the design and manufacture of computers that were not targeted at military, academic, or business applications, but rather directly at consumers. These home computers, or *personal computers* as they became known, were at first extremely expensive, but as their popularity grew, and manufacturing costs decreased as volumes increased, their prices dropped to the point where it was very common for any given household to have at least one computer in it. Around this time Bill Gates and Paul Allen founded Microsoft, developing a BASIC language interpreter for one of the very first personal computers from Altair; in 1977 Steve Wozniak and Steve Jobs founded Apple Computer in Jobs's garage, and in 1980 IBM introduced the IBM PC, cementing that term in the annals of history; that original PC included an operating system developed by Microsoft and licensed back to IBM. In 1984 Apple countered with its own personal computer, the Macintosh, based on early work that Jobs had done at a company called NextStep, and building on the success of the Apple II computer. The Macintosh introduced a modern graphical user interface, including windows and a mouse for input, which had been primarily developed at Xerox at their Palo Alto Research Center (PARC).

What's Next?

From a computer architecture standpoint, not much has changed since 1984. Computers have become smaller, faster, and less expensive, but the underlying design is unchanged.

The next big thing in computing seems to be the network. Even more so than computing, the network has become a major disrupter of industries and businesses that have existed for hundreds of years. In just the past 10 years we've moved from a world where music was something that you purchased at a record store to a world where music is all around us, streaming constantly, with millions upon millions of songs available on demand wherever we are. We wear computers on our wrist that not only talk to us but link with satellites to pinpoint our location anywhere on Earth to just a few feet. The network has become the computer, and the laptops and desktops and phones have become just a way to access that universal computer.

Just as the technologies of the 1800s gave way to the Industrial Revolution and the incredible advances of the mid-1900s, so it is now with the astonishing pace of development and innovation that we're seeing in the 2000s, primarily driven by ubiquitous, powerful computing resources. As Clarke predicted, our technology is practically indistinguishable from magic.

Bottom Line

We have become so used to having access to incredible computational resources, but it is sobering to look back on those early attempts at computation; sticks and stones, gears and steam engines, all driving toward the same goal; the reality is that the techniques that we use now for computation really are not much different from those that have been used for thousands and thousands of years. We compute faster, we store more information, and we are more dependent on computation than ever before, but the foundations of the computers that are ubiquitous in our lives now were laid down in prior centuries, and it seems unlikely that we will move on to a different path anytime soon.

Figure Credits

Figure Credits

2

Numbers and Bases

Your computer isn't very smart. We like to think computers are smart; after all, they can land a tiny probe on a comet hurtling through space, keep people alive with sophisticated medical applications, and even drop an angry bird onto a pile of thieving pigs. But in reality, the computer hardware is capable of only performing a very few operations. It deals exclusively in numbers, not pigs or birds, and it can add numbers together, move those numbers from one place to another in its memory, and shift numbers to the right or to the left. That's about it.

This makes sense when you recall how we got from Jacquard's loom to modern-day machines. The early computers were designed to solve mathematical problems, such as the equations used to predict the path of a mortar shell on the battlefield or the tabulations needed for the federal census. These were numeric problems that resulted in machines that could do math. Even after Von Neumann described the requirements for a general-purpose computer in his 1945 paper, the underlying mechanism of working with numbers remained unchanged.

Here's the problem, though. When you and I think of a number, we treat it as, well, a number. Take *42*. What makes it 42? What is the essence of 42-ness that makes it different from 41 or 43? In our minds we understand what numbers represent and we're capable of doing some pretty amazing things with those concepts. While we often talk about the computer having a "brain" of sorts, in reality the arithmetic processing unit is just a collection of switches, very similar to the light switches on your wall. The switch can be either on or off. How can we relate a switch like that to the concept of the number 42? That's the problem we want to solve in this chapter. In getting to the solution, we'll look at four different ways to represent numbers: decimal, binary, octal, and hexadecimal.

What a Number Is

Before we can solve this problem we need to pause and consider what a number really is. The number 42 is an *integer*, or counting number. We could lay out 42 marshmallows on a table and proudly say, "There, that's forty-two things. Any questions?" Counting, or measuring, or weighing things gives us some result that we express as a number.

When we write the number 42 down on a piece of paper, we are using a standard notation to represent the 42 marshmallows on the table. You probably haven't thought much about this since third grade, but we write symbols like 4 and 2 in a specific order so that we can effectively communicate numeric information. The format that we use in most of our daily communications is called *decimal*. The English word decimal comes from the Latin *decimus*, meaning tenth, and so decimal numbers use units of ten. While we are most familiar with decimal numbers, there are several other formats in common use in technical and scientific fields.

Using Exponents

Before we dive into the various formats we can use to represent numbers, we'll need a refresher on exponential notation. An exponent is the little number that we write above and to the right of a number to indicate that we want to multiply the number with itself a certain number of times. For example, when we write 5^4, what we're really saying is $5 \times 5 \times 5 \times 5$. We say, "five raised to the fourth power," or just, "five to the fourth." Likewise, "three to the fifth" is 3^5, or $3 \times 3 \times 3 \times 3 \times 3$.

A number raised to the "zero" power is defined to be the number 1. So, $5^0 = 1$, and $4,765,442^0 = 1$. Similarly, a number raised to the "first" power is defined to be the number itself; $3^1 = 3$, $42^1 = 42$, and so on.

Symbols, Numbers, and Bases

We use *symbols* as a way to represent numbers, and each numbering system uses its own set of symbols. We use the term *base* to indicate how many symbols are being used. Decimal numbers, for example, are base 10 and use 10 symbols: 0, 1, 2, 3, 4, 5, 6, 7, 8, and 9. A single decimal number can be any of ten values. Binary numbers are base 2 and use two symbols: 0 and 1. A single binary number can be either of those two values.

We now have the tools we need to tackle decimal numbers and any other numbering system we might be interested in.

Decimal Numbers

Let's return to our good friend, the number 42. When we write it down, we first jot down the 4 and then the 2 to the right of the 4. This very specific arrangement lets us represent the value in decimal, or powers-of-ten notation. Each number, from right to left, represents quantities of a power of ten. We start on the right with 10^0; the next column to the left is 10^1, the column to the left of that is 10^2, and so on. We say that we are working in *base 10* or decimal. It looks like this:

10^3	10^2	10^1	10^0
		4	2

What we're really indicating is that we have 4 of the 10^1 units, and 2 of the 10^0 units, and we can add them up:

$$(4 \times 10^1) + (2 \times 10^0) = (4 \times 10) + (2 \times 1) = 42$$

Let's try another example. We'd write the number 4,096 like this:

10^3	10^2	10^1	10^0
4	0	9	6

$$(4 \times 10^3) + (0 \times 10^2) + (9 \times 10^1) + (6 \times 10^0) = (4 \times 1000) + (20 \times 100) + (9 \times 10) + (6 \times 1) = 4{,}096$$

We do these steps automatically in our heads when we work with decimal numbers. The computer hardware, though, can't deal at all with decimal numbers; its circuits can only mange to be either on or off. Fortunately there's an easy way to solve this problem: The computer works in powers of 2 rather than powers of 10.

Here's another way to look at decimal numbers. Figure 2-1 shows how the number 924 is represented as a sum of powers of 10.

FIGURE 2-1 Decimal 924

10^2	10^1	10^0
9	2	4
9×10^2 +	2×10^1 +	4×10^0
9×100 +	2×10 +	4×1
900 +	20 +	4
	924	

Binary Numbers

Decimal numbers use ten symbols, 0, 1, 2, 3, 4, 5, 6, 7, 8, and 9, to represent values. When we represent values using powers of 2, there are only two symbols available: 0 and 1. A one might represent the "on" condition of a switch and zero the "off" condition. Maybe someday someone will invent a computer that uses dimmer switches with many values between on and off, but for now we're stuck with this either-or, or *binary*, arrangement.

You might think that being limited to just two symbols would not be all that useful, but nearly every electronic device that we use has at its heart hardware that operates exclusively on binary numbers.

Just as we did with decimal numbers, we can write out values expressed in powers of two. For example, the decimal number 42 looks like this in binary:

2^7	2^6	2^5	2^4	2^3	2^2	2^1	2^0
0	0	1	0	1	0	1	0

As before, this becomes a series of additions, but this time with powers of 2:

$$(0 \times 2^7) + (0 \times 2^6) + (1 \times 2^5) + (0 \times 2^4) + (1 \times 2^3) + (0 \times 2^2) + (1 \times 2^1) + (0 \times 2^0)$$
$$= (0 \times 128) + (0 \times 64) + (1 \times 32) + (0 \times 16) + (1 \times 8) + (0 \times 4) + (1 \times 2) + (0 \times 1)$$
$$= 32 + 8 + 2$$
$$= 42$$

FIGURE 2-2   Converting a binary number to decimal

2^3	2^2	2^1	2^0
1	1	1	0
1×2^3 +	1×2^2 +	1×2^1 +	0×2^0
1×8 +	1×4 +	1×2 +	0×1
8 +	4 +	2 +	0

14 (fourteen)

We typically would write the binary value as one continuous group of digits: $42_{10} = 00101010_2$. In this notation, the subscripts indicate the base we are using, either base 10 (decimal) or base 2.

Figure 2-2 shows a quick way to calculate the value of a binary number.

Note that moving one column to the left multiples the column value by 2, so $2^3 = 8$, and $2^4 = 16$. Moving to the right halves each value. Decimal works the same way, so that a column to the left is ten times the value of the one to the right; moving to the right divides the value by 10. This table shows the powers of 2 up to 2^{15}.

Power of 2	Decimal Value	Power of 2	Decimal Value
2^0	1	2^8	256
2^1	2	2^9	512
2^2	4	2^{10}	1024
2^3	8	2^{11}	2048
2^4	16	2^{12}	4096
2^5	32	2^{13}	8192
2^6	64	2^{14}	16,384
2^7	128	2^{15}	32,768

Here's a hint to help you use powers of 2 using your fingers, but don't let anyone see you doing it! Start with a closed fist for 2^0, and say, "one." Then double the number and raise a finger, repeating until you have as many fingers up as the power you are calculating. For example, to calculate 2^7, say, "one" with a closed fist, raise a finger for 2^1 and say, "two," raise a second finger for 2^2 and say, "four," and so on as you work your way up. When you have seven fingers in the air, you'll have just said the correct value, "one hundred twenty eight."

Bits and Bytes

When working with binary numbers, the symbols 1 and 0 are called *binary digits*. We contract this to the single word *bit*. One bit is one binary digit, either a 1 or a 0.

It is convenient to group these bits together. Most computer hardware works on bits in groups of 4, 8, and 16 (and sometimes larger groups), so it's natural to have a term to represent each grouping. In 1956, Werner Buchholz at IBM coined the term *byte* to represent a group of 8 bits. David Benson is credited with light-heartedly using the term *nibble* (sometimes spelled *nybble*) for a group of 4 bits, or half of a byte, around 1958. Who says that computer scientists are dull?

For groups of bits larger than a byte, the term *word* is commonly used, and it can represent two, three, four, or more bytes. One word might be two bytes, or 16 bits, long. The following table summarizes the relationships.

Term	Length (bits)
bit	1
nibble	4
byte	8
word	multiple bytes

The Units K, M, G, and T

Some binary values come up over and over as we work in binary, and we use shortcut notations for them. Unfortunately, other fields use the same notations but with different meanings. In the SI (International Scientific) units commonly used in engineering physics and other sciences, the suffix *k* or the prefix *kilo* denotes 1,000 of something. When we write 1 *kilo*meter, we mean 1,000 meters.

In computer science we typically work in powers of 2, and so the suffix *k* or prefix *kilo* denotes 1,024 (2^{10}) of something. When we write 1 *kilobyte*, we mean 1,024 bytes, *not* 1,000 bytes. The same applies to other SI units, as shown in the table below. Usually it's clear in the context of our discussion whether we mean 1,000 or 1,024. In casual conversation precision often doesn't matter, and so we might say that a solid-state storage device has 500Gb (gigabits) of storage and not care that much about whether it's 500,000,000 bits or 524,288,000 bits.

Term	Abbreviation	Common term	SI value	Computer Science value
kilo	K	thousand	1,000	1,024
mega	M	million	1,000,000	1,048,576
giga	G	billion	1,000,000,000	1,073,741,824
tera	T	trillion	1,000,000,000,000	1,099,511,627,776
peta	P	quadrillion	1,000,000,000,000,000	1,125,899,906,842,624

One time that we *do* care about the unit is when we are buying storage, such as a hard disk or a solid-state disk. You might find two brands in the store, each with 500G of storage, but one is a slightly better deal. Check the tiny print on the box of each and make certain that both use the same unit of storage; one might hold 500,000,000 bytes while the other holds 524,288,000 bytes.

Practically speaking, 500 billion bytes is quite a bit of storage space, whether it's 500,000,000 or 524,288,000!

The Units b and B

Things get a little murky when we are discussing bits and bytes, because both start with the same letter, B. The rule of thumb is that the lower-case b refers to bits, and the upper-case B refers to bytes. You can remember that the "smaller" letter is for the smaller unit.

Just as with disk storage, you should be careful when comparing units that use bits or bytes. Network speeds, such as for a wireless router or cable modem, describe how fast data is transmitted or received and might be expressed in either. At a casual glance, a 100Mbps router and a 100MBps router might appear to run at the same speed, but 100MBps is 100 million *bytes* per second, nearly ten times faster than the 100Mbps device at 100 million *bits* per second. Even worse, in conversation we sometimes just say, "one hundred meg," shortening the units into ambiguity, though we typically can assign a value in context.

Converting Decimal Numbers to Binary

We often need to convert a decimal, or base 10, number to its binary, or base 2, equivalent. For small decimal numbers under a few hundred you'll find that, with practice, it's straightforward to do the conversion in your head. Using paper, to convert 14210 to binary, you know that $2^7 = 128$, and so you immediately know that you can represent the decimal number in just eight bits since 128 is smaller than 142. Write a line of powers of 2 from 2^7 to 2^0:

$$2^7 \qquad 2^6 \qquad 2^5 \qquad 2^4 \qquad 2^3 \qquad 2^2 \qquad 2^1 \qquad 2^0$$

Since 2^7 is the largest power of 2 that is smaller than 142, write down a 1 in the 2^7 position and subtract its value, 128, from 142 to get 14.

$$2^7 \qquad 2^6 \qquad 2^5 \qquad 2^4 \qquad 2^3 \qquad 2^2 \qquad 2^1 \qquad 2^0$$
$$1$$

Working from left to right, consider each power of 2. Is 2^6 less than 14? No, since $2^6 = 64$ (half of 2^7). Write down a zero for the 2^6 position.

$$2^7 \qquad 2^6 \qquad 2^5 \qquad 2^4 \qquad 2^3 \qquad 2^2 \qquad 2^1 \qquad 2^0$$
$$1 \qquad \;\, 0$$

Next up is 2^5. We are moving to the right, so each value is half of the previous one; $2^5 = 32$. Is 32 less than 14? No, so write down a 0 in that position.

2^7	2^6	2^5	2^4	2^3	2^2	2^1	2^0
1	0	0					

Now consider 2^4, or 16, which is larger than 14. Place a 0 in that position.

2^7	2^6	2^5	2^4	2^3	2^2	2^1	2^0
1	0	0	0				

$2^3 = 8$, smaller than 14, and we'll place a 1 in that position and subtract 8 from 14 to get 6.

2^7	2^6	2^5	2^4	2^3	2^2	2^1	2^0
1	0	0	0	1			

Moving again to the right, $2^2 = 4$, which is smaller than 6; a 1 goes into that position, and we'll subtract 4 from 6 to get 2.

2^7	2^6	2^5	2^4	2^3	2^2	2^1	2^0
1	0	0	0	1	1		

The next value to check is $2^1 = 2$, which is equal to 2, and we'll place a 1 in the position. Subtract 2 from 2 to get zero. When we hit zero, we're all done, and the remaining positions are filled with 0s.

2^7	2^6	2^5	2^4	2^3	2^2	2^1	2^0
1	0	0	0	1	1	1	0

The conversion is compete: $142_{10} = 10001110_2$.

While this works well for small numbers, it's useful to have a more formal method to convert larger numbers. Figure 2-3 shows one method that records the remainder of divisions by 2; the converted binary number is then read from bottom to top.

To check your result, use the same method that we used earlier when working with decimal numbers; add up all of the powers of 2 to determine the decimal equivalent. Figure 2-4 shows how to convert 111100101 back to decimal.

Octal Numbers

Sometimes it is convenient to work in base 8, or *octal*, rather than in decimal or binary. The reasons for this are somewhat historical; several early computers organized bits into groups of three, and ubiquitous seven-segment displays, similar to those shown in Figure 2-5, need only three bits to control the segments (since $2^3 = 8$). UNIX-style operating systems such as Linux use octal numbering for setting and displaying permissions on files and directories.

FIGURE 2-3 Converting decimal to binary

485	/ 2 = 242	remainder:	1
242	/ 2 = 121	remainder:	0
121	/ 2 = 60	remainder:	1
60	/ 2 = 30	remainder:	0
30	/ 2 = 15	remainder:	0
15	/ 2 = 7	remainder:	1
7	/ 2 = 3	remainder:	1
3	/ 2 = 1	remainder:	1
1	/ 2 = 0	remainder:	1

To get the result, start with the bottom digit and go up the column

485 = 111100101

FIGURE 2-4 Converting binary to decimal to check work

$$1 \times 2^0 = 1$$
$$0 \times 2^1 = 0$$
$$1 \times 2^2 = 4$$
$$0 \times 2^3 = 0$$
$$0 \times 2^4 = 0$$
$$1 \times 2^5 = 32$$
$$1 \times 2^6 = 64$$
$$1 \times 2^7 = 128$$
$$1 \times 2^8 = 256$$

$+$

$$485$$

Octal numbers are represented using 8 symbols: 0, 1, 2, 3, 4, 5, 6, and 7. Just as base 2 numbers are evaluated using powers of 2, base 8 numbers are evaluated using powers of 8. To convert an octal number to decimal, follow the same procedure as with decimal and binary numbers, but use powers of 8 instead of powers of 10 or of 2. For example, to convert 243_8 to decimal:

8^3	8^2	8^1	8^0
0	2	4	3

$$= (0 \times 8^3) + (2 \times 8^2) + (4 \times 8^1) + (3 \times 8^0)$$
$$= (0 \times 512) + (2 \times 64) + (4 \times 8) + (3 \times 1)$$
$$= 128 + 32 + 3$$
$$= 163$$

It's very easy to convert from octal to binary and back again by working in groups of three bits. To convert 243_8 to binary, for example, work from left to right, writing down the three-bit binary number for each of the digits of the octal value. The first digit is a 2; convert 2 to binary:

    010

The next octal digit to the right is 4; place the binary equivalent to the right of the first group:

    010 100

Finally, write the binary number for the final octal digit, which is 3:

    010 100 011

The binary equivalent of 243_8 is 010100011.

Similarly, to convert from binary to octal, group the binary number into groups of three bits, starting from the right and working left. Then write down the octal number corresponding to each group of three. For example, to convert 101110111001 to octal, first break it into threes (if there are only one or two binary digits in the left-most grouping, add 0s to the left to make it a group of three):

101110111001 becomes

101	110	111	001
5	6	7	1

and so $101110111001 = 5671_8$.

FIGURE 2-5   A seven-segment display, with a decimal point

Hexadecimal Numbers

The three numbering systems we've seen so far, decimal, binary, and octal, are commonly used in computer science. It isn't unusual to bounce among them several times during the course of daily work. There's a fourth numbering system, though, that is even more common than the other three. It is *hexadecimal*, or base 16. Hexadecimal uses 16 symbols to represent numbers: 0, 1, 2, 3, 4, 5, 6, 7, 8, 9, 0, A, B, C, D, E, and F. The decimal equivalents are shown in the table below.

Hexadecimal	Decimal	Hexadecimal	Decimal
0	0	8	8
1	1	9	9
2	2	A	10
3	3	B	11
4	4	C	12
5	5	D	13
6	6	E	14
7	7	F	15

Why in the world would we so often use such an unusual numbering system? The answer lies in the hardware: We normally work with bits (binary digits) in groups of eight, sixteen, or thirty-two, and it's convenient to work in a numbering system that reflects that underlying structure. Because each hexadecimal character is the equivalent of 4 bits (one nibble), two hexadecimal characters can represent a full byte (8 bits). It also is easier to remember short hexadecimal numbers rather than their longer binary equivalents. For example, DA16 = 110110102—which would you rather remember?

We often use the characters "0x" (zero-ex) in front of a number to indicate that it is written in hexadecimal, which is easier than typing a superscripted "16." The "0x" isn't part of the number; it is simply a label. Thus we would write 0xDA = 11011010. In everyday conversations we refer to hexadecimal as simply "hex."

Converting Binary to Hexadecimal

Each hexadecimal digit has 16 possible values, from 0 to F. In binary, we can use 4 bits to represent 16 different values, from 0000 to 1111. This means that we can express any hexadecimal digit in four binary bits. To convert from binary to hex, break the binary number into groups of four bits starting from the right. As you work to the left, if you end up with a final group of binary digits that isn't exactly four bits, add 0s to the left. Then, simply convert each group of four bits into the equivalent decimal value, and then to the appropriate hex digit.

For example, convert the binary number 10111001011001 to hex.

Step 1: Break the binary number into groups of four, starting from the right, and adding 0s to the left to make the last group exactly four bits.

0010   1110   0101   1001

Step 2: Convert the groups of four bits to decimal.

2   14   5   9

Step 3: Convert the decimal values to the appropriate hex digit.

2   E   5   9

So the binary number 10111001011001 is 0×2E59.

Converting Hexadecimal to Binary

Converting hex to binary works on the same principle as converting binary to hex, that each hex digit can be represented in four bits. To convert from hex to binary, convert each hex digit to decimal, and then write the 4-bit binary equivalent of each decimal value.

For example, convert 0xBEEF to binary.

Step 1: Convert each hex digit to its decimal value.

11   14   14   15

Step 2: Convert each decimal value to its 4-bit binary equivalent.

1011   1110   1110   1111

So 0×BEEF is 1011111011101111 in binary.

Converting Hexadecimal to Decimal

Hexadecimal numbers are written in base 16, just as decimal numbers are written in base 10. We can convert from hex to decimal in the same way that we converted binary to decimal, using powers of 16 rather than powers of 2. Figure 2-6 shows the conversion of 0x3E6 to decimal.

FIGURE 2-6 Converting hexadecimal to decimal

16^2		16^1		16^0
3		E		6
3×16^2	+	14×16^1	+	6×16^0
9 X 256	+	14 X 16	+	6 X 1
2304	+	224	+	6
		2534		

Bottom Line

Both computers and humans work with numbers, but because the computer is made up of switches that are either on or off, it is limited to being able to understand only numbers that are in base two (representing on or off). We are terrible at working in base two, or in fact any other base, preferring to work with decimals.

To make things a little easier, we can work in hexadecimal or octal, both of which map easily onto the computer's hardware. Most users, though, will simply write documents, visit web pages, upload photos, and interact with the computer in a natural way. For its part, the computer translates all of these things to and from a format that it understands: binary numbers.

Figure Credit

- **Fig. 2.5:** Copyright © Pengo (CC BY-SA 3.0) at https://commons.wikimedia.org/wiki/File:Seven_segment_02_Pengo.jpg.

Data Representation
TEXT AND COLOR

3

Working with computers presents an interesting problem. Internally, as we've discovered, the computer operates only on binary numbers—ones and zeros—that are represented by the presence or absence of voltage on a switch. Outside the computer, though, the world is most definitely not a binary, on-or-off sort of place. We experience sounds and colors and subtle changes in light and temperature that are analog in nature; their values vary smoothly over an infinite gradation.

This is the problem. We have two vastly different systems of representing the world: One, binary, uses only two values; the other uses an infinitely variable range.

How is it possible to store music, video, and images on a computer that only understands two levels of information? Before we jump into that discussion, we'll need to examine ways of expressing values in numbering systems other than binary, and that information will help us develop ways to save a digital copy of Pomplamoose's latest mashup.

Storing Characters

We know that the computer only works with binary numbers—zeros and ones. Even at that, the binary numbers that we write down and convert and manipulate are themselves just a numeric representation of what is really happening inside the computer's circuits, which is simply hundreds of millions of switches turning on and off in predetermined patterns.

Working with numbers in any base intuitively makes sense. The computer, after all, was built to compute. But what if we need to write a paper for class? Or send an e-mail to a friend? This poses a new problem, which is that we need some way to map the characters that we understand onto something that the computer understands. We know the two endpoints: The computer works with numbers, and we want to work with text. What we need is a way to convert between the two.

FIGURE 3-1   Semaphores in use by the US Navy at sea

Encoding Schemes

The computer science term for this mapping of characters onto numbers is *encoding*. It isn't a new idea; the ancient Greeks, around the 3rd century BC, used a system of torches lit in specific patterns to transmit messages one character or phrase at a time over distances of 40 to 50 miles. The idea was further developed into a system of communicating by flags; the position of two flags held in a skilled person's hands stand characters and numbers, which could be used as an index into a shared book of messages (for example, the semaphores "B-6" would allow the receiver to look up message 6 in section B). Morse code uses patterns of sounds to represent individual letters. For computers, most encoding systems map one character to one number.

Paper Tape

During the early decades of the computing age, from 1950 to 1970, permanent storage was extremely expensive. We are used to buying USB thumb drives capable of holding gigabytes of data in blister packs at the drugstore, but in the 1970s you were lucky to afford a floppy disk that would store 110 *kilo*bytes. Disk drives were the size of washing machines and only the larger companies and government agencies had a budget for them.

A much cheaper alternative, paper tape, was used for permanent storage of data. Figure 3-2 shows an example of this kind of tape. The holes in the tape are arranged in vertical columns and are punched by a special machine attached to a keyboard. A seven- or eight-bit code is used to represent letters and numbers. To read the tape, it is fed into a device that uses either lights or mechanical switches to sense where the holes appear.

There are two significant problems with paper tape. Since the material is paper, it is relatively easy to tear. Most tapes were made of reinforced material, but it still had to be flexible enough to either fold or be wound on a spool for storage. Most computer rooms kept splicing kits handy to fix breaks in the tape or to add additional tape to one that was too short.

FIGURE 3-2   Punched paper tapes

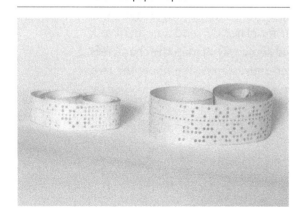

The second problem is that when a tape was punched, it created chad, the material ejected from a hole when it was punched. Usually this was collected in a small bin under the tape punch, but it was a common occurrence to have the bin overflow or be dropped, which would result in tiny bits of paper being strewn around the computer room. Normally this was just a nuisance, but once in a while the chad would get sucked into a machine through its cooling fans and cause major havoc.

Chad also played a starring role in the US presidential election in 2000. In that election, the national vote was neck-and-neck in the Electoral College, evenly split between candidates Al Gore and George W. Bush.

It came down to Florida, which also was too close to call, and so a manual vote recount was undertaken. At the time, Florida used an election ballot on which a voter would poke a hole next to the candidate's name for whom they were casting a vote. During the recount a significant number of ballots came under question because the chad had not completely separated; was a hanging chad a vote or not? And what about ballots on which there was a dimple in the paper but no chad? The entire country learned about the nuances of chad. In the end the vote, and so the election, was decided by the US Supreme Court in favor of George W. Bush.

ASCII

One early seven-bit encoding system for representing text was the American Standard Code for Information Interchange, or *ASCII*. In it, a seven-bit binary number represents a letter, number, or special character such as a carriage return. When a letter is typed on the computer keyboard, it is converted by the computer into the equivalent ASCII code and then stored. When you type the letter *a*, for example, what is stored is 1100001, the binary ASCII code for the letter *a*. Figure 3-3 shows the different ASCII values for each character.

The paper tape system that we looked at earlier used the same ASCII code, and the tape would have a hole to represent a 1 and the absence of a hole to represent a 0.

ASCII reigned the computer world from its introduction in 1963 until as late as 2007. It wasn't intended to be a universal standard, hence the "American" part of its name. The expectation was that countries would adopt their own version of the code for their specific needs, and many did; YUSCII, for example, is a variant used for many years in what was then Yugoslavia.

While it's a simple matter to encode *cat* as 63 71 74 in hexadecimal using ASCII, what if we wanted to encode "Joyeux Noël" or "圣诞快乐" ("Merry Christmas" in French and Chinese)? There are no French diacritical marks in the table, let alone any Chinese glyphs. It is, after all, the *American* standard for storing text. We know that ASCII is a binary code, and that it encodes characters using seven bits. We can calculate the number of unique characters that ASCII can represent: 2^7 or 128. This is a very small number of characters (and numbers) for languages such as Chinese or Japanese or Russian, or just about any language that isn't English. Even countries such as the former Yugoslavia that adopted their own variant of the code were hindered by the small alphabet available.

The length of the code, seven bits, was a very deliberate decision, and it was based on the snail's pace of computer networks in the late 1950s and early 1960s as well as the high cost of computer memory and storage. An eight-bit code would handle 2^8 or 256 different characters, which is enough for many languages, but an eight-bit code is 14% longer than a seven-bit code; it would take 14% more time to send each character over a network, and would consume 14% more storage. These were not insignificant numbers at the time.

There were some early attempts to patch the problem. Microsoft and IBM used a "code page" to switch character sets; if you wanted to work in Cyrillic, for example, you could load the Cyrillic code page into your computer and type away. Switching back to English meant loading a new code page. It worked, but it was cumbersome and really only a stopgap.

FIGURE 3-3 ASCII table

Decimal	Hexadecimal	Binary	Octal	Char	Decimal	Hexadecimal	Binary	Octal	Char	Decimal	Hexadecimal	Binary	Octal	Char
0	0	0	0	[NULL]	48	30	110000	60	0	96	60	1100000	140	`
1	1	1	1	[START OF HEADING]	49	31	110001	61	1	97	61	1100001	141	a
2	2	10	2	[START OF TEXT]	50	32	110010	62	2	98	62	1100010	142	b
3	3	11	3	[END OF TEXT]	51	33	110011	63	3	99	63	1100011	143	c
4	4	100	4	[END OF TRANSMISSION]	52	34	110100	64	4	100	64	1100100	144	d
5	5	101	5	[ENQUIRY]	53	35	110101	65	5	101	65	1100101	145	e
6	6	110	6	[ACKNOWLEDGE]	54	36	110110	66	6	102	66	1100110	146	f
7	7	111	7	[BELL]	55	37	110111	67	7	103	67	1100111	147	g
8	8	1000	10	[BACKSPACE]	56	38	111000	70	8	104	68	1101000	150	h
9	9	1001	11	[HORIZONTAL TAB]	57	39	111001	71	9	105	69	1101001	151	i
10	A	1010	12	[LINE FEED]	58	3A	111010	72	:	106	6A	1101010	152	j
11	B	1011	13	[VERTICAL TAB]	59	3B	111011	73	;	107	6B	1101011	153	k
12	C	1100	14	[FORM FEED]	60	3C	111100	74	<	108	6C	1101100	154	l
13	D	1101	15	[CARRIAGE RETURN]	61	3D	111101	75	=	109	6D	1101101	155	m
14	E	1110	16	[SHIFT OUT]	62	3E	111110	76	>	110	6E	1101110	156	n
15	F	1111	17	[SHIFT IN]	63	3F	111111	77	?	111	6F	1101111	157	o
16	10	10000	20	[DATA LINK ESCAPE]	64	40	1000000	100	@	112	70	1110000	160	p
17	11	10001	21	[DEVICE CONTROL 1]	65	41	1000001	101	A	113	71	1110001	161	q
18	12	10010	22	[DEVICE CONTROL 2]	66	42	1000010	102	B	114	72	1110010	162	r
19	13	10011	23	[DEVICE CONTROL 3]	67	43	1000011	103	C	115	73	1110011	163	s
20	14	10100	24	[DEVICE CONTROL 4]	68	44	1000100	104	D	116	74	1110100	164	t
21	15	10101	25	[NEGATIVE ACKNOWLEDGE]	69	45	1000101	105	E	117	75	1110101	165	u
22	16	10110	26	[SYNCHRONOUS IDLE]	70	46	1000110	106	F	118	76	1110110	166	v
23	17	10111	27	[END OF TRANS. BLOCK]	71	47	1000111	107	G	119	77	1110111	167	w
24	18	11000	30	[CANCEL]	72	48	1001000	110	H	120	78	1111000	170	x
25	19	11001	31	[END OF MEDIUM]	73	49	1001001	111	I	121	79	1111001	171	y
26	1A	11010	32	[SUBSTITUTE]	74	4A	1001010	112	J	122	7A	1111010	172	z
27	1B	11011	33	[ESCAPE]	75	4B	1001011	113	K	123	7B	1111011	173	{
28	1C	11100	34	[FILE SEPARATOR]	76	4C	1001100	114	L	124	7C	1111100	174		
29	1D	11101	35	[GROUP SEPARATOR]	77	4D	1001101	115	M	125	7D	1111101	175	}
30	1E	11110	36	[RECORD SEPARATOR]	78	4E	1001110	116	N	126	7E	1111110	176	~
31	1F	11111	37	[UNIT SEPARATOR]	79	4F	1001111	117	O	127	7F	1111111	177	[DEL]
32	20	100000	40	[SPACE]	80	50	1010000	120	P					
33	21	100001	41	!	81	51	1010001	121	Q					
34	22	100010	42	"	82	52	1010010	122	R					
35	23	100011	43	#	83	53	1010011	123	S					
36	24	100100	44	$	84	54	1010100	124	T					
37	25	100101	45	%	85	55	1010101	125	U					
38	26	100110	46	&	86	56	1010110	126	V					
39	27	100111	47	'	87	57	1010111	127	W					
40	28	101000	50	(	88	58	1011000	130	X					
41	29	101001	51	)	89	59	1011001	131	Y					
42	2A	101010	52	*	90	5A	1011010	132	Z					
43	2B	101011	53	+	91	5B	1011011	133	[					
44	2C	101100	54	,	92	5C	1011100	134	\					
45	2D	101101	55	-	93	5D	1011101	135	]					
46	2E	101110	56	.	94	5E	1011110	136	^					
47	2F	101111	57	/	95	5F	1011111	137	_					

Unicode

It wasn't until 1991 that a universal solution to the character encoding problem would be unveiled. In that year the first version of the Unicode standard was introduced; the standard is actively maintained and improved. The current standard, version 9, was released in 2016.

Unicode solves the character limitation of ASCII by using a larger number of bits to encode characters. In all there are 1,112,064 characters available in a large number of alphabets in Unicode, designed to encompass the languages of the world, as well as special symbols used in fields such as mathematics, chemistry, astronomy, and so on. While there are several encoding schemes defined by the standard, three are in common use and are described in the document by their Unicode Transformation Formats (UTFs).

UTF-8

UTF-8 uses one to four 8-bit "chunks" to encode its character set. Characters with smaller encoded values use fewer chunks. The first 128 characters correspond to the original

7-bit ASCII encoding map, which means that ASCII and UTF-8 are compatible with each other—an older file that stores its data using ASCII can be read by a newer UTF-8 program. UTF-8 sees widespread use on the Internet; it is the recommended encoding scheme for both e-mail programs and web pages.

UTF-16

UTF-16 also uses "chunks" of bits to encode the 1,112,064 characters in Unicode, but it uses 16-bit chunks rather than the 8-bit chunks of UTF-8. Like UTF-8 the number of chunks varies with the numeric value of the character being encoded. One notable user of UTF-16 is Microsoft Windows. It is also used as the default character encoding for programming languages such as Java and JavaScript. Since they differ only in chunk size, UTF-8 and UTF-16 are compatible with each other.

UTF-32

UTF-32 differs from UTF-8 and UTF-16 in that it is a fixed-size code. Any character, whether it has a very small encoded value or a very large one, is encoded in exactly 32 bits. The advantage is that the values stored are always exactly the same size, and so there is no need to determine the start and end of a character value as in UTF-8 or UTF-16, which may vary in length. The disadvantage is that a given text could potentially take significantly more space to store in the computer since no "shrinking" of the code takes place for small values.

While UTF-32 isn't typically used on the Internet (for web pages, e-mail, and the like), it does see use in computer programs. A game, for example, might use UTF-32 encoding to store information about the graphics being displayed during game play.

Storing Colors

We now have a way to map characters that we type—in an e-mail, or an assignment for class, for example—to binary numbers that the computer can understand and store. Fortunately, text is pretty easy to encode; the letter *B* is always going to be 01000010. But what about colors?

The computer, remember, is made up of hundreds of millions of switches. Just like the light switch on your wall, the computer's switches have two positions: on and off. There isn't a position on the switch for "burnt orange." Once again we need a way to map individual colors onto numbers that the computer can understand. To understand the way that we'll do this requires a peek into the history of the computer monitor.

Early Computer Monitors: Monochrome

The first of what we might think of as modern computer displays were single-color (monochrome) devices that used a chemical, known as a phosphor, that glows when it is illuminated by a beam of electrons. In this kind of display the phosphor is deposited in small dots, called *pixels*, along the inside of the screen, and an electron gun mounted in the back of the monitor uses a magnetic aiming device to sweep its beam across the

FIGURE 3-4   A monochrome computer monitor, 1984

phosphors, one line at a time. A typical monitor might have 600 horizontal lines of phosphors, with each line holding 800 individual phosphor dots (an 800x600 display).

In this kind of monitor, the phosphor dot is either lit up or not, and so we only need to store either a 1 (lit) or a 0 (not lit) for each phosphor dot on the screen. The color of the displayed image is a function of the chemicals used in the phosphor. Two common phosphors of the time were zinc sulfide mixed with copper, which fluoresces green, and zinc cadmium sulfide, which fluoresces yellow/amber. Green and amber were the colors of choice, and we still talk about green screen monitors (and, in fact, many places such as banks and insurance companies still use them).

The next innovation was to vary the intensity of the electron beam, which provided a way to dim or brighten individual phosphor dots as the electron beam swept across them; in this way some rudimentary shaded graphics could be displayed. However, it meant that a single bit (on or off) per pixel was no longer sufficient; there had to be a way to store the intensity of the beam at each pixel. Most computers of the time used an 8-bit byte as the smallest unit of storage, and so it made sense to store an 8-bit value for the shade of each pixel. In eight bits we can represent 2^8 or 256 different values, from 0 to 255.

Early Computer Monitors: Color

Many chemical compounds have fluorescent properties that make them suitable for building a computer display, and the idea of a full-color monitor in which individual pixels of different fluorescent material would be placed so close together as to be indistinguishable predated the first working devices.

The problem was red. You might recall the principle of primary colors from grade school; colors that, when mixed together, produce other colors. On the printed page the primary colors are cyan (a shade of blue), magenta, and yellow; when combined in different percentages an entire spectrum of color can be produced. Typically a black pigment is included to introduce shading. This is the CMYK color system that is common on ink-jet printers as well as in the print industry. In this scheme the colors are *subtractive*.

On a screen, though, it's a slightly different story. The colors are *additive*—they are being transmitted from the screen to our eye, unlike a printed page on which light is absorbed by the pigment and the result is that color is subtracted. In an additive system such as a computer display we use the sum of three colors: red, green, and blue. Figure 3-5 shows the result of the additive color process. By varying the intensity of red, green, and blue we can produce a nearly full spectrum of intermediate colors.

FIGURE 3-5   The additive color process

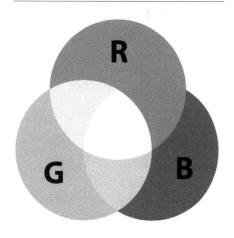

Blue and green phosphors were known in the early years of monitor development, but red remained difficult. As color televisions advanced in the 1960s into the 1970s, work on computer monitors kept pace, and by the early 1980s they became available to consumers. Most computer programs of the time were text-based, though, and so most of the demand for color systems was driven by computer games.

You might recall seeing televisions (and monitors) that have a deep cabinet extending backward from the screen. They also tend to be quite heavy. Inside the cabinet were three electron guns and the circuitry necessary to operate them. The guns emitted a stream of electrons and could be precisely aimed at tiny spots on the back of the screen, each of them containing a small bit of phosphor, which glowed when excited by electrons. The phosphors were made in a way that caused them to glow with either red, green, or blue light and were arranged in stripes or small groups of three called *triads*. While the triads were tiny, if you stood quite close to the screen you could see the individual dots of phosphor. Figure 3-6 shows the arrangement. The phosphors were deposited on the inside face of a large vacuum tube called a cathode ray tube, or CRT, which is what we also called the monitors.

FIGURE 3-6   A color cathode-ray tube (CRT). 1. Red, green, and blue electron guns. 2. Electron beams. 3. Focusing coils. 4. Deflection coils. 5. Connection for final anodes. 6. Mask for separating beams for red, green, and blue part of displayed image. 7. Phosphor layer with red, green, and blue pixels. 8. Close-up of the inside of the CRT screen.

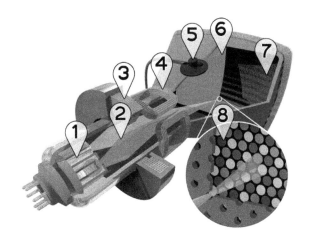

By varying the strength of the electron beams, the phosphors on the CRT would light up in varying brightness. One downside of this method is that an alarming number of X-rays are produced as the electron beams collide with the phosphors and their associated structure—sitting too close to early color TVs or monitors was definitely a health hazard! For this reason, lead glass (similar to the material in lead crystal goblets) was used to construct the front part of the screen, significantly contributing to the monitor's weight and making the monitors themselves hazardous waste.

Even though CRT technology was capable of producing a wide range of color, early color graphics cards, and the computers themselves, were limited by the amount of video data that could be stored, and the speed of retrieving and displaying that data. Color computers made baby steps, from displaying at first 16 colors at a time, then 256, and finally to the millions of colors we now take for granted. On those fledgling color systems, if you played a game that used a specific set of 16 colors, the computer had to be set up to use that color palette. Every other program running on the machine had to use those same 16 colors—it made for some interesting (and frustrating, at times) work!

The *resolution* of the screen—the spacing between the pixels and the number of rows—followed a similar path, with resolution increasing and price decreasing over time. Early color computers offered 640 horizontal pixels in 480 rows (640x480 or VGA); today's high-resolution displays measure 5120 horizontal pixels in 2880 rows (5120x2880, marketed as 5K).

FIGURE 3-7   Color pixels on a flat-screen computer monitor (detail)

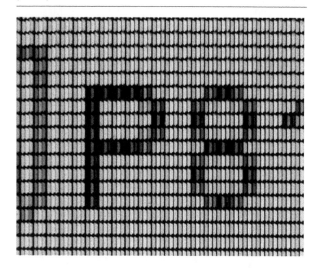

RGB

Modern LCD and OLED computer displays no longer use guns that shoot electron beams at glowing phosphors. Instead, individual pixels emit their own light, or vary the intensity of a light directly behind them on the screen. What hasn't changed is that each color unit is a combination of three pixels: one red, one green, and one blue. Figure 3-7 shows the arrangement of pixels on a typical display.

Each pixel, be it red, green, or blue, varies in intensity to blend together into a single color. If the red pixel is fully on, and the blue and green pixels are off, for example, we see red on the screen. If the red and blue pixels are fully on and green is dark, we see purple, and so on. Each of the three pixels can be adjusted in intensity in steps from 0 (off) to 255 (fully on). Since each pixel has 256 intensity levels, and we have three pixels, the number of combinations of the three is $256^3 = 16,277,216$ discrete colors. We often see this marketed as "16 million" colors. Further, each of the three colors' values can be stored in 8 bits, or one byte, since $2^8 = 256$. Color information using RGB is stored as a sequence of three bytes for a total of 24 bits.

RGB Hexadecimal Notation

The computer stores each of the three RGB values for red, green, and blue as a binary number. Pure red, for example, would be 111111110000000000000000. This is not a convenient way for humans to think about color!

One common way to represent color data is by converting each of the RGB color levels into a hexadecimal value. Since the R, G, and B information is contained in 8 bits each, we can use a two-digit hex number for them. In hexadecimal the values from 0 to 255 are written as 0x00 to 0xFF. (Recall that the leading 0x just indicates a hexadecimal number follows.) Pure red, then, would be 0xFF0000, and neutral gray 0xCCCCCC (128-128-128). You'll often find colors expressed in hexadecimal in the code of web pages; however, rather than a leading 0x, those values have a leading #, so that for neutral gray we would write #CCCCCC.

Most of the time we don't work directly with hex values for RGB colors; it is just too difficult to either remember more than a few RGB hex values, or to determine a precise color using them. Instead, we use a tool that displays color in a wheel or other type of chart, typically called a *color picker,* and can choose a color from it, which is then converted for us to hex for use in a program or web page.

RGB Names

It might be true that 0xCCCCCC is easier to remember than 100000001000000010000000, but it would be nice if there was *some* sort of notation that more closely resembled actual colors. Fortunately, for many colors we can use a name rather than a numeric value. For

FIGURE 3-8   A selection of RGB color names

Color	Hex	Color	Hex	Color	Hex
aliceblue	#F0F8FF	gainsboro	#DCDCDC	mistyrose	#FFE4E1
antiquewhite	#FAEBD7	ghostwhite	#F8F8FF	moccasin	#FFE4B5
aqua	#00FFFF	gold	#FFD700	navajowhite	#FFDEAD
aquamarine	#7FFFD4	goldenrod	#DAA520	navy	#000080
azure	#F0FFFF	gray	#808080	oldlace	#FDF5E6
beige	#F5F5DC	grey	#808080	olive	#808000
bisque	#FFE4C4	green	#008000	olivedrab	#6B8E23
black	#000000	greenyellow	#ADFF2F	orange	#FFA500
blanchedalmond	#FFEBCD	honeydew	#F0FFF0	orangered	#FF4500
blue	#0000FF	hotpink	#FF69B4	orchid	#DA70D6
blueviolet	#8A2BE2	indianred	#CD5C5C	palegoldenrod	#EEE8AA
brown	#A52A2A	indigo	#4B0082	palegreen	#98FB98
burlywood	#DEB887	ivory	#FFFFF0	paleturquoise	#AFEEEE
cadetblue	#5F9EA0	khaki	#F0E68C	palevioletred	#DB7093
chartreuse	#7FFF00	lavender	#E6E6FA	papayawhip	#FFEFD5
chocolate	#D2691E	lavenderblush	#FFF0F5	peachpuff	#FFDAB9
coral	#FF7F50	lawngreen	#7CFC00	peru	#CD853F
cornflowerblue	#6495ED	lemonchiffon	#FFFACD	pink	#FFC0CB
cornsilk	#FFF8DC	lightblue	#ADD8E6	plum	#DDA0DD
crimson	#DC143C	lightcoral	#F08080	powderblue	#B0E0E6
cyan	#00FFFF	lightcyan	#E0FFFF	purple	#800080
darkblue	#00008B	lightgoldenrodyellow	#FAFAD2	red	#FF0000
darkcyan	#008B8B	lightgray	#D3D3D3	rosybrown	#BC8F8F
darkgoldenrod	#B8860B	lightgreen	#90EE90	royalblue	#4169E1
darkgray	#A9A9A9	lightgrey	#D3D3D3	saddlebrown	#8B4513
darkgreen	#006400	lightpink	#FFB6C1	salmon	#FA8072
darkgrey	#A9A9A9	lightsalmon	#FFA07A	sandybrown	#F4A460
darkkhaki	#BDB76B	lightseagreen	#20B2AA	seagreen	#2E8B57
darkmagenta	#8B008B	lightskyblue	#87CEFA	seashell	#2E8857
darkolivegreen	#556B2F	lightslategray	#778899	sienna	#A0522D
darkorange	#FF8C00	lightslategrey	#778899	silver	#C0C0C0
darkorchid	#9932CC	lightsteelblue	#B0C4DE	skyblue	#87CEEB
darkred	#8B0000	lightyellow	#FFFFE0	slateblue	#6A5ACD
darksalmon	#E9967A	lime	#00FF00	slategray	#708090
darkseagreen	#8FBC8F	limegreen	#32CD32	slategrey	#708090
darkslateblue	#483D8B	linen	#FAF0E6	snow	#FFFAFA
darkslategray	#2F4F4F	magenta	#FF00FF	springgreen	#00FF7F
darkslategrey	#2F4F4F	maroon	#800000	steelblue	#4682B4
darkturquoise	#00CED1	mediumaquamarine	#66CDAA	tan	#D2B48C
darkviolet	#9400D3	mediumblue	#0000CD	teal	#008080
deeppink	#FF1493	mediumorchid	#BA55D3	thistle	#D8BFD8
deepskyblue	#00BFFF	mediumpurple	#9370DB	tomato	#FF6347
dimgray	#696969	mediumseagreen	#3CB371	turquoise	#40E0D0
dimgrey	#696969	mediumslateblue	#7B68EE	violet	#EE82EE
dodgerblue	#1E90FF	mediumspringgreen	#00FA9A	wheat	#F5DEB3
firebrick	#B22222	mediumturquoise	#48D1CC	white	#FFFFFF
floralwhite	#FFFAF0	mediumvioletred	#C71585	whitesmoke	#F5F5F5
forestgreen	#228B22	midnightblue	#191970	yellow	#FFFF00
fuchsia	#FF00FF	mintcream	#F5FFFA	yellowgreen	#9ACD32

example, Lemon Chiffon is defined to be 0xFFFACD and Dark Goldenrod is defined to be 0xB8860B.

The current standard for web colors as defined by the World Wide Web Consortium (W3C) includes only a few hundred named colors out of the 16 million possible combinations. A small subset of 16 colors are marked "web safe" as they are guaranteed to be supported in all web browsers. Figure 3-8 shows a collection of named colors. Web designers often start with a named color and then adjust it as necessary to get the desired shade. For example, you might start with "HotPink" (0xff69b4) and subtract a little red to cool it off.

A Word about Print versus Screen Colors

The RGB color combinations are only a small subset of the colors that occur in the natural world. Even more important, the process used to create color on the printed page is very different from that used on a computer screen. In the case of print, colors are created with the primary colors cyan, magenta, and yellow in a subtractive way: Light is absorbed by the pigments on the paper, and the resulting reflected light is the result of the removal from the white light striking the image of various shades.

On a computer screen the color is being transmitted to our eye rather than reflected as it is on paper, and the process used to combine colors is additive, using the red, green, and blue values of RGB.

This presents two problems to designers who use computer software to create artwork destined for print media. What they see on the screen uses a different technology to represent color than a printing press; the colors displayed in their software are not identical to what will appear on the printed page. Professional graphic designers and artists use special calibration devices to tune their monitors to match as closely as possible the print-based color spectrum.

The second problem is that the range of colors available, called the *gamut*, is different between print and screen. There are colors that a printing press can reproduce that simply aren't available in software, and vice versa. When working with images in Adobe Photoshop, for example, a designer can specify what kind of printing equipment will be used, and overlay the gamut of the press on top of their image to see if any colors are not printable (called a gamut check). When working on color-critical projects, it is often possible to specify custom printing inks to match a certain range or group of colors that might not ordinarily be reproducible.

Bottom Line

Whether we are working with text or color, internally the computer is only operating on binary information—ones and zeros. The representations that we apply to the data—Unicode, color names, and the like—are really only a convenience for humans, since we aren't well suited to remembering or manipulating longs sets of binary numbers. When we store information on the computer or send it over the network, it is just binary data being stored or sent. That data is interpreted using a standard such as Unicode or RGB to transform it into the format that is needed for whatever the application is—letters, numbers, colors, sound, and so on.

The translation from one representation to another isn't free; it takes some small amount of time and computer resources to accomplish. In the past, when computers were very slow, the translation time was significant. Our computers are now fast enough that we don't notice any delay, even though work is still being done behind the scenes.

Figure Credits

- **Fig. 3.1:** Source: https://commons.wikimedia.org/wiki/File:US_Navy_051129-N-0685C-007_Quarter-master_Seaman_Ryan_Ruona_signals_with_semaphore_flags_during_a_replenishment_at_sea.jpg.
- **Fig. 3.2:** Source: https://commons.wikimedia.org/wiki/File:PaperTapes-5and8Hole.jpg.
- **Fig. 3.3:** Source: https://commons.wikimedia.org/wiki/File%3AASCII-Table.svg.
- **Fig. 3.4:** Source: https://commons.wikimedia.org/wiki/File%3ADesktop_Computer_-_The_Future_for_Medicine_(FDA_095)_(8249708093).jpg.
- **Fig. 3.5:** Source: https://commons.wikimedia.org/wiki/File%3AAdditiveColor.svg.

Data Conversion and Compression

We take it for granted that we can effortlessly listen to music, watch a movie, read a book or an e-mail, or browse the web on our computers. In reality there's an enormous problem to solve before any of those activities can take place: The computer, as we know, only understands binary information, just ones and zeros. The real world, on the other hand, is not at all a binary place.

To move back and forth between these two worlds we'll need to convert from one type of information to another. Music, for example, is full of tone and rhythm and nuance; we must take the essence of a song and represent it as binary data in order to store it and manipulate it on a computer. If we want to play that song back, the opposite must occur, translating a stream of cold ones and zeros back into a rich musical experience.

This process of conversion comes at a price, which is the amount of data necessary to represent even the simplest sound. Our storage devices—thumb drives, disk drives, and so on—have a finite amount of space. To solve this problem we compress the digital files to make them smaller.

This chapter explores both the conversion and the compression techniques that we use to bridge the large divide between the computer and our world.

Audio: Some Definitions

Before we can talk about how to capture and store real-word information like audio on a computer, we need to define a few terms.

When we talk casually about sound we often describe its pitch or tone, which is how high or low a note sounds. We might also be interested in how loud or soft the sound is. Sound is an *analog* signal, which means that the tone and volume change smoothly from one level to the next in a continuous way; Figure 4-1 shows such a signal. Sound travels in waves, which oscillate up and down like ripples on a body of water.

The pitch or tone of an audio signal, be it a very high note or a very low one, is determined by the frequency of the signal, which is how rapidly the signal is oscillating up and down.

FIGURE 4-1   An analog wave

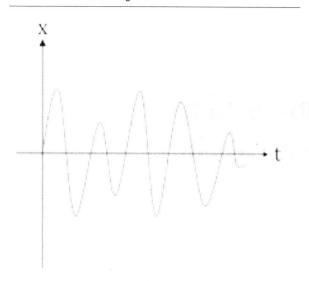

We measure frequency in *hertz*; 1 hertz is equal to 1 oscillation per second.

The volume of an audio signal can be described by its amplitude, which is the distance from the top to the bottom of an oscillation. The larger the distance, the louder the sound at that point in time. A convenient unit to measure amplitude is voltage. Pitch and amplitude are illustrated in Figure 4-2.

Signals like audio can't be directly stored on a computer. The switches that make up the computer's circuitry have just two settings: on and off. There isn't a setting for "a little loud" or "a really high pitch." To work with analog signals like audio on a computer, they must first be converted into a binary, or digital, format.

FIGURE 4-2   Audio definitions

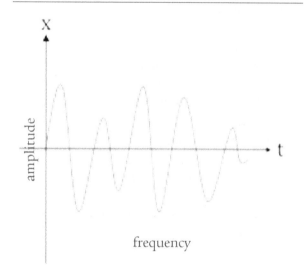

Analog to Digital Conversion

Fortunately we can describe an audio signal numerically by using units such as hertz for frequency and voltage for amplitude. If we can turn the audio into numbers, we'll have something that the computer can store and work with. The technique we'll use is to sample the signal at regular intervals and record the voltage (representing the amplitude) at that point. Figure 4-3 illustrates the principle. At each sample, the amplitude, which is measured as one of several levels, is recorded as a numeric value. The computer then stores the value as a binary number. Typically a special integrated circuit, or chip, called an A/D converter (ADC) handles the process; an analog signal is fed in on one side, and a digital value is produced on the other side at each sampling interval.

For the analog signal in Figure 4-3, the amplitude value at each interval from left to right would be recorded; this is the *sampling frequency*. There are eight possible amplitude values, from level 0 to level 8. For this signal, the amplitude at sample 0 is 0; at sample 1 it is 4; at sample 2 it is 5; and so on. The data collected would be similar to:

0	1	2	3	4	5	6	7	8	9	10	11	12	13
0	4	5	4	3	4	6	7	5	3	3	4	4	3

Each amplitude value would be stored as a binary number. Since there are 8 possible values, from 0 to 7, we can use a three-bit value for each (since $2^3 = 8$). The amplitude at sample 4 would be 011 (3), that at sample 7 would be 111 (7), and that at sample 12 would be 100 (4). Now that the values are in binary, the computer can store, retrieve, and manipulate them. If we wanted to make this particular sound a little softer, for example, we could direct the computer to subtract 2 from each sample.

FIGURE 4-3   Sampling an analog signal

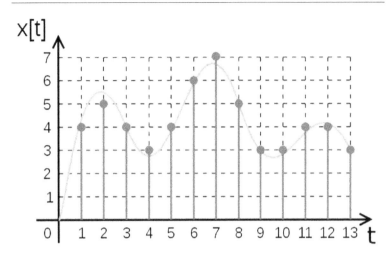

Digital to Analog Conversion

If we have a file containing the digital values produced by an ADC, another conversion can be done, this time in the opposite direction, from digital to analog, to reproduce the original sound. Like A/D conversion, a special chip called a D/A converter (DAC) is used for this function. The playback rate is set to be the same as the original sampling rate, and the DAC outputs the recorded voltage at each interval. Figure 4-4 shows the process.

There are two things that we can control: The number of levels to record and the sampling rate. Both of these affect the quality of the music that we will hear when a digital file is played back.

FIGURE 4-4   Audio conversion process

Sampling Levels

At each sample interval the amplitude of the input signal is measured and recorded. The value is stored as a binary value, and so the number of different levels that we can measure is limited by the number of bits in that binary value. For example, if we use a three-bit binary number to store the measurement, there would be only 2^3 or 8 different values that could be stored. When the file is played back, the resulting restored audio will jump from one level to the next. Figure 4-5 shows the result.

This is not an ideal situation; as you can see, the audio that is played

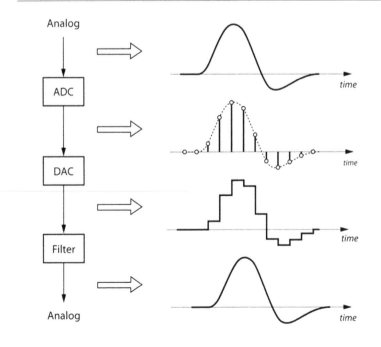

FIGURE 4-5   Playing back three-bit audio

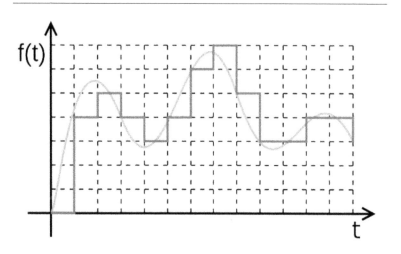

back is not a very good representation of the original sound. An obvious solution is to increase the number of levels that can be measured by increasing the number of bits in the binary value. For example, if instead of three bits we use eight bits, the number of levels increases to 2^8 or 256. The trade-off is the size of the file. By increasing the samples from three bits to eight, we must store five extra bits for each sample, making the resulting file 166% larger than the one using three-bit samples.

CD audio uses a 16-bit value for each sample, which provides $2^{16} = 65,536$ different levels. This number was arrived at partly due to a constraint of the technology used to record information on a CD, which limits the amount of stored data to about 700 megabytes. Audio CDs were originally designed to hold an hour of music.

Sample Rate

The second thing we can control when recording audio is the sample rate, or how often a sample of the original sound is taken. The goal is to capture as much of the original sound as possible, but not too much. When the sample rate is multiplied by the size of each sample in bits, the result is the size or amount of data that must be stored. For example, if we use a sample rate of once each second and a sample size of 16 bits, we would store 16 bits for each second of audio, and a 60-second audio clip would take up 16 bits * 60 seconds * 1 sample/second = 960 bits, or just under 1 kilobit.

FIGURE 4-6   Sampling at a rate that is too low

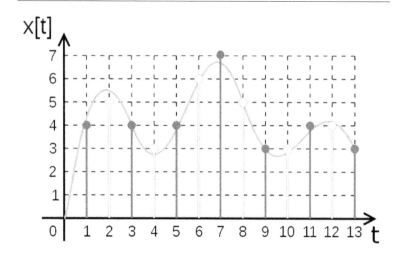

The challenge is that we want to sample often enough to capture high-frequency parts of the audio (those that oscillate rapidly) but not so often that the size of the resulting file is too large to store. Figure 4-6 shows the result of a too-low sample rate.

We can place an upper limit on the sample rate by considering how humans hear sound. Most of us can hear sounds in a range from a low of 20 hertz to a high of 20 kilohertz (20,000 hertz). Research in this field by Claude Shannon, and expanded on by Harry Nyquist in the 1920s, revealed that it is sufficient to use a sample rate of just twice the highest frequency to be recorded in order to faithfully reproduce the original signal. Since humans can hear sounds of up to 20,000 hertz, a sample rate of twice that, or 40,000 samples each second, is a good upper limit. To provide for a smoother playback, CDs add a buffer of about 10% that results in a sample rate of 44,100 sample per second. (An interesting aside—44,100 is the sum of the squares of the first four prime numbers: 22 + 32 + 52 + 72 = 44,100.)

Sampled File Size

For CD audio using 16-bit samples at 44,100 samples per second, the size of a one-minute audio clip is 16 bits * 60 seconds * 44,1000 samples/second or 42,336,000 bits, which is equivalent to 5,292,000 bytes (recall that 8 bits = one byte). We can round this off to 5 megabytes per minute. Since most music is recorded in stereo, there are two recorded channels of audio, right and left, and so a minute of stereo music can be stored in 2 * 5 megabytes, or 10MB.

A typical song is roughly three to four minutes long. Since a CD can store 640MB of data, we can calculate that it will hold 640MB / 40MB per song or 16 songs for a total of 64 minutes, about an hour's worth of music.

Data Compression

When it was introduced in the 1980s, and well into the 1990s, the CD could hold much more data than the hard drive in a typical PC, which for consumers peaked at around 40MB. PC storage was not only limited, it was expensive: In 1990 that 40MB hard drive would cost $300 or more. By contrast, thumb drives, which we now can buy in blister packs for $20, hold 16 gigabytes or more! There was a strong need in the early days of computing to reduce the size of stored files. The answer was to compress those files, to make them smaller.

Slow network speeds also were a factor. Dial-up modems were common, and transferring a large file across a network could take quite a bit of time. It was a common practice to start a download, then go and have lunch; when you were finished eating, the download would be just about done. Streaming music, such as Apple Music or Spotify, was for the most part out of the question due to the slowness of the network.

While compression seems like an obvious solution, it isn't that simple. If we make a file smaller, doesn't it follow that some information has been lost? Wouldn't it ruin the experience if some of the music was removed?

The answer is, in many cases, "Not necessarily."

Think about how you listen to music. Much of the time it's through earbuds, or a phone, laptop, or tablet speaker, none of which has the frequency response necessary to reproduce the full 20Hz to 20kHz range recorded on a CD. Unless you are listening carefully on an expensive playback system, you probably won't notice if some of the high notes are missing in your favorite song.

We can take advantage of this by removing information from a recorded audio file; the highest highs, the lowest lows, and by resampling at lower rates. The result is a file that, when played back, sounds very close to the original recording but is significantly smaller.

Lossy Compression and MP3

When the size of a file is reduced by removing information from it, we say that the compression is *lossy*. The MP3 compression format takes advantage of a few features of human hearing, including:

- When two sounds are playing at the same time, we only hear the louder of the two.
- Short, loud sounds will temporarily cover up softer sounds.
- We hear some ranges of sounds better than others; the better ones can be scaled back.

In addition, the sampling rate can be adjusted to reproduce just enough, but not more, sound.

Extra processing is used to reduce the size of each group of bits in the file. The result of MP3 encoding is a file that sounds close to the original CD audio but that is 10 to 15 times smaller. A typical three-minute song that occupies 32MB on a CD can be stored as a 3MB MP3.

The MP3 specification is more formally known as the Motion Picture Experts Group (1) Audio Layer 3 and it was developed in the early 1990s for a wide range of uses, including DVD and television audio. Other compression formats have been introduced both before and since, but MP3 is the one that most people are familiar with.

Lossless Compression

Reducing the size of a file by removing information isn't always an acceptable solution. What if the file you are trying to compress is a document or an e-mail? It wouldn't do to remove characters or words from this kind of file. There are some audio hobbyists who would argue that the same holds true for audio files. Yet the fundamental problems, that storage is finite and networks are slow, haven't gone away.

Several approaches have been developed that satisfy both the need for a smaller file and for faithful reproduction; these are the lossless compression algorithms. While they vary in their approaches, most accomplish compression by storing the instructions to reproduce the original file instead of removing information. You might have heard of many of these algorithms, including Ogg/Vorbis, FLAC, and ZIP.

Dictionaries

Dictionary trees demonstrate a common approach to lossless compression. Take a look at this sentence:

The rain in Spain falls mainly in the plain.

It comprises 44 characters, including the spaces between words and the final punctuation. In a dictionary-style algorithm we look for repeating patterns of data. In our sample sentence, the patterns **ain[space]**, **he[space]**, and **in[space]** each appear more than once. Using this information, we can devise a code such as this:

Code	Value
1	ain
2	he[space]
3	in[space]

Substituting code numbers for their values in the original sentence yields:

T2r1 3Sp1 falls m1ly 3 t2 pl1.

The number of characters has been reduced from 44 to 30. The code tables also need to be stored, and they take up another 9 characters. The total file needed to store the instructions for recreating the original sentence would be 30 coded characters + 9 coded strings = 39 characters, an 11% reduction. A larger file would yield more and longer repeated sequences and thus a greater compression ratio. Even so, saving 10% of the space required to store a text file could be significant, and for large text files, many compression algorithms (7z, ZIP, and so on) can produce files that are 10 to 20% the size of the original.

Trees

A technique similar to dictionaries is to arrange the words in a file in an upside-down tree and store just the unique words in the file along with instructions on how to traverse the tree in order to reproduce the original. Figure 4-7 illustrates such a tree.

In this kind of compression, the instructions for reproduction are a sequence of left- or right-turn instructions, each starting at the top of the tree. For example, to retrieve the word **incredulity**, the instructions, from the top, consist of three turns: right-left-right (RLR). What famous phrase does this sequence of 49 characters encode, if each hyphen indicates a return to the top of the tree? **L-LL-R-L-LR-R-L-RR-RRR-L-RR-LRL-L-RL-RLL-L-RL-RLR**

The answer: *It was the best of times, it was the worst of times, it was the age of wisdom, it was the age of foolishness, it was the epoch of belief, it was the epoch of incredulity.*

The decoded phrase has 170 characters, and the tree created from it has 85. The code, L-LL and so on, is 49 characters long. Adding the tree and the code results in 134 characters, a reduction of about 21%. A longer text would provide more opportunities for finding longer sequences to encode.

An interesting note: Because of the way this kind of tree, known as a binary search tree, is constructed, the number of right- or left-turn instructions needed to arrive at any location in the tree is no more than $\log_2 n$, where n is the number of locations. For example,

FIGURE 4-7 Compression using a tree

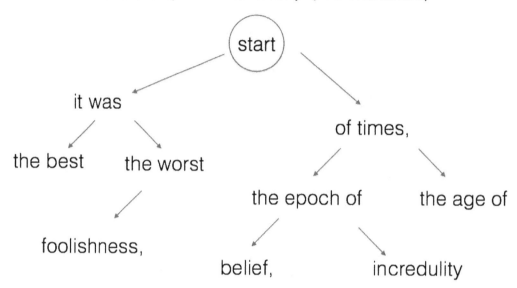

It was the best of times, it was the worst of times, it was the age of wisdom, it was the age of foolishness, it was the epoch of belief, it was the epoch of incredulity (170 characters)

1,024 different phrases could be encoded in a binary tree that requires 10 or fewer steps to find any phrase, since $\log_2 1024 = 10$. Similarly, over a million phrases could be encoded in a tree requiring a maximum of 20 lefts and rights, since $\log_2 1,048,576 = 20$.

Compressing Images

Like audio and text files, image files can become quite large. You've probably seen advertisements for smartphones and other devices that promote the number of pixels that the included camera can capture; 8 megapixels, 12 megapixels, and so on. A pixel is one tiny dot of color, and so a megapixel is 1 million of those dots. A 12 megapixel camera has an image sensor that can capture 12 million pixels of information in each photo.

We know from Chapter 3 that images are typically displayed on a computer monitor in RGB format. Each of the colors captured—red, green, and blue—uses 8 bits of data, so each pixel in RGB uses 24 bits, 8 for each color. A 12 megapixel camera would therefore create a file that is 12,000,000 * 24 = 288,000,000 bits, or 36,000,000 bytes (since 8 bits = 1 byte). We'd say that the file size is 36MB.

It's a relatively rare situation in which we'd need to use the full-resolution, large file coming straight off of the camera. An exception might be a photographer who is using the raw camera image sensor data as a "digital negative" and intends to process the file in a photo manipulation package such as Adobe Lightroom or Photoshop. Perhaps the camera is being used to record astronomical images in the search for new asteroids; another case where we might want the original raw data from the camera.

For most uses, though, a smaller file that is close to the original suffices, and a smaller file means that we can store more of them on a disk, or send and receive them faster across a network. Maybe the image is part of a web page, in which case we might only want to show a smaller version of the original.

For all of these reasons, we can apply compression algorithms to the original file in order to reduce its size.

JPEG Compression

Compression algorithms for images fall into two categories: lossless, which retains all of the original information in the image, and lossy, which sacrifices data in order to reduce the final file size. JPEG compression is in the latter category, and is a common algorithm used to produce image files for print, web, and other uses. You can recognize a JPEG compressed file by its .jpg or .jpeg file extension.

The name JPEG comes from the group that wrote the standards for this type of file compression: the Joint Photographic Experts Group. Committees such as JPEG are responsible for many of the standards that we use every day on our computers and across our networks. The JPEG standard was designed specifically for the compression of still images (as opposed to motion pictures). A still image stored in a computer file is a collection of pixels arranged in a grid. We might, for example, say that an image is 640x480, which means that it has 480 rows of 640 pixels each. Each pixel typically represents a combination of red, green, and blue values (RGB).

Most video compression algorithms rely on a few fundamental facts about how humans perceive images. One is that if two adjacent pixels have color values that are very close, they can be averaged into a single color without a significant loss in perception. Another is that the colors themselves can be flattened somewhat without changing the original in a noticeable way. The image can be sampled in a manner similar to audio files, looking at every other pixel, for example, to further reduce the amount of data that will be required to reproduce the image.

Figure 4-8 shows the effect of sampling; a low rate on the left of the picture results in large blocks of color, and as the sampling rate is increased to the right, the image becomes clearer.

All of the compression techniques described above are lossy, in that some of the original information is lost. Once these reductions are made, the JPEG algorithm performs an additional step to further reduce the file size using a lossless algorithm such as a binary tree dictionary. We normally don't see the original and the compressed versions of a file next to each other; since we don't have the original to compare, the compressed file usually looks "good enough."

Figure 4-9 shows how a large amount of compression can be achieved without significant loss of detail. The file for the original image on the left is 372,000 bytes, while the image on the right is just 61,000 bytes, an

FIGURE 4-8   Effect of sample rate on image quality

FIGURE 4-9 Original (left) versus heavily compressed image (right)

83.6% reduction in size. Without the original to reference, the compressed version would look just fine.

Compressing Video

Video files are essentially a collection of still images that are played back quickly enough that our eye sees continuous motion. In a film that you might see at the cinema, the individual frames are projected at a rate of 24 frames per second (24fps), which is fast enough that we see no flickering. A shutter closes over the frame as the next frame is pulled to position to avoid a blur; the shutter is typically cycled twice as fast as the film (at 48fps) to avoid it being seen as a flicker, too.

For computer video, we can apply techniques similar to those used in JPEG compression, since what we perceive as motion is really just individual images being displayed quickly. We can further take advantage of opportunities unique to video. Imagine a video of a newscaster delivering the evening's news in front of a backdrop. There are many instances in which not much is changing; the newscaster's mouth and head might be moving slightly between frames, but perhaps the backdrop isn't. There's no reason to store information about the backdrop in each frame; it can be repeated until the backdrop changes. Storing just the parts of the scene that are in motion can significantly reduce the size of the video file.

Bottom Line

We live in an analog world, but the computer only sees things in a digital way. Analog-to-digital (A/D) and digital-to-analog (D/A) conversions, usually done by specialized hardware, bridge the gap between the two. There are inherent inefficiencies in this process, and the result is that it is difficult to accurately record and reproduce sounds and images, although we can come close.

A more pressing problem is that A/D conversion creates files that can be quite large, and computer storage is a finite resource. We use compression techniques like MPEG for audio and JPEG for images to reduce the size of the digital files, accepting that there will be a loss of information.

Sometimes a lossy compression technique is unacceptable; we certainly wouldn't want to remove words in a document to make the file smaller. For these applications we can employ lossless techniques such as dictionaries and trees in order to reduce file size.

Figure Credits

- **Fig. 4.3:** Source: https://commons.wikimedia.org/wiki/File:Digital.signal.discret.svg.
- **Fig. 4.8:** Copyright © AzaToth (CC by 3.0) at https://commons.wikimedia.org/wiki/File%3AFelis_silvestris_silvestris_small_gradual_decrease_of_quality.png.

CHAPTER

5

Binary Logic and Hardware

A t the heart of every computer is its central processing unit, or CPU. Inside the CPU are hundreds of millions of switches, arranged into electronic circuits that implement the logical operations that the computer must perform. Taken as a whole, the design seems utterly complicated, but broken down into its smallest parts it becomes easy to understand.

All of the switches are designed to do one thing: turn electricity on or off, just like the light switch on your wall. As we saw in our discussion of numbering schemes, the computer works on binary numbers, which have two states: on or off. These binary states map directly onto the state of any individual switch in the computer. Unlike our light switches, however, the computer's switches are connected together to form circuits. In this chapter we will look at various ways of combining switches to create logical circuits, which themselves can be combined to perform higher-order operations in the computer.

Electricity and Switches

When we think of electricity, the first thing that comes to mind is plugging things into the sockets on our walls. Electricity coming out of wall sockets has two important properties: *voltage*, which is a measure of the force provided by the flow of electrons through the wires in our circuit; and *current*, which is a measure of the number of electrons flowing past a given point each second. Current is measured in a unit called amperes, or amps, and a standard wall socket produces 15 to 20 amps of current. In the United States, the standard voltage at a wall socket is 110 to 120 volts.

When we plug things like a lamp into a wall socket, electricity is delivered to the device through one or more wires, which are made from a material that conducts electricity easily, such as copper. In general, metals like copper, silver, and gold are excellent conductors of the electrons, and other materials such as glass and pure water are insulators, extremely poor conductors. A third class of material, called a *semiconductor*, varies its ability to conduct electricity based on a controlling current or voltage. Semiconductors are what make up the

FIGURE 5-1   Operation of a PMOS transistor

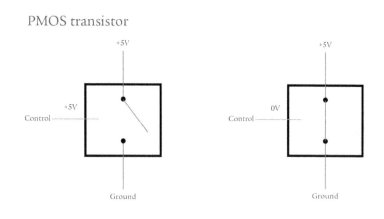

PMOS transistor

majority of the electronic circuits that we find in our computers.

Transistors

Even in the early days of computing, electricity was used; for instance, in the 1930s electromagnetic relays served as switches that controlled the flow of electricity, and were replaced in the 1940s by vacuum tubes, which were orders of magnitude faster because they had no moving parts. In vacuum tubes electrons flowed across the vacuum between two terminals.

Transistors, invented in 1948 and developed over the next few decades, improved on the vacuum tube by eliminating the fragile glass envelope required to hold a vacuum and the large power requirements for heating up components to generate electrons. In addition, transistors were tiny—hundreds of them could be packed into the space taken up by a single vacuum tube. Transistors are made out of silicon, a semiconducting material that is further enhanced by the addition of atoms of boron and phosphorus to create miniaturized, solid-state switches.

In its simplest form, a transistor operates exactly like a light switch. While there are many configurations of transistors in use today, we will focus on a single type, the metal-oxide semiconductor (MOS) transistor. MOS transistors come in two flavors: PMOS transistors and NMOS transistors. The PMOS transistor is infused with atoms that cause it to allow the flow of electricity if no voltage is present on a control wire, as shown in Figure 5-1. When a control voltage is present, the switch opens, and no electricity can flow through the switch.

FIGURE 5-2   Operation of an NMOS transistor

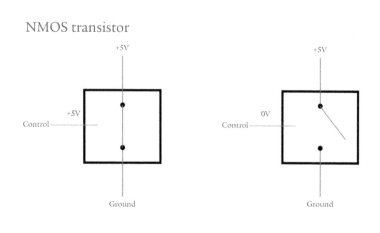

NMOS transistor

Similarly, an NMOS transistor is created in the opposite fashion, so that electricity flows through the switch when voltage is present on a control wire, and no voltage flows through when the control voltage is absent, as shown in Figure 5-2.

By themselves, single transistors are not all that useful for designing computers; it is when we combine them together to form circuits that we can begin to build the foundation of logic necessary to perform complex operations in the CPU. These combinations of transistors are called *gates*.

FIGURE 5-3   Two transistors arranged in a NOT gate

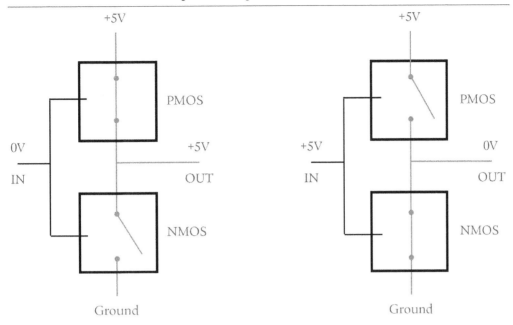

Gates

The simplest logical gate uses two transistors, one PMOS and one NMOS, as shown in Figure 5-3. In this arrangement, the control wire is used as an input. If we represent a binary zero as 0V or a binary one as 5V on the input, we can observe what happens on the output wire of the gate. As you can see in the diagram, when 0V is applied to the input of this gate, the PMOS transistor closes, allowing voltage to flow from the power supply at the top through the transistor, to the top of the NMOS transistor at the bottom. However, the NMOS transistor acts in the opposite fashion from the PMOS; since it has 0V on its input, or control wire, the NMOS switch opens, preventing the electricity from flowing through the transistor into ground. The result is that 5V appears on the output, coming through the PMOS transistor at the top of the gate.

Reversing the situation, applying a binary 1, or 5V, on the input of the gate causes the PMOS transistor to open up, preventing electricity from flowing from the power supply at the top through the transistor. It also closes the NMOS transistor on the bottom, attaching the output wire directly to ground, or 0V. Thus, when a binary 1 is present on the input of the gate, a binary 0 appears on the output.

The result of this combination of transistors is a negation of the input value. If there is a 0 on the input, a 1 appears on the output, and so for the reverse, when a 1 is present on the input, 0 is present on the output.

The NOT Gate and Truth Tables

This simple arrangement of two transistors results in a very powerful logical operator, called NOT, which is a gate that inverts its input. We can represent the states of this device in tabular form, called a *truth table*, which lists the inputs to the device on one side, and the output of the device on the other. The truth table for a NOT gate is shown in

FIGURE 5-4   Truth table for a NOT operation

X	Y
0	1
1	0

Figure 5-4. The symbol for the NOT gate is also shown in the diagram; it consists of an input side, a triangle representing the gate, a small circle representing negation, and the output line.

While truth tables will always show the inputs and outputs of a specific gate or collection of gates, the inputs and outputs can be expressed either as binary values (1 or 0), or "truthy" values (true and false). Generally, true represents a binary one and false represents a binary zero. You'll see both notations in literature, although when discussing electronic circuits we tend to see the binary version; the true and false version often appears when we are speaking strictly of the logic behind the circuit.

Binary Logic

The two-transistor NOT gate is an extremely simple circuit. Even so, it is widely used, since it is often the case that we need to process the negation of a particular logical operation, whether it be an input value or an output value. There are several other logic gates entrusted to us in computer science, and will look at each in turn:

- AND
- OR
- NAND (not AND)
- NOR (not OR)
- XOR (exclusive OR)

The AND Gate

An AND gate is shown in Figure 5-6 along with its truth table. You can see that the output of an AND gate is 1 only when both of its inputs are 1. We might also say that the output is true only when all of the inputs are true. When we write an AND operation in an equation, the symbol used is a small solid circle, such as A•B, or we can also just place the inputs side-by-side like this: $Y = AB$.

FIGURE 5-5   AND gate with multiple inputs

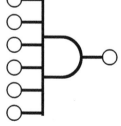

We are not restricted to having just two inputs to an AND gate, or for that matter any other logical gate, with the exception of the NOT. As shown in Figure 5-5, we can have several inputs, and for an AND operation all of them need to be true, or 1, for the output to also be true or 1. It's easy to remember the operation of an AND gate; just say to yourself, "This one *and* that one must be true."

The OR Gate

The OR gate implements the logical OR operation. Its symbol and truth table are shown in Figure 5-7. The OR gate produces a 1, or true, on its output if one or the other or *both* of its inputs are also 1 or true. When working with an OR

FIGURE 5-6   An AND gate and its truth table

A	B	Y
0	0	0
0	1	0
1	0	0
1	1	1

FIGURE 5-7   An OR gate and its truth table

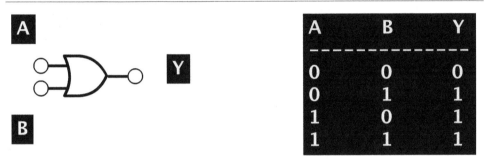

A	B	Y
0	0	0
0	1	1
1	0	1
1	1	1

operation in a written equation, we use the + symbol between the inputs, so we might say that **Y** = **A+B**. Like the AND, we are not limited to just two inputs, and so we might have an OR gate with, say, eight inputs; its output will be true if any combination of its inputs are true, from a single input, to all eight.

The NOR Gate

Placing a logical NOT operator at the output of an OR gate creates a NOT OR gate, commonly contracted to NOR. In practice, the NOT operation is part of the logic circuit, and so we consider the NOR gate to be a separate circuit even though we could accomplish the same thing with two gates, an OR and a NOT. Its symbol and truth table are shown in Figure 5-8. The small circle on the output side of the gate indicates a NOT operator.

FIGURE 5-8   A NOR gate and its truth table

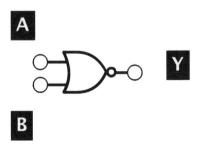

A	B	Y
0	0	1
0	1	0
1	0	0
1	1	0

The Exclusive OR Gate

The exclusive OR (written XOR) is related to the OR gate but adds a small twist. Its symbol and truth table are shown in Figure 5-9. In an XOR operation, the output is true or one or either of the inputs are true, but not all of them. For a multiple input exclusive or gate, any combination of true inputs will result in a true output, *unless* all of the inputs are true. The symbol used in equations for an XOR is a + in a circle: $\oplus$.

FIGURE 5-9 An XOR gate and its truth table

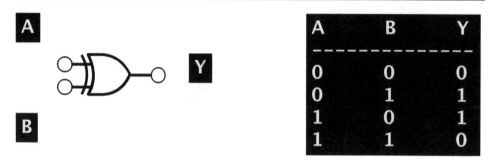

A	B	Y
0	0	0
0	1	1
1	0	1
1	1	0

The NAND Gate

Like the NOR gate, we can negate the output of an AND operation by placing a logical NOT on the output. The symbol and truth table for a NAND gate is shown in Figure 5-10. Since the NAND is the opposite of AND, its output will be true or one when its inputs are not both true.

FIGURE 5-10 A NAND gate and its truth table

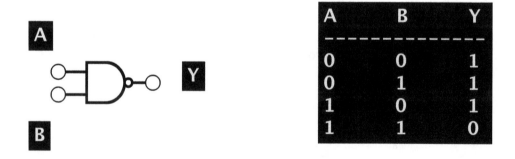

A	B	Y
0	0	1
0	1	1
1	0	1
1	1	0

De Morgan's Law

An important concept in binary logic was codified by Augustus De Morgan, an English mathematician working in the mid-1800s. DeMorgan expanded on work by mathematician George Boole, who laid down the fundamentals of an algebra specifically for logic, later called Boolean algebra. Using Boole's notation, De Morgan described a relationship that had been known since Greek times, but not formally applied to Boole's new algebra:

The negation of a conjunction is the disjunction of the negations;
The negation of a disjunction is the conjunction of the negations.

In our terms, negation is the NOT operator, disjunction is an AND operation, and conjunction is an OR operation. We can say that $\overline{AB}$ is equivalent to $\overline{A} + \overline{B}$, and similarly $\overline{A + B}$ is equivalent to $\overline{A} \cdot \overline{B}$:

$$\overline{AB} = \overline{A} + \overline{B}$$
$$\overline{A + B} = \overline{A} \cdot \overline{B}$$

The bar over a symbol indicates a NOT, or negation. The reason that this is so important is that it allows us to construct any logical operator using only NAND gates or only NOR gates. Consider a CPU chip that has 100 million transistors. From a manufacturing perspective, if we had to design circuits for the CPU in such a way that it was a combination of AND, OR, NOT, NOR, and XOR gates it would best be a complicated design, and in reality would be very difficult to manufacture. Each of those types of logic circuits is manufactured in a different way; so that if we had a mixture of all of them across the CPU chip, it might become so difficult to build the circuit in silicon as to be impossible.

Applying De Morgan's Law, however, allows us to reduce the number of types of logic circuits that we have to build on the CPU chip. Since any logical operation can be made from only NAND or only NOR gates, it's possible to create a CPU circuit design that is almost exclusively NAND or NOR gates in various combinations to supply the logic necessary for the CPU's operations. From a manufacturing standpoint this uniformity is an enormous win, and the yield of our chips, that is, the number of good chips that we can produce out of a batch, increases dramatically. We say that the NAND and the NOR gates are *universal gates* for this reason. Figure 5-11 shows an OR gate constructed from NANDs, and Figure 5-12 an XOR gate. Note that in a few cases we tie two inputs of a NAND gate together; this creates the equivalent of a single NOT gate or inverter.

FIGURE 5-11   Applying the universal NAND gate to build an OR circuit

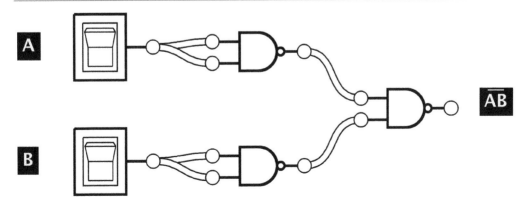

FIGURE 5-12   Applying the universal NAND gate to build an XOR circuit

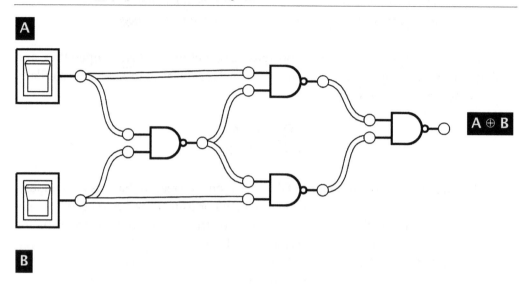

Expressing Logical Equations with Gates

When an engineer is designing a new computer, often the operations are expressed as Boolean equations. It's a relatively simple matter to go from a Boolean equation to the equivalent logical circuit. The first step is to write down the equation, like this one:

$$R = X \cdot Y \cdot \overline{Z}$$

In this equation, R will be the output of the circuit, and X, Y, and Z will be inputs. There are two operations being performed: an AND operation on X, Y, and Z, and a NOT operation on Z. For a simple equation like this, we can simply sketch out the logical circuit, as shown in Figure 5-13.

For a slightly more complicated circuit, consider this equation:

$$R = X + \overline{Y} \cdot Z$$

FIGURE 5-13   A circuit for $R = X \cdot Y \cdot \overline{Z}$

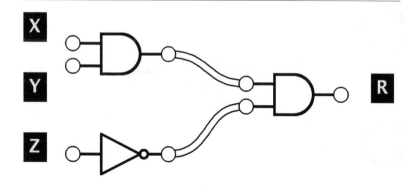

Here, there are three logical operations: an AND between Y and Z, a NOT on input Y, and an OR between X, Y, and Z. This equation illustrates a bit of a problem. Are we looking for X OR'd with $\overline{Y}$ AND Z, or are we looking for Z ANDed with X OR $\overline{Y}$?

Just as there is an order of operations for mathematical equations, there is an order of operations for logical equations as well. The order of operations specifies which symbol

FIGURE 5-14   A circuit for R = X + $\overline{Y}$ • Z

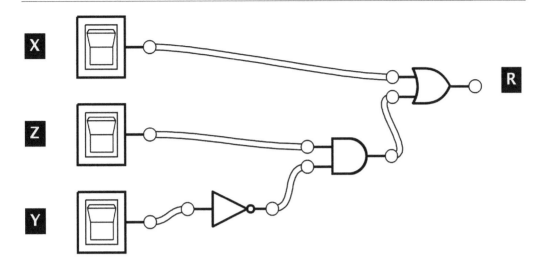

has a higher priority, that is, which will be done first, and then second, and so on. In Boolean logic, NOT has the highest priority, then AND, and then OR, so that this equation specifies X OR'd with the result of $\overline{Y}$ AND Z. The circuit is shown in Figure 5-14.

Just as in ordinary mathematics, we can make our intent clear by enclosing the parts of our equation that should be evaluated first in parentheses. Expressions inside parentheses are evaluated first, regardless of the order of operations, and then the other operators are applied according to the rules of order. We would better have expressed the equation of Figure 5-14 as:

$$R = X + (\overline{Y} \cdot Z)$$

Here's an example that shows parentheses in action:

$$R = ((A \cdot B) + (C \cdot D)) \cdot \overline{\overline{E}}$$

In this equation, it's much clearer which elements are grouped together, and so it is easier to draw the corresponding logic circuit, shown in Figure 5-15.

From Gates to Circuits

It is not typical to see individual logic circuits such as AND or XOR on a computer chip; rather, we see hundreds, or thousands, of gates combined together to provide some high-level function. For example, Figure 5-16 shows a binary adding circuit. It adds two four-bit numbers together and outputs a five-bit binary value that is the sum of the two inputs.

Before we can understand what's going on inside this adding circuit, we need to understand how to add two numbers together in binary.

FIGURE 5-15 A circuit for $R = ((A \bullet B) + (C \bullet D)) \bullet \overline{E}$

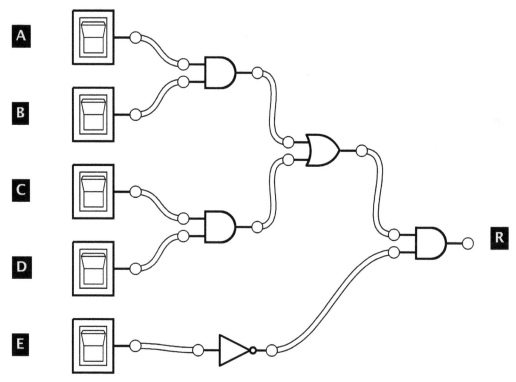

FIGURE 5-16 Four-bit binary adder

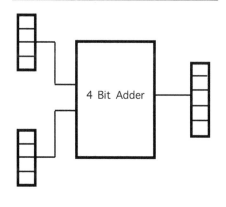

Adding Binary Numbers

One great thing about adding binary numbers together is that there are fewer symbols to deal with, since we only have zeros and ones. Just like adding decimal numbers together, we can write an addition with one number on top of the other, and then simply add the columns up. Also just like decimal numbers, we have to be concerned about carrying a remainder. For example, if I add the decimal numbers 17 and 5, we intuitively know that the result is 22; however, what has really happened is that shown in Figure 5-17. Notice that we have to carry a 10 in this case to the column to the left; that 10 then gets added to whatever is below it in the column, in this case zero, and the result is 12.

Similarly, with binary numbers, we have to be concerned about carrying a binary digit to the left as the result of an addition. Here are the rules for binary addition:

FIGURE 5-17 Adding decimal numbers, showing a carry operation

$$^{1}1\ 7$$
$$+\quad 5$$
$$\overline{\quad\quad}$$
$$2\ 2$$

$$0 + 0 = 0$$
$$0 + 1 = 1$$
$$1 + 0 = 0$$
$$1 + 1 = 10$$

All but the last case are simple, since zero plus zero is zero and zero plus one is one in every number base. The last case makes sense when you recall that $2_{10} = 10_2$, so one plus one is two. For example, if we add the binary numbers 101 and 11, the result is 1000, as shown in Figure 5-18; it requires two carries.

It's pretty simple to write a truth table for single-bit binary addition, and one is shown in Figure 5-19. This truth table is one that you have seen before; it is identical to an XOR operation. It does not take the carry bit into account, however.

Figure 5-20 shows the truth table for the carry bit. The only time that the carry bit is 1 is when adding two 1s together; this truth table is identical to the one for the AND operator.

Combining these two operations allows us to design a circuit to handle one-bit addition using an XOR gate and an AND gate. The circuit is shown in Figure 5-21.

This simple circuit, with just two gates, is known as a *half adder*. It's only a half adder because it does not include an input for the carry bit of a prior operation. This means that we are limited in this circuit to adding only two one-bit numbers together. If we combine two half adders together, however, we can build what is called a *full adder* circuit that does take into account the carry bit from a prior operation; this is shown in Figure 5-22.

We now have a small electrical circuit that correctly adds two binary bits together along with a carry. We still are limited to just one-bit values, however. If we combine full adder circuits together, we can increase the number of bits that we can add together, using one full adder per bit that we want to sum. The circuit is shown in Figure 5-23; it adds to four-bit numbers together using four full adders, and produces a five-bit result. We need the fifth bit because the result of the four-bit addition might result in a carry.

FIGURE 5-18 Adding binary numbers, showing a carry operation

FIGURE 5-19 Truth table for single-bit binary addition

A	B	Sum
0	0	0
0	1	1
1	0	1
1	1	0 (and a carry)

FIGURE 5-20 Truth table for a single-bit carry

A	B	Carry
0	0	0
0	1	0
1	0	0
1	1	1

FIGURE 5-21 A half-adder circuit

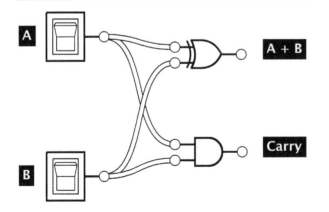

FIGURE 5-22 Full adder made up of two half adders

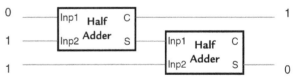

FIGURE 5-23 A four-bit adder

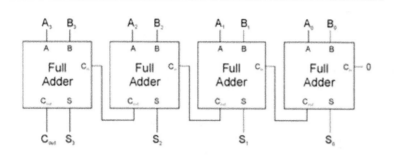

Our four-bit adder is an extremely simple circuit, but it illustrates exactly the way that engineers design more complex circuits that will be manufactured into a CPU chip. Starting with Boolean equations to express logic, we can move directly into circuitry, applying De Morgan's Law along the way so that the result is a combination of easier-to-manufacture NAND or NOR gates. In the early days of microprocessor design this was done by hand, but now the task is left to software; a computer designing a computer!

Bottom Line

Everything that we see on our computers, whether it be streaming video, or text chats, or e-mail, or websites, is the result of logical operations being performed by simple transistor-based circuits. These simple logic circuits are combined into complex arrangements by chip designers, and then manufactured using primarily NAND or NOR gates to increase the production yield.

The real estate, or available space, on a CPU chip is limited by the manufacturing processes used; the larger the chip is, the more likely something on it will fail during manufacture, and so there is an upper limit on the physical size of the chip. What has happened over the past 40 years, as embodied in Moore's Law, is that we have discovered how to shrink the size of individual transistors, which means that individual logic gates are also smaller, to the point where about every 18 months we can double the number of transistors on a chip of a given size. With more transistors come more gates, and with more gates come more complex operations that can be done in single steps on the CPU chip rather than having to do a sequence of steps for the same result.

The question facing chip manufacturers today is whether or not Moore's Law will continue to hold for the next 10 to 20 years; some indications are that we are reaching physical limits that will prevent us from manufacturing ever smaller transistors. For example Intel's core i7 chip uses what is known as a 14 nm process, which means that leads coming out of the individual transistors are only 14 nm (nanometers) wide. This is only 70 silicon atoms wide. Recent news from IBM indicates that they have developed a process that will reduce this size by a factor of four, so that the width of individual leads coming out of transistors will be on the order of 3 nm, or just 15 silicon atoms. Research is also being done in new materials and new manufacturing processes to see if Moore's Law can be extended into the next decade. At the end of the day, however, the internal workings of these very complex chips comes down to simple logical operations performed by tiny gates, operating on binary values.

Networking

AN INTRODUCTION

6

W hen writing software, whether it be an application, an operating system, or networking code, a common pattern is to write the software in a layered fashion. Software isn't the only layered item that we interact with. For example, there isn't one specific thing that is a car; rather it is made up of hundreds or even thousands of individual components, and each of those components does one thing and does it really well. It's the same with computer network software, there is no one "networking thing" in the computer; instead the network is made up of many smaller layers, and each of those layers does some specific task. This layered networking software is commonly called a *network stack*.

Another advantage to layering is that we can take a layer out and replace it with something else, and the layers above and below the replaced layer don't necessarily know that we've done anything at all.

The networks that we use have five layers, shown in Figure 6-1. You probably have heard of some of them: Ethernet, TCP/IP, and so on. The layers are arranged vertically, with the lowest layers handling very basic tasks, such as what sort of wire (or wireless signal) we are using to connect devices together, and how we will represent the binary ones and zeros that the computer needs to send and receive. The upper layers manage connections across the Internet and how applications such as your browser will use networked services. We'll look at each layer in turn, starting from the bottom, working our way up.

Protocols

Because each of the layers is independent of the others, and each has its own way of formatting data, moving bits around, and addressing, we need some common way for them to speak to one another. Also, you might buy an Ethernet card from any of hundreds of different manufacturers and it wouldn't make sense for each of them to have their own way of formatting bits, addressing, and sending and receiving. What we need is some standard way for all of these devices to communicate with one another.

FIGURE 6-1 The five layers of the network stack

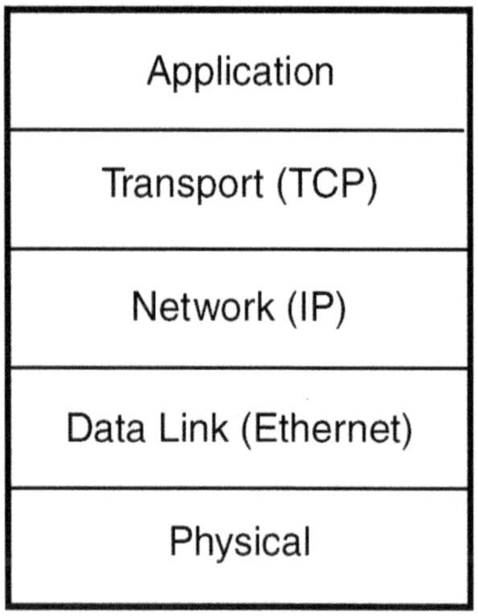

```
┌─────────────────────────────┐
│        Application          │
├─────────────────────────────┤
│      Transport (TCP)        │
├─────────────────────────────┤
│       Network (IP)          │
├─────────────────────────────┤
│    Data Link (Ethernet)     │
├─────────────────────────────┤
│         Physical            │
└─────────────────────────────┘
```

A *protocol* is a set of rules that allows network devices to talk to one another. Each layer in the network stack has its own set of protocols, and also a set of interfaces that allow the layers above and below to communicate with it. At the lowest levels of the stack the protocols are concerned about what exactly a one or a zero looks like; is it a pulse of voltage, a flash of light, a sound, or something else? As we move up the stack protocols are more involved in connecting computers together, for example the TCP and IP layers handle Internet connections. At the top of the stack applications use protocols to get access to network services.

You can think of a protocol as a common language that the devices and software in the layer share, or as being similar to the rules of a card game. At a poker tournament the players, even though they might never have met, all know and understand the rules of how to play poker and so are able to sit down and immediately start playing cards. So it is with protocols at each layer.

Protocols also include the inputs and outputs of a particular layer. Each computer or network device manufacturer might write their own software for the Ethernet layer, but each also follows the rules, including how to send data into the Ethernet layer and how to retrieve data from it.

For example, when you browse a web page your browser is in the application layer. It makes a request of the layer below it, TCP, to connect to a website. The TCP layer sends a request to the layer below it, IP, which figures out the address of the website that you're going to and then asks the layer below it, usually Ethernet, to transmit a message to your home router or access point. Finally, at the very bottom of the network stack, your website request goes out either a wire to the wall if you're using Ethernet, or wirelessly to an access point or router in your home or office, and then from there starts the process all over again to work its way across the Internet to the website.

As the data leaves your computer, it has to be encoded in some way so that the various devices that your message will be sent to can understand the difference between a one and a zero. Up until that point, the data is being managed inside the computer's software, which treats it as binary numbers. Once the data leaves the computer, though, what is a one and a zero are defined by the medium that is being used to connect to the rest of the network. If the cable coming out the back of the computer is fiber optic, ones and zeros will be encoded as pulses of light; if it is a wired Ethernet cable, they will be levels of electric voltage; wireless devices use radio signals for encoding. This encoding is the responsibility of the very bottom layer of the stack. Each of these has its own unique properties, which dictates how we encode the individual bits.

Wired Networks

The simplest way to connect two computers together is with a wire. Not just any wire, though; we use a special networking cable, designed to transmit and receive bits at high speeds. At the store you'll see these cables labeled Cat (for Category) 5, Cat 7, Cat 7e, and so on. The various categories are an indication of how how fast the cable has been designed to send and receive bits; generally speaking, the higher the category, the faster the cable is, and the more expensive it will be.

These cables, though designed specifically for networking, are not without their faults. One problem they exhibit is that they resist the flow of electricity through them, and this resistance increases the faster we send bits. This kind of resistance is known as *impedance*. Because impedance increases with speed, there's an upper limit on how fast we can send bits over this kind of wire.

Another problem with wire is that if you put two wires close together send data across them, the bits in one wire will induce a sort of ghost signal in the other wire, called *crosstalk*. If you've ever used an old style telephone, you might have experienced this firsthand. In these old-style systems, you would occasionally hear a faint voice behind your own conversation, induced on your circuit by a pair of wires nearby in the cable.

Twisting the wires together can provide some measure of shielding from this kind of crosstalk. Additionally, we can add physical shielding on the outside of the wire in the form of a metal sheath, often made of aluminum, which further reduces crosstalk. When the wires are twisted, and a shield is in place, the cable is called a *shielded twisted pair*.

Because of the impedance of the wire and its natural resistance to signals, and also to some extent crosstalk, the length of the wire also has an upper limit. As the wire gets longer and longer, the signal gets weaker and weaker, and at some point disappears altogether. Practically speaking this means that the length of the wires used to build a network are limited to a few hundred feet in most situations. We can build LANs that are larger than this by using devices such as switches and bridges, which receive a stream of bits on one side, clean up any noise or weakness, and send clean bits out the other side.

Encoding Data

There are many ways to encode ones and zeros on a wire. One simple method is to use the presence of voltage, often 5 volts (5V), to represent a one, and the absence of voltage, 0 volts (0V) to represent a zero as show in Figure 6-2.

This is not a bad scheme, and very simple systems can be built using it. One problem though is that if somebody plugs the wires in backwards, now we have a situation where 5V represents a zero, and 0V represents a one. Unfortunately we can't trust people to plug things in the right way 100% of the time!

We can take care of this problem by focusing not on the absolute voltage on the wire (either 0V or 5V) to represent a 1 or a 0, but instead looking at the *transition* at the beginning of each bit. So, if a zero is being sent we might say this is represented by a transition from one voltage to the other ... the two endpoints don't matter, it is just the transition that is of interest. For a one, the voltage remains steady. This approach, known as a *differential* signal,

FIGURE 6-2 A simple way to encode 0 and 1 using voltage

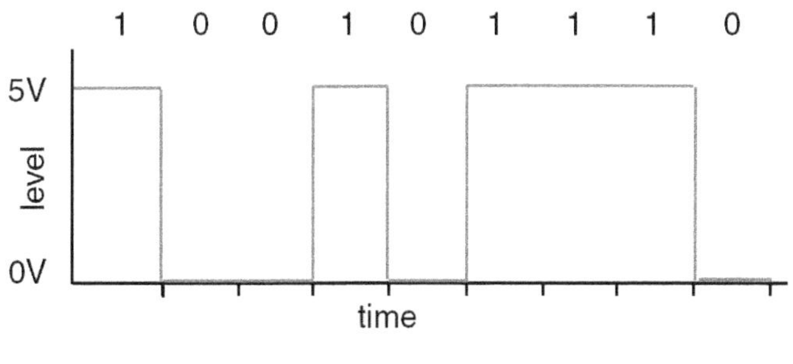

FIGURE 6-3   A differential encoding scheme

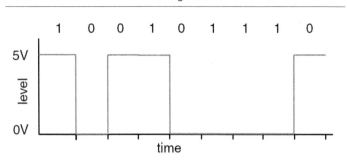

is shown in Figure 6-3. Notice that for the long series of ones, there is no transition.

Bits on a network are sent and received at a specific rate. For example, you might have a 100Mb (one hundred million bits) per second connection (100Mbps). That means that the bits are being sent at the rate of 100 million per second. But now we have a new problem! The rate of transmission and reception is being controlled by a clock. Every computer has at least one clock, and sometimes several clocks, built into it. These clocks are very precise within a given computer, but the clock in another computer might be slightly different. For example, the clock on the receiving side of a network connection might run a little fast or a little slow, just like the clocks in your kitchen or bedroom.

The challenge is that we are sending bits from a transmitter to a receiver at a very precise rate, but how does the receiver, where the clock is either a little slower or a little faster than the transmitter's, know exactly when a bit is starting? The differential protocol we came up with to solve the problem of a connector plugged in backwards creates a new problem … what if the transmitting network card is sending a long string of ones? According to our protocol, the absence of a transition from one voltage to another signals a one, but a long string of ones would result in no transitions *at all* on the wire for a period of time. If the clocks at the transmitter and receiver are drifting apart, at some point the receiver will get out of sync with the transmitter and will start missing bits.

To solve *this* problem, we can embed a clock signal along with the bits that we are sending and use it to synchronize the receiver's clock with the transmitter's. Figure 6-4 shows how this is done. You'll note that in the center of every bit is a transition *regardless* of whether a one or a zero is being sent. This transition gives a hard edge moving from one voltage to another, which is easy to detect on the receiving side. When the receiver sees that edge in the middle of the bit it uses the edge to adjust its clock slightly to match that of the transmitted clock. This method of embedding the clock along with the bit stream is known as *differential Manchester encoding*. The differential part just means that we're looking at transitions from one voltage to another, and not some specific value like 0V or 5V to represent a zero or one. The Manchester part is the clock being embedded in the bit stream. The transition scheme … a transition for a 0, none for a 1, remains the same.

FIGURE 6-4   Differential Manchester encoding

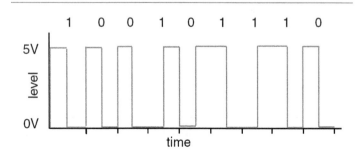

This very neatly solves the problem of somebody plugging the wires in backwards, and also the problem of clocks running faster or slower on either the transmitting or receiving end. But, of course, it introduces a new problem—the wire itself. You might recall that the impedance of a wire, that is, the resistance it presents to signal flowing through it, varies with the speed or frequency of the signal being sent. The higher the frequency of the signal, the higher the impedance and the more resistance the wire presents. When we talk about the frequency of a signal we are interested in the number of transitions the signal makes in one second. One transition per second is defined as one hertz, a unit named after Heinrich Hertz, a pioneer in electromagnetic wave theory.

Those extra transitions in the center of each bit, used for clock synchronization in Manchester encoding, effectively increase the number of transitions, or frequency, on the wire over that which would be normal just for sending ones and zeros. From the wire's perspective, it looks like we're sending a faster signal than we really are. You can see this yourself by comparing Figures 6-3 and 6-4. If we're sending 100 million bits per second (100Mbps) over the wire, the wire itself might see that as 120Mbps to 150Mbps because of all the extra transitions. As the frequency increases, so does the impedance exhibited by the wire.

This means that there's a practical upper limit, based on the physics of the wire, to how fast we can send bits across the network cable. It turns out that for normal twisted-pair networking cable this limit is around 250Mbps. The cable that you would use at home or in the office has eight wires grouped into four pairs, and each pair is twisted together. Each of those pairs can handle a 250Mbps data rate.

If a twisted pair can manage only 250Mbps, how is it that most computers have a "Gigabit Ethernet" port? One gigabit is 1 billion bits per second. The trick is to use all four pairs in the cable simultaneously; each has a rate of 250Mbps, and so the aggregate rate is 250 × 4 = 1,000Mbps or 1Gbps.

If you were to go to the store to buy networking cable, you would see that they offer different "categories" of performance (shortened to the word Cat); Cat 5, Cat 5e, Cat 7, and so on. The category is just an indicator of how fast the cable can go and how long the runs can be; higher-quality cables can sustain higher speeds and have longer runs. For home use, Cat 5 is typically just fine, and is a little less expensive than the higher-quality Cat 7.

Fiber-Optic Cable

We've seen how to define ones and zeros on a copper wire; for an Ethernet LAN we'll use Manchester encoding, a differential scheme where a transition from one voltage to another is a zero and no transition is a one at each bit time, and we also embed the clock in the center of each bit clocks to synchronize the transmitting and receiving computers.

Another way to connect computers together is with the fiber-optic cable. Optical fiber is extremely thin—think human hair—and is made of glass or very high-quality plastic. It has the property of transmitting light with very little loss. It also has a property of not being susceptible to crosstalk. Optical fiber is extremely lightweight, made of inexpensive materials, has little to no loss, and so allows us to have extremely long runs of cable connecting devices together. A typical cable bundling several fibers is shown in Figure 6-5.

FIGURE 6-5 Optical fibers bundled in a cable

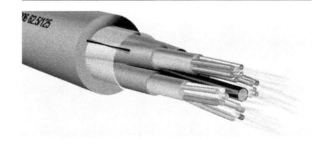

There are many ways to represent ones and zeros when using optical fiber. Sometimes it's just the presence of light or not: The light is on if there's a one, and a zero if the light is off. We can also use the frequency or color of the light to encode ones and zeros, and we can use coding schemes that combine colors or light to represent entire groups of bits.

When fiber was introduced 20 years ago, the hope was that all networks, including those at home, at the office, and the data center would be connected together with inexpensive, ultrafast fiber. This didn't happen, and today we still use copper for most networks at the more local levels such as in your home. However, some progress has been made in running fiber to the home or to the office; Verizon's FiOS, for example, provides high-speed Internet connectivity and cable television signals right to the home.

Part of the reason for the slow adoption at the consumer level is that connecting and maintaining fiber is somewhat specialized, so we couldn't expect regular consumers to be able to build and maintain complex home networks using fiber because it might be too difficult. At the same time, copper cables used on Ethernet have evolved; 20 years ago 10Mbps was just about all you could get for consumer use, and now most computers and most network equipment for the home come standard with 1Gbps Ethernet, 1000% faster. Copper twisted-pair Ethernet cables are also much easier to use. Most home and small-office networks are underutilized and so wouldn't benefit from faster, more expensive fiber.

Encoding with Audio Tones

Another way to encode binary information is to use audio tones. Do you remember the popular movie *You've Got Mail*? Several times in the movie Tom Hanks and Meg Ryan connect to their e-mail service on AOL. During the scenes you'll hear "BEEbop-BOOOOOObeeeebrzzzz." Those beeps and bops are an audio encoding of the ones and zeros being sent across the telephone line. This older-style networking, which some still use today, relies on the existing telephone network to send audio tones back and forth between two computers using a device called a *modem*. The word modem is a mash-up of modulator and demodulator; the transmitting side takes bits and converts them into a series of audio tones; this is the modulation part. On the receiving end the demodulator converts the audio tones back into bits and sends them up the network stack. Older modems such as the Hayes Smartmodem shown in Figure 6-6 measure transmission speed in baud (named after French telecommunication pioneer Jean-Maurice-Émile Baudot), which indicates how many symbols per second are being sent or received. It's also common to see speed measured in bits per second.

The telephone system was designed to carry voice conversations, and it doesn't work all that well for carrying binary data. A slightly more advanced version of the old dial-up system, called digital subscriber line or *DSL*, was introduced in the late 1990s; it used the unoccupied bandwidth of the

FIGURE 6-6 The Hayes 300 Smartmodem (1981)

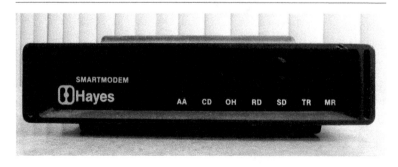

telephone line to send digital data, though it was still encoding the bits with audio tones. Old-style modems topped out at about 128,000 bits per second (128kbps), but DSL, as it had more bandwidth to work with, was able to send and receive at about 1 million bits per second (1Mbps). Quite a bit of the world, especially in rural areas, still uses DSL as it's often the only kind of networking available. In order to use both the voice part of the telephone line and the data part at the same time, a DSL filter is installed on each modem to separate the two.

Connecting Devices

A key concept in computer networking is that the devices on the network are connected directly to each other. Every time we send data across the network, that data is sent from one machine to the next, so that all connections are only between two devices. If we need to send a message to a computer that's on a different network or physically far away from where you are, the message is sent like a relay race, from one computer to the next to the next, to the next, and so on until it reaches its destination. We say that the network is made up of a series of *point-to-point connections*.

A point-to-point connection between two computers is fine if you're only ever going to send messages between those two computers. But what if I have three computers or five computers or 5,000 computers? How do I connect all of these devices together in such a way that they can all talk with each other? We need some sort of device that we can plug all of our computers into that can decide how to deliver messages to those individual computers.

Addressing

Another key concept of networks is that every device on the network needs to have a unique address. This makes sense, if you think about it. If two computers have the same address, how would the network know which one of the two to deliver a message to? This is very similar to street addresses. Imagine that a street with houses along it is the network. Each house on the street has a street address that uniquely identifies it on that street. Further, the street itself is part of a town, which is part of a state, which is part of a country, and all of these things uniquely identify that specific location on the planet with its address. It is just the same with computer networks; every device that sits on the network is similar to a house that sits on the street in that it must have a unique address.

In computer networking, each of the layers in the networking stack uses its own kind of address. Down at the bottom of the stack, which is what we're looking at right now, the addressing scheme is specified by Ethernet. Addresses are unique to each Ethernet card or interface that's attached to the computer. There are several more types of addresses in use as we move up and down the networking stack, and we'll examine several n the course of our discussion.

Local Area Networks

Most homes and offices these days have a network in them. When the network is physically close to you, and everything is connected together on it, we call it a local area network, or LAN. For example, you might have a printer, a laptop computer, maybe a desktop computer, a streaming device attached to your television; all of these are connected together and can talk to each other on the LAN. These small, local networks are designed for devices on them to speak with each other, and are isolated from the Internet. It isn't unusual to have a LAN that never connects to the Internet at all. This isn't to say that a device on a LAN can never access the Internet, in fact we do it all the time, but it takes a special gateway device to make that access possible.

The physical connection, be it wire, fiber, or wireless access on a network is really only part of the story in the lower layers. Once we've figured out a way to encode ones and zeros, we then need to figure out a way to format them so that both the sender and the receiver know when the start of the message is happening, what part of the message is the address, when the end of the message is, and so on. This is the responsibility of the second layer of the network stack, the data link layer. A good analogy is that in the first layer we developed the idea of an alphabet, and now in the second layer we need to define a common set of words.

Token Ring LANs

A fundamental problem of networks in the early days was that the physical network was made via a single piece of wire shared by multiple computers, printers, and other devices. If you had 50 computers all trying to send and receive messages at the same time, it could become chaotic quite quickly! Layer 2 protocols tried to address this by specifying a set of rules regarding which computer can send data at any given time. The goal is to provide fair access to a limited resource, which is the network.

There are two major ways to approach LANs: orderly and disorderly. One very orderly layer 2 LAN protocol is called Token Ring, which was introduced in the 1970s by IBM Corporation along with several of its partners.

Token Ring took the approach of only allowing one computer to send data at any given time. Devices were connected together in a ring structure, and access to the network was controlled by passing around a special piece of data called a token. The rule was simple: If you had the token you were allowed to send your traffic onto the network. In order to avoid one particular station having unlimited access to the network, essentially hogging the bandwidth, the token had a timer on it, typically around 100 ms. When a device received a token from its neighbor, it could start sending data up to the limit of the timer. Once the timer went off the device had to stop sending data and pass the token to the next to device in line. A Token Ring network is shown in Figure 6-7; the MAU is a Media Access Unit, and is where the network wires attach.

This kind of orderly process makes a lot of sense, since it provides for fair access to the network resources, and special rules can allow stations that have critical traffic to take control temporarily. Since only one station is

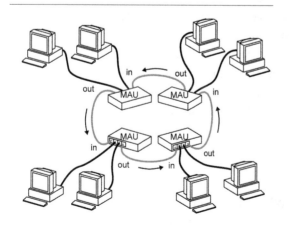

FIGURE 6-7   A Token Ring network

transmitting at a time, there's no chance that some other station will be transmitting and interfere with any other station's transmission.

Ethernet LANs

About the same time that the Token Ring was being developed, a rival technology was being designed by partners Digital Equipment Corporation, Xerox, and Intel. It was based on work done by Robert Metcalf at Xerox's Palo Alto Research Center (PARC). Bob had been given the task of placing a laser printer on the network so that everyone could access it. This was the original laser printer, and there were only one or two of them, so as you can imagine everybody wanted to use them. Rather than invent yet another protocol, Metcalf looked at work that had been done in the Hawaiian Islands for a network called ALOHA, which had been designed to solve a very interesting problem, somewhat unique to Hawaii. Researchers there wanted to be able to communicate on a computer network from island to island; however, there were no cables at the time or wires of any sort running between the islands.

ALOHA (which stood for Additive Links On-line Hawaii Area, an early example of a backronym) used radio signals to move data back and forth. Transmitters and receivers were set up on each island and a set of rules established to enable the exchange of digital traffic. The rule was simple: If you had traffic to send you would just send it. As you can imagine, this created a lot of chaos on the airways: As one station would start transmitting, another station on another island, perhaps not hearing the original station, would start transmitting its own data, and the two data streams would collide and interfere with each other, resulting in a garbled message. The protocol handled these inevitable collisions by specifying a rule that allowed for messages to be resent, sometimes several times, until they were successfully received.

Metcalf added an additional rule to the ALOHA protocol which stated that a computer that wanted to send data first had to listen to the network to see if any other station was sending data at that time. This was called *carrier sense*. Once the device started sending data, it would continue to listen for collisions on the network; this was called *collision detection*. If a collision was detected, the sending device would immediately stop sending, wait for a random period of time, and then start the process all over again. The full name of the protocol is Carrier Sense Multiple Access / Collision Detection (CSMA/CD).

One would think that a protocol in which devices listened before they spoke would result in something similar to Token Ring in which only one station would be transmitting at any particular time, since all of the others would hear a station sending data and not send their own until it was done. In practice, that was almost never the case. This kind of network, which Metcalf dubbed *Ethernet*, had so many collisions that about 40% of the activity on the network was taken up just by collisions, meaning that only 60% of the time data actually got through successfully! And that was on a good day.

The protocol acknowledges this by stating that if a device's transmission is garbled, and it has to try again, it will only do so 16 times before giving up completely. When that happens, it isn't the case that the message is just completely discarded; another message is sent up the network stack to the application that was originally trying to send the data indicating that there was a problem with the network and that the message should be resent.

FIGURE 6-8 An Ethernet LAN

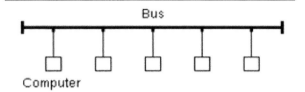

In essence, the lower-level layer is telling the upper-level layer that *it* needs to take care of the problem. An Ethernet network is shown in Figure 6-8. This configuration is an early network; the Ethernet cable is arranged in a line as a bus, and computers using the network connect directly to it.

Comparing the Two

Ethernet and Token Ring were introduced around the same time. They took radically different approaches; IBM's Token Ring was designed to work in offices by using existing telephone wiring. The idea was that each office had excess capacity in its walls for telephones, and the network could take advantage of that by using those unused wires to form a network. Ethernet, on the other hand, required businesses to completely rewire their buildings for this new network, using thick, hard-to-work-with coaxial cable. The cable was difficult to bend, it was difficult to attach to devices, it was difficult to maintain. However, because it used special cabling, rather than phone wires, Ethernet was able to transmit data faster than Token Ring.

Ethernet won the marketing battle between the two companies, and it really was more of a marketing battle than a technical one. IBM's Token Ring topped out at about 4Mbps using existing telephone wires; Ethernet advertised maximum speeds of 10Mbps. The reality, however, was that Token Ring was almost 100% efficient in how it sent data on the network; since only one device could send data at any given time, that device had complete access to the network, and there were no collisions to have to deal with. That lack of collisions meant that when data was being sent it was almost always being received properly, and so there were no repeats. Because it was an orderly process, moving a token from one station to the next, to the next, and so on, the network achieved almost 100% utilization.

Ethernet, on the other hand, even though it advertised a 10Mbps maximum transmission speed, spent most of its time in collisions. About half of the time, data was being collided with and had to be repeated. The effective throughput of the network was around 50%, which works out to 5Mbps, very close to the maximum speed that a Token Ring network could go. It really became a business decision; would a company rather use existing phone lines, saving cabling costs but limiting the possibility of future speed increases, or spend the money to refit an office with special cable for Ethernet? Token Ring was the superior technology, but the original design decision to use existing infrastructure, meaning the telephone wires already in the wall, limited its usefulness.

Framing the Bits

One of the major tasks of Layer 2 protocols like Ethernet is to organize bits into a standard format, including a way to add addresses to the data. Figure 6-9 shows an Ethernet frame. The term *frame* just means the way that the bits are organized; which bit positions are addresses, which are data, and which positions include information about the frame

FIGURE 6-9   An Ethernet frame

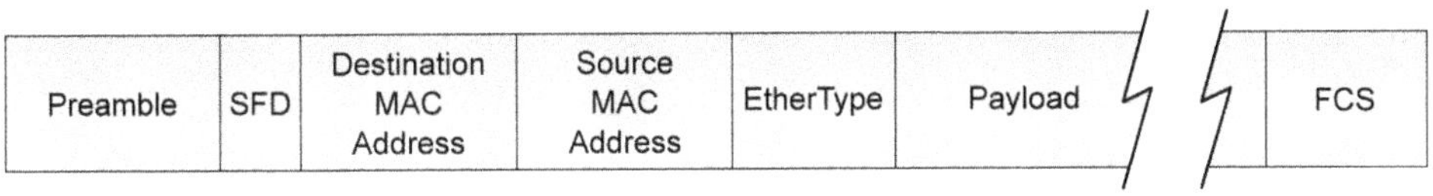

Preamble	SFD	Destination MAC Address	Source MAC Address	EtherType	Payload		FCS

itself. As you can see, the protocol is extremely simple, consisting mainly of two addresses (a To and From address) and the data itself.

The first eight bytes (64 bits) of the frame is a preamble; alternating ones and zeros, which, in Manchester encoding provides plenty of transitions between low and high voltage, used to synchronize the receiving clock. A Start of Frame Delimiter (SFD) signals that the preamble is complete, and the next byte will be the beginning of the frame.

After the SFD, the first 48 bits on the network are the destination address, i.e., where this message is going to. This is followed by a 48-bit source address, or where the message came from. Next are a few bytes of metadata, or information about the data, that indicate the version of the protocol being used, what's inside the data itself, and a few other items of interest. This is followed by about 1500 bytes of data in the payload, and finally some error-correcting code in the Frame Check Sequence (FCS) that allows the receiving device to determine whether or not the message was received correctly. 1500 bytes doesn't sound like a lot, and in some cases it isn't; if the message from the application layer, say a web page, or streaming video, is larger than that, then multiple Ethernet frames are sent across the network.

While it would certainly be possible to construct and read these frames in software, as Ethernet speeds increased from 10Mbps to 100Mbps, and then 1Gbps and beyond, it became more efficient to handle the processing of each frame in specialized hardware. Special chips built into Ethernet network cards or into the main board of a computer or other device handle all of the processing for each Ethernet frame.

Comparing Ethernet and Token Ring Frames

The Ethernet frame is extremely simple. The corresponding Token Ring frame is, too, and if you think about it they really have to be. At this lower level of the networking stack, with bits coming in and out of the machine at 1 billion bits per second, if the protocol was complicated it would significantly slow down network traffic. Each of these lower-level protocols, whether it be Ethernet or Token Ring or something else, uses only enough complication to get the job done and no more. Look at the Token Ring frame in Figure 6-10. You'll see that it is almost identical to an Ethernet frame; really there's just a to and from address, the data itself, and a little bit of error checking and metadata about what is inside the frame. We'll see this repeated as we work our way up the stack, into the Internet layers and even into the application layer.

FIGURE 6-10   A Token Ring frame

Start Delimiter	Control	Dest Addr	Source Addr	Data	Frame Check	End Delimiter

Like many areas in computer science, what we perceive as complex systems are really just many very simple systems working together.

Connecting Devices Together

Local area networks today are almost entirely made up of Ethernet devices. Any laptop or desktop computer that you purchase will include an Ethernet port on the back, or a wireless Ethernet chip embedded in it. In a wired network, all of the wires coming out of all of the computers need to attach to something; in this kind of LAN that device is called a *switch*. As you can see in Figure 6-11, a switch has dozens of ports to connect Ethernet cables to. The switch itself handles the task of determining how to deliver a message on the LAN; it does this by examining the destination (the To:) address in the header of each Ethernet frame and then looking at its ports to see where the device with that address is attached.

An interesting thing about switches is that internally they must run many times faster than the Ethernet itself is running. Let's say that you have ten devices attached to the switch, and each of those devices is running at 100Mbps. In the worst case for the switch, five of those devices are transmitting data to five of the other devices. In other words, there are five simultaneous connections occurring through the switch. In order to maintain the full 100Mbps throughput for each of the five connections, the switch itself has to run five times that speed, or 500Mbps. This internal network inside the switch is called the *switching fabric*, and the faster the fabric has to go, the more difficult and expensive it is to manufacture. This is why switches with a very large number of ports, or extremely high-speed, or both, are also very expensive.

In a wireless network, the switch is replaced by an access point. It serves the same purpose, except that instead of wires connecting each device on the LAN, wireless radio signals handle the task. The access point accomplishes the same job of delivering messages based on the destination address as the switch does.

One big advantage of a switch over older-style Ethernet networking is that in a switch each connection is between only two devices, a sender and a receiver. Old-style Ethernet networks relied on a single cable that all of the LAN devices attached to, and so when one device wanted to send data the chances were good that some other device was sending at the same time. Collisions were frequent, and the overall throughput of the network was decreased because of all the time spent resending data and receiving garbled messages. The switch, on the other hand, connects two devices directly with each other through the switch. This means that the chance of a collision is almost zero. As a result, switches allow Ethernet networks to run at almost their full rated speed.

FIGURE 6-11 A typical Ethernet switch

Switches definitely offer many advantages to a network designer; however, there are still limits. For example, the number of ports is limited because of the difficulty of providing fabric that runs fast enough to support all of the devices utilizing the switch simultaneously.

Designers get around this by stacking one switch on top of another. For example, two eight-port switches can be connected together to form what looks to the network like a single 16-port switch.

What about Wireless?

Wireless networks such as the one you might run in your home or connect to at school use radios rather than wires to communicate with each other. These radios operate not that much differently from the one you might use to tune in to the latest beach music on your portable AM/FM radio when you go on holiday. The transmitters operate in a special part of the radio frequency spectrum called the industrial, scientific, and medical (ISM) spectrum. This part of the radio spectrum was set aside in the United States by the FCC, and internationally by International Telecommunications Union, to allow for low-power devices in industries such as medicine and consumer electronics to operate without a license.

In most countries, operating a transmitter requires a license from a government agency. Here in the United States, broadcast radio stations must apply for, and pay for, a license to operate the transmitter from the Federal Communications Commission (FCC). When consumer devices such as microwave ovens, baby monitors, and garage-door openers became popular, it quickly became clear that it didn't make sense to require every consumer to purchase or apply for a license for all of their cordless devices. And so, small chunks of unlicensed radio frequency spectrum were set aside just for this purpose. Devices using these frequencies are restricted to a very small amount of power so that their signal does not extend more than a few hundred meters.

Unfortunately, the ISM spectrum is used by just about every cordless device you can imagine. Your microwave oven, for example, operates on the same set of frequencies as does your wireless router at home. In fact, it wasn't uncommon in the early days of wireless for your network to completely stop working when you ran your microwave, because they interfered with each other. Baby monitors, cordless phones, cameras, garage-door openers, and more all use the ISM spectrum. Many discovered to their horror (or delight) that their cordless phone could easily pick up signals from the neighbor's baby monitor!

FIGURE 6-12   Hedy Lamarr in 1944

This potential for massive interference among dozens of consumer devices all using radios on the same set of frequencies meant that some other way of communicating over those frequencies was necessary. As it turns out, a technology already existed, and had been in use since the Second World War. Invented by film star Hedy Lamarr (Figure 6-12) and composer George Anthiel, the system, called frequency hopping, was adapted for use by wireless networks and other devices that needed to operate on these ISM frequencies.

The problem that Hedy and her friends was trying to solve was that in World War II when Allied ships would speak to each other over radio frequencies, enemy subs would surface and listen to the conversations, break codes if they could, or jam the communication entirely. Hedy got the idea of giving each ship radio operator a small booklet with a set of frequencies that were listed in a random order, organized by minutes of the hour. The radio operator would open the book to the given day and the time of transmission, and every 10 seconds or so change the channel on his transmitter to correspond to what was listed in the book.

On the receiving side the radio operator had the same book and would so follow the same set of frequencies. So for example, the transmission might go from Channel 4 to Channel 2, then Channels 9, 1, 3, and 8. Enemy subs would only hear small snippets of conversation, most likely encoded, and would have difficulty not only following them but decoding the message since many pieces would be missing. Jamming was similarly difficult.

This is exactly the technique that wireless devices on wireless networks use. Called frequency hopping, the WiFi standards specify a set of channel-hopping sequences that are performed thousands of time each second. Each device follows the same sequence according to the set of protocols that it is running, and because all are using the same set, they can communicate with one another. The set used by your microwave is different than the set used by your wireless access point, and so the two don't interfere. Even if they do appear on the same channel, it is for such a brief period of time, that the interference is minimal. In fact, if you were to listen across all of these channels with a broadband radio you would most likely hear just what appeared to be a soft static hiss.

There are many wireless protocols in use, almost all of them falling under the 802.11 specification. You probably have seen these at the store on boxes that are labeled with numbers such as 802.11b, 802.11z, 802.11bg, and so on. The numbers just indicate which protocols the device can use, and it's common now for wireless devices to be able to speak to all of these protocols so that they are compatible with one another. It used to be that you had to build wireless networks using devices that all used the same protocol, but these days you can just buy any commercial devices off the shelf and they all should work together. Figure 6-13 shows a typical model of wireless access point that includes a router.

FIGURE 6-13   A common wireless access point and router

From a networking standpoint, Ethernet LANs operate very similarly whether they are wired or wireless. In most cases, especially for home networks, the wireless access point includes a routing function that is typically provided by a separate device in wired networks. Wireless LANs have become so simple to set up that a large majority of new installations are strictly wire-free. We are even starting to see automobiles come standard with their own wireless networks!

Bluetooth

Bluetooth is ubiquitous. You probably have several devices on you right now that use the Bluetooth protocol. Is it a network? It is a LAN? The short answer is: yes and no. Bluetooth was originally designed to replace the wires running from keyboards and mice to your computer. It was intended to be a low-speed protocol that strictly was for connecting peripherals to computers. The protocol was named for the Scandinavian King Harald

Bluetooth (c. 970 CE) and the symbol for Bluetooth, shown in Figure 6-14, is derived from the runes representing Harald's initials.

FIGURE 6-14   Bluetooth logo featuring King Harald's runes

Bluetooth devices, like other wireless devices, use radios to send and receive data in a frequency-hopping scheme. However these radios are extremely low-power, which significantly limits the range of each device. While an 802.11n access point signal might span an entire floor of a building, Bluetooth devices typically only have a range of 10 to 15 feet. Even within this limited range, however, it's possible to send and receive a large variety of data; we might use Bluetooth devices to stream music, act as a microphone and speaker for our phone, send photos back and forth, or even control other devices. The practical differences between Bluetooth and 802-style wireless networking really is just the range and the speed offered by each.

Other Protocols

LAN protocols aren't limited to just electricity, light, and radio waves. In the past we've seen networks built out of technologies such as infrared, which uses pulses of infrared light to encode ones and zeros in a local area, usually a single room. Work is currently being done on ways to use smart LED lightbulbs to create LANs; the idea is that the lightbulb can flash on and off to encode ones and zeros, but so quickly that humans don't even notice the flicker. Similar to infrared networks, a light-based network such as this would be limited to the line of sight for the device being used; so if you can't see the lightbulb, you're not going to be able to use that network. On an even smaller scale work is being done to use the galvanic response of skin to create the kind of a network in which data can be sent across the surface of a person's body; this is often called a Personal Area Network (PAN).

Leaving the LAN

A local network is only useful to a point. While it's convenient to be able to communicate among devices in a room or on the floor of the building or even in a large office building, at some point we want to send and receive messages to and from outside of our local area. We would like to visit websites, place videoconferencing calls, get data from remote sites, and many other things. In order to accomplish this we have to have some way for the data to leave our local area network and go out into the Internet. The answer, of course, is to use additional protocols in upper-level layers and additional devices to move data from the local area out into the world.

Bottom Line

The bottom two layers of the network stack implement protocols that allow us to encode bits to be placed on the network. In some cases the encoding is done with electricity, such as that used on a wired Ethernet; sometimes it is with radio signals on a WiFi network, and other times it might be light signals. All of these protocols have one thing in common:

They must be as efficient as possible because data is being sent and received so quickly that anything complicated would slow things down.

In addition to determining how a one or a zero is encoded on the device, low-level protocols provide fair access to the network medium, and they also provide for local device addressing. On the network, just like on a city street, addresses are unique. This allows the networking devices to easily determine where a message should be delivered, and where it came from. The networks that we commonly interact with at the LAN level are almost all running the Ethernet protocol, whether it be wired or wireless.

Regardless of the protocol being used, each connection across the network is between two individual devices; this means that if we need to send a message to a remote device, it is relayed from one device to another until it gets to its final destination.

Figure Credits

- **Fig. 6.5:** Copyright © Srleffler (CC-BY-SA 3.0) at https://commons.wikimedia.org/wiki/File%3AOptical_breakout_cable.jpg.
- **Fig. 6.6:** Copyright © Michael Pereckas (CC BY-SA 2.0) at https://commons.wikimedia.org/wiki/File%3A-Hayes_300_Baud_Smartmodem_02.jpg.
- **Fig. 6.7:** Copyright © Andrew28913 (CC BY-SA 3.0) at https://commons.wikimedia.org/wiki/File%3ATo-ken_ring.svg.
- **Fig. 6.8:** Copyright © Tomateus (CC BY-SA 3.0) at https://commons.wikimedia.org/wiki/File%3ABusto-pologie.png.
- **Fig. 6.9:** Source: https://commons.wikimedia.org/wiki/File%3AEthernet_frame.svg.
- **Fig. 6.11:** Copyright © Geek2003 (CC BY-SA 3.0) at https://commons.wikimedia.org/wiki/File%3A2550T-PWR-Front.jpg.
- **Fig. 6.12:** Source: https://commons.wikimedia.org/wiki/File%3AHedy_Lamarr_Publicity_Photo_for_The_Heavenly_Body_1944.jpg.
- **Fig. 6.13:** Source: https://commons.wikimedia.org/wiki/File%3ALinksys-Wireless-G-Router.jpg.
- **Fig. 6.14:** Source: https://commons.wikimedia.org/wiki/File%3ABluetoothLogo.svg.

Networking

THE INTERNET

A local area network, or LAN, connects devices that typically are physically close to each other. This might be a group of computers in an office; your laptop, desktop, and printer in your dorm room; or even devices that are connected to a network on a bus traveling down the road. LANs are useful for moving ones and zeros short distances. In the early days of computing, the local network was all that existed. Machines and devices, often simple terminals, were connected together to form a computing network that was contained within a building, or a small portion of a campus. If you wanted to send data to another LAN, you would use a dial-up connection to send the data over normal telephone lines. Remember the *bee-doop-BEESH* sound in the movie *You've Got Mail*? That was a modem connecting.

We still use local area networks every day, but what if we want to go beyond the LAN? Maybe you want to send an instant message to a friend in another country, or send an e-mail home to your mom, or browse a website that your friend told you about. To make this sort of connection, we'll need to move up a layer or two in the network stack and examine the protocols that make up the Internet.

Three Ways to Connect

Generally speaking, there are three ways to connect computers together so that they can exchange information. The simplest way is to run a wire between the two, and send data back and forth between them. Adding a third computer to this simple network is quite easy; all we have to do is run a wire from the new computer to each of the other two computers. In this way each computer is connected to every other computer in the network. Figure 7-1 is an example.

This works surprisingly well for a small number of devices that want to exchange data, but what if we have hundreds or thousands of computers scattered all over a large area and we want them to talk to each other? With this method we would have to run a wire from each device to each other device, so that each computer would have hundreds or thousands

FIGURE 7-1   Three computers directly connected in a network

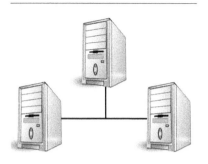

FIGURE 7-2   A fully connected network of six computers

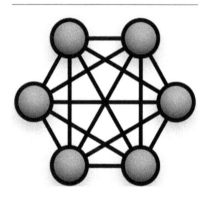

FIGURE 7-3   A telephone switchboard at USAF SAC HQ, 1967

of wires coming out the back running to all of the various machines in the network. As you can imagine this gets very messy very quickly. This form of connection is called a mesh network, sometimes known as a fully connected network, as shown in Figure 7-2. Here there are only six devices represented, and you can see that the number of connections has risen dramatically. In this kind of network the number of connections is governed by the equation

$$connections = n(n - 1) / 2$$

so for six devices, we have 6 (6 − 1) / 2 = 15 connections. For only 100 devices, the number jumps to 100 (100 − 9) / 2 = 4,950 connections! Clearly this is not a practical way to build a large network.

Another way to connect computers together is to replace the wires that would run from each device to all of the other devices, as in a fully connected network, with a central connection point. This is the way that the old telephone systems worked (Figure 7-3). When you wanted to make a call, you would pick up your handset, dial the operator (who seemed to always be named Mabel or Blanche), and ask her to connect you with the number that you wanted to talk with. Blanche would make a physical connection between your phone line and the phone that you wanted to speak to by connecting a patch cord between sockets that represented the ends of each phone line. The telephone switchboard in this case was the central connection point.

This kind of networking is called *circuit switching*. In the case of the telephone network, the devices were of course telephones, and when the connection was made the operator would send a special signal to the receiving telephone to cause it to ring, indicating that you wanted to speak to somebody.

When a circuit-switched connection is made we say that it has been *nailed up*, in reference to the telegraph systems of the late 1800s and early 1900s. In those days, when people wanted to be able to send messages between two adjacent towns, a worker would ride down the road on a horse, climb a tree, and string a wire between the two towns. That wire was then available to send messages back and forth. The circuit was "nailed up" because the worker literally nailed the wire to the tree or pole or whatever was handy to get it off of the ground.

Circuit switching has a lot of advantages. One advantage of this kind of network is that it is very easy to characterize the properties of the connection. Since the circuit is always up, we can analyze it for things like noise, or delay, or crosstalk, or any other sort of information that we are interested in. Another advantage, and this might seem obvious, is that messages that are sent will arrive in the same order. If, for example, we send A, B, C on the network, on the receiving side we will see A, B, C.

There's one distinct disadvantage to a circuit-switched network: It is nailed up. This means that when a connection is made between two devices, it remains connected even if no data is being exchanged. To revisit the telephone system analogy this would be like calling your friend up on the telephone, realizing that you had something burning on the stove, and asking the friend to hold on for a minute while you run to the kitchen to attend to it. During the time that you are away, the circuit is still occupied, even though you are not talking, and that means that no one else can use that circuit through the switchboard. A circuit-switched network is quite similar to a fully connected network, the difference being that in the fully connected network the connections are permanent.

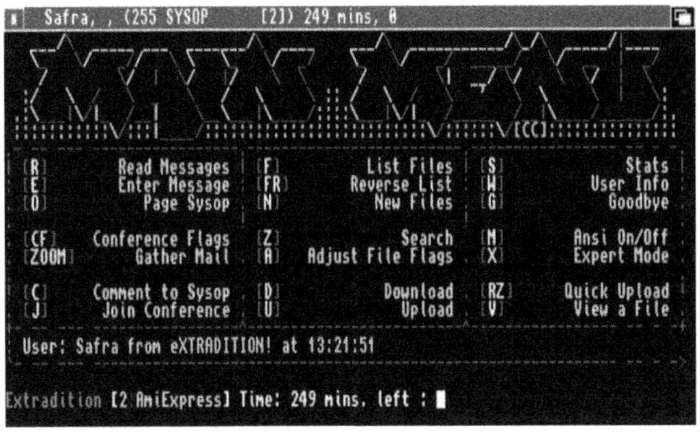

Circuit switching like this was quite common in the pre-Internet days of dial-up bulletin board systems and services such as AOL (Figure 7-4). Those old enough can remember the frustration of wanting to make a call while a family member was online, or the agony of losing your connection when the phone rang.

FIGURE 7-4   A typical early dial-up bulletin board service (BBS)

Packet Switching

A third way of connecting devices across a large area is very similar to sending a series of postcards through the post office. Let's say that you wanted to send a letter to a friend across the country. Rather than writing the entire message on one sheet of paper, you instead would write one sentence on one postcard, the next sentence on another postcard, and so on, until your entire message had been written onto a series of postcards. You would address each postcard to your friend, and then drive around town and drop your postcards into random postboxes on the street.

At some point during the day, each postbox would be visited by a postman, who would pick up some of your postcards and take them to a central sorting facility. Because you drove all over town, that central sorting facility might not be the same as one that another postman took other cards to.

At the local sorting facility, postcards that could not be delivered locally would be gathered together and sent to a larger sorting facility that served several smaller sorting facilities. For example, all of the post office sorting facilities in a town might send their nonlocal postcards to a single sorting facility that serves the entire state. Since your letter is going all the way across the country, your postcards would probably end up in a very large sorting facility that served a region of the country, and from there they would travel to a similar facility on the other side of the country, at which point the reverse process would begin of sorting the postcards back into regional groups, and then city-based groups, and finally down to a local post office that would deliver them.

This might seem like a really inefficient way to send a letter, and there are several significant disadvantages. One is that because you are dropping your postcards off at several different locations around town, there's absolutely no guarantee that once the postcards reach a sorting facility they will be in the correct order. In fact, because each postcard has the potential of taking a different route through the postal system, they probably will arrive at your friend's house completely out of order, possibly not even on the same day. Your friend will have to put them all back together into the correct sequence in order to read the message. Even worse, what happens if there's a hole in the bag that a postman uses and one of your postcards falls out? Or maybe one gets stuck in a sorting machine, or even is sent to the wrong address. Now your friend not only has to reassemble the message from individual postcards, she has to deal with the missing parts of the message.

To fix this kind of problem, it would be wise to number each postcard. For example, if you had 100 postcards containing your message, you could label the first one 1 of 100, the second one 2 of 100, and so on until the last one, which would be labeled 100 of 100. That way when your friend received all the postcards it would be simpler to put them all back together into sequence. And, if one was missing it would be easy to either phone you up or send another postcard back to you. If one of the postcards was missing, it would be obvious, and your friend could send you a postcard back requesting the missing part of the message.

This is clearly a really complicated way of sending messages, and there are many disadvantages to it. The biggest is that we just aren't guaranteed that a particular message will get through to the destination in one piece. On the receiving side, there's work involved in reassembling a message from its parts back into the original, and we also have to deal with missing parts of the message itself. This kind of connection is called *packet switching*, and despite its many disadvantages, this is the way that the Internet is connected together. All of the disadvantages are outweighed by one very large advantage: there are no nailed-up circuits.

To use the telephone switchboard analogy, in packet switching the wire that the operator uses to connect you and your friend's phones can be reused when you pause between words. If there's a pause in the conversation, the operator simply uses that physical wire to connect two other telephones until there's a pause on that circuit, and then connects another set and so on. This lets us put together a network with fewer physical connections than we might otherwise need, and that are utilized very efficiently. Each digital message going through them is extremely short, just a few thousand bytes, and they move very quickly.

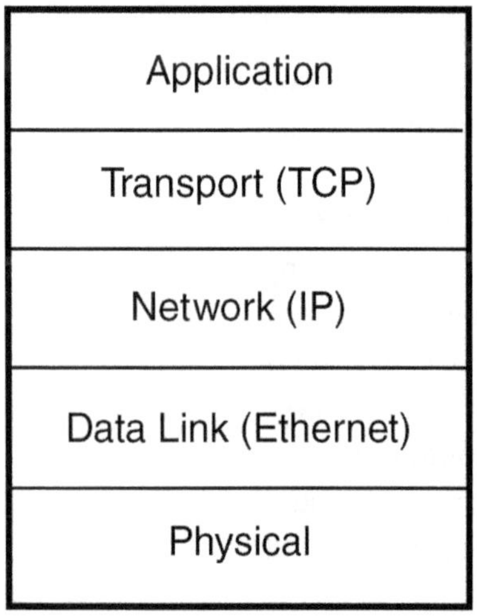

The task of breaking a long message into very small pieces, numbering them, keeping track of those that are received, reassembling them into the correct order, looking for missing messages, and so on are taken up by two layers in our network stack: TCP and IP. You probably have heard these referred to together as simply TCP/IP. TCP stands for Transmission Control Protocol, and IP stands for Internet Protocol. TCP and IP are in the middle layers of the network stack, shown in Figure 7-5. We'll look at each of these in turn, mainly from a perspective of how they get messages from one spot to another.

FIGURE 7-5   The network stack

| Application |
| Transport (TCP) |
| Network (IP) |
| Data Link (Ethernet) |
| Physical |

Internet Addresses

On a local area network, devices are typically connected together with the Ethernet. This might be wired or wireless, but in both cases each device has a unique Ethernet address on the network. Remember, it's important for each device to have its own unique address, so that when a message is being delivered, it's clear where it should go to. If there were two houses on the street that had the same address, the postman wouldn't know which house a particular letter was going to, and it is just the same in a network.

We also use addresses on the Internet, and they're different from the Ethernet addresses that individual devices use on the local area network but serve a similar purpose. Just as in a local area network, each device on the Internet has a unique IP address. There is an exception to this rule, and we will look at that in a bit, but generally speaking each has a unique address.

You probably have seen IP addresses in the past; they consist of four decimal numbers separated by periods. An example would be 192.168.14.42. This kind of notation for an address is strictly a convenience for humans; from the computer's perspective an address consists entirely of ones and zeros. An IP address is a 32-bit binary number; that is, it consists of a sequence of 32 ones and zeros. How many Internet addresses are there? Since we're dealing with binary numbers, the answer is 2^{32}, or roughly 4 billion.

You would think that 4 billion addresses would be plenty to give each computer in the world its own unique address, but it turns out that is hardly adequate. In fact, many countries are running out of Internet addresses, which means that we have to come up with some better solution. North America ran out of large address blocks in 2015 (though it still can allocate small sets of addresses), and Africa is on track to run out in 2018.

There are actually two solutions to this problem. The first is a new Internet address protocol called IP version 6, or IPv6. In this new version, addresses are 128 bits long, which means that there are 2^{128} or approximately 3.4×10^{38} (340 undecillion or 340,282,366, 920,938,463,463,374,607,431,768,211,456) possible unique addresses. This is an extremely large number; it is enough addresses to assign each atom on the surface of the earth an IP address and still have enough left over to do another 100 Earths!

IPv6 is a great solution, and it offers many more new features than simply an increased address space. You would think that it would be ubiquitous at this point—why wait?—but the reality is that adoption of the protocol has been extremely slow. Introduced in 2001, for many years it was restricted to universities and other research facilities. Adoption by consumer devices is still very sluggish, although some progress has been made. The problem is that there are so many devices currently running the older version of the protocol, from older personal computers to high-level Internet infrastructure, that it would be prohibitively expensive to just replace everything. And so, IP version 6 was designed to be backward compatible with the older version, IPv4, meaning that as new devices are manufactured and deployed, running the new protocol, they will still work with older devices. At some point the roll-out will be complete, and every new device will ship with IPv6.

The second solution is called Network Address Translation.

FIGURE 7-6 Network address translation (NAT)

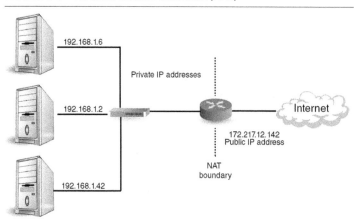

Network Address Translation (NAT)

One reason for the slow adoption of IPv6 is that around the same time as it was being released, a new technique for preserving Internet addresses was developed and deployed widely. Called *Network Address Translation* (NAT), it is a way to create "hidden" networks that are not visible to the Internet as a whole, but can still access the Internet through a special device called the network address translation bridge. This bridge has two sides; one side faces the Internet and has a public IP address. The other side faces the hidden network and has an address on the hidden, local IP network. When a device on the network wants to access the Internet, it asks the network address translation bridge for assistance, and the NAT bridge/request to the Internet. When the response comes back, it is then forwarded to the device that made the original request. We say that the bridge acts as a proxy—it performs requests on behalf of another device. You can see this in action in Figure 7-6.

There are three groups of private IP addresses used for NAT; together they comprise nearly 18 million addresses. Most large companies, as well as most consumer, home-based networks, use private IP networks behind NAT routers.

Many of the consumer networking devices that you might buy off-the-shelf implement network address translation, which means that there are literally hundreds of millions of devices sitting on hidden networks at home, offices, and schools. This is taking a lot of pressure off of IPv4, because it allows us to preserve IPv4 network addresses. Nevertheless, the future of the Internet is IPv6, and we hope that as years go by we will see more and more networks switching completely to the new protocol.

Routers

Just as we can build local area networks with Ethernet switches, there's a device that is used to connect the Internet (IP) layer together. These devices, called *routers*, connect smaller networks together into larger networks. Take a look at Figure 7-7. Here we have one router which has three smaller networks attached to it. Each of the smaller networks is self-contained, in that each is a local area network (LAN) unto itself. To send a message from LAN 1 of this network to LAN 3, the message is first passed to the router, which determines if it can deliver the message to one of the networks that it is directly attached to. If it can, it will send its message to the switch on the second network for delivery. Routers can have many smaller networks attached to them.

FIGURE 7-7 A router with three subnetworks

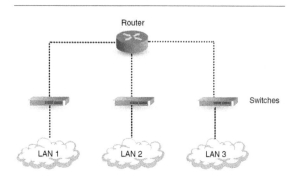

FIGURE 7-8   Multiple routers in a hierarchy

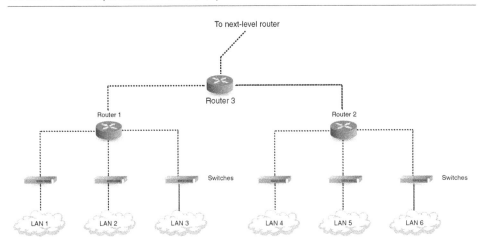

As shown in Figure 7-8, we can set up a router that is connected to other routers. In this diagram, Router 1 is responsible for three subnetworks (subnets), and Router 2 has another three subnets. When a message is sent from LAN 1 to LAN 5, Router 1, examines all of the networks that are directly attached to it and decides whether or not it can deliver this message. Since this message is going to LAN 5, and LAN 5 is connected to another router, Router 1 can't deliver the message directly and so sends it to the next-higher router in the network hierarchy, Router 3.

This upper-level router directly connects Routers 1 and 2, effectively aggregating all of the smaller LANs that are attached to both of the lower-level routers. Router 3 receives the message from Router 1 and looks at its own connections to see if LAN 5 is directly attached to it. It doesn't have a direct connection to network, but Router 2 does, and Router 3 is connected to Router 2; the message is passed down to Router 2. Upon receiving the message, Router 2 looks at its directly connected networks, sees that LAN 5 is directly attached, and passes the message to the switch implementing LAN 5.

Practically speaking, those smaller networks are Ethernet LANs built out of switches. The routers are specially built devices that are designed to handle large volumes of traffic very efficiently. The basic structure of the Internet is a tree of routers, with low-level routers handling small networks, and higher-level routers managing the flow of messages across those networks.

At the lowest level we have local area networks, connected through their switches to routers. Those local routers are connected to larger routers that aggregate multiple lower-level routers, and those routers are connected to even larger routers. As we work our way up the tree the number of smaller networks and routers that are aggregated grows larger and larger, so we get to the very top of the Internet. At this top level extremely large amounts of traffic are passed between very fast, very efficient machines that handle the backbone of the Internet. There aren't a lot of these machines, and in some cases a country might only have a small handful of them. These backbone routers typically use fiber-optic connections between themselves and run special high-speed protocols to move traffic around the world efficiently. There are currently six multinational telecommunication entities that make up the top level of the Internet: Level 3 Communications, Telia Carrier, NTT, Cogent, GTT, and Tata Communications.

The messages being sent between the mid-level and lower-level routers are packet-switched. This means that larger messages are broken up into smaller pieces and sent along various routes across the network; we don't necessarily know at any given moment which part of which messages are being passed through any particular router. One important advantage of this scheme is that if one router becomes congested or breaks down, messages can flow through a different router until the first one is back in service. There's an old joke that the Internet sees censorship as an error and routes around it; this is in some cases quite true, and certainly any time there's a problem in the network, packet switching means that a new route can be found to bypass the problem until it is resolved. To manage this, routers at all levels constantly send messages to each other describing the networks and routers that they know about, essentially building a fresh map of the Internet every few seconds.

Each time you click a link on a web page, send an e-mail or IM, or really anything that involves the network, your message moves from router to router, working its way up the hierarchical tree, and at some point moves down through the tree until it reaches its destination. We call each connection a hop, and you can use the command line tool `traceroute` (`tracert` on Windows) to see each hop. Figure 7-9 shows a sample trace from Boston to Universal Hub's servers. Each numbered line is a hop; hops marked with asterisks (*) are routers that are configured to not report their IP address or name. It's often possible to make an educated guess about where a particular router is physically located by its name; for example, b3332.bstnma-lcr-22.verizon-gni.net is likely located somewhere in Boston, on Verizon's network.

The times displayed to the right of each hop is the round-trip time it takes to communicate with the router on that hop. Hop 6 to Newark takes 14.816 milliseconds, 7.4 ms in each direction.

FIGURE 7-9   Output of running traceroute to www.universalhub.com

```
traceroute to www.universalhub.com (104.20.11.66), 64 hops max, 52 byte packets
 1  bb1-kidpub-com (192.168.1.1)  1.695 ms  0.938 ms  1.555 ms
 2  lo0-100.bstnma-vfttp-332.verizon-gni.net (71.174.60.1)  4.414 ms  3.859 ms  4.504 ms
 3  b3332.bstnma-lcr-22.verizon-gni.net (100.41.140.34)  5.756 ms
    b3332.bstnma-lcr-21.verizon-gni.net (100.41.140.32)  9.321 ms
    b3332.bstnma-lcr-22.verizon-gni.net (100.41.140.34)  5.997 ms
 4  * * *
 5  0.xe-4-0-0.il1.nyc41.alter.net (140.222.238.91)  13.541 ms
    0.xe-4-0-0.il2.nyc41.alter.net (140.222.238.95)  13.450 ms
    0.xe-10-1-0.il1.nyc9.alter.net (140.222.236.23)  14.067 ms
 6  0.ae7.gw10.ewr6.alter.net (140.222.231.129)  14.816 ms
    0.ae8.gw10.ewr6.alter.net (140.222.231.131)  14.464 ms
    0.ae12.gw10.ewr6.alter.net (140.222.235.119)  16.328 ms
 7  157.130.91.86 (157.130.91.86)  15.086 ms  15.896 ms  15.803 ms
 8  cloudflare-ic-301663-nyk-b2.c.telia.net (213.248.77.162)  19.269 ms  22.377 ms  17.286 ms
 9  104.20.11.66 (104.20.11.66)  17.384 ms  17.240 ms  17.693 ms
```

Intercontinental Traffic

What about messages that are going from one country to another, or between continents? There has to be some sort of connection between the United States, for example and Europe, if we are to read our favorite blogs in France. There are two primary ways to make this long-distance connection. The first is by satellite; messages can be beamed to orbiting satellites by radio, from one continent to another. This method is not widely used, as radio signals are not always 100% reliable, and can be affected by things like solar storms, weather, and of course are subject to interference or eavesdropping by any number of third parties.

A second way, and the one most widely used, is to send messages over fiber-optic cables that run under the ocean. These cables, laid about one meter below the ocean floor between continents, carry the bulk of intercontinental traffic on the Internet. The cables come ashore near population centers such as New York City or London or Tokyo, and once the messages emerge from the oceanic cables they are placed onto high-level routers in each continent or country. There the message is treated just as a normal message would be, routed from place to place until it is finally delivered.

As you might guess, laying cables across an entire ocean is a very expensive process, and so there aren't that many of these intercontinental cables. Current cables are shown in the map in Figure 7-10. Before fiber became prevalent, the cables were made of copper and were heavy, prone to breakage, and also susceptible to surveillance. New fiber-optic

FIGURE 7-10 Map of current undersea communication cables

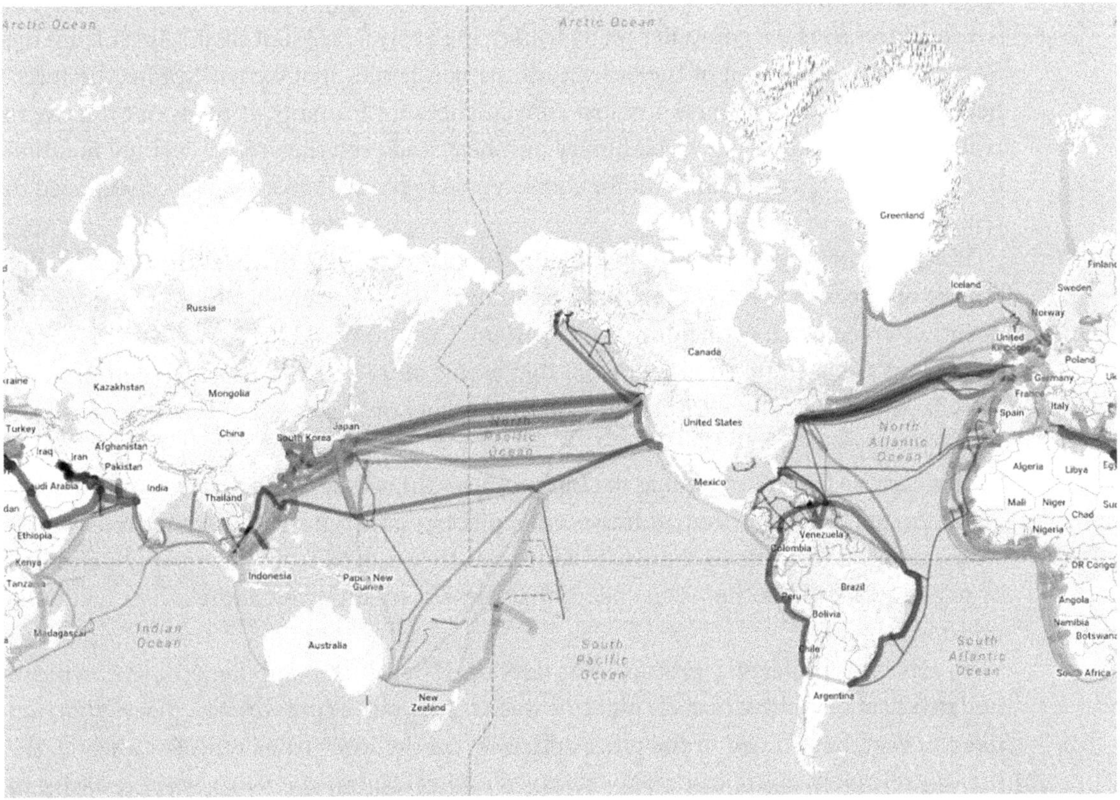

cables laid in the past 10 to 25 years have vastly increased the capacity of the network between continents, they are smaller, lighter, less expensive to manufacture and deploy, and are not susceptible to normal forms of surveillance.

One thing that we don't think about much is that it takes a finite amount of time, albeit small, for a signal to get from a computer on one side of the world to one on the other. The fundamental limit here is the speed of light, which is roughly 300 kilometers per second (186,000 miles per second) in a vacuum; it is a bit slower in fiber-optic cables, and quite a bit slower in copper cables. It might take several hundred milliseconds or even longer in some cases for a message to get from your computer in the United States to a computer in, say, China, and the same for the response.

The same holds true for satellite communications. Most of these links are made using geosynchronous satellites which orbit the earth at an altitude of roughly 26,000 miles, and it takes several hundred milliseconds for a transmission from the earth's surface to reach a satellite and be beamed back to Earth. This is why you sometimes see foreign news correspondents standing silently for a few moments when the anchor asks a question; it simply takes a bit of time for that signal to get from the studio to the reporter in the field.

Internet Names

Let's say that we want to visit Electronic Frontier Foundation (EFF). We open up a browser or computer, type in the URL https://www.eff.org and hit enter. But wait a minute: eff.org is not an Internet protocol (IP) address; it certainly doesn't look like 192.168.12.42. We also know that the computer itself sees the address as simply a 32-bit binary number. So, which addresses is the computer really using? The answer is: All of them. Apart from the 32-bit binary address, all of the other addressing schemes that we will see for the Internet, and networks in general, are just conveniences for humans. It turns out that we're really bad at remembering 32-bit binary numbers, and even the dotted-decimal notation like 192.168.12.42 can be difficult for some people to remember, especially if you need to remember a lot of them.

When the Internet was young, though, we actually did exactly that. Most people kept a piece of paper in their drawer that had a dozen or two addresses that were used frequently. Remember, it wasn't until the mid-1990s that the World Wide Web was born, and IP networks existed for decades before that event. Most network users were in military installations or on college campuses, and the number of sites or e-mail addresses needed was relatively small.

This wasn't a bad system, but as the Internet grew things started to get a bit cumbersome. What started out as a dozen addresses on a piece of paper grew to the hundreds, and it wasn't unusual for a site to change its address as they moved from one server to another, or one network to another. This meant that these manually kept address lists had to be updated frequently.

To solve this problem, a protocol was developed by which computers could download updated lists of addresses each night; it wasn't just your addresses, the places that you liked to visit, but also all of the other addresses on the Internet as well. For a while, the list was relatively small, just a few thousand addresses, but even so it was expensive to send this list all over the Internet once a day. What if you got a new list every day of tens of thousands of addresses, and never used it? It would be a waste of time to send this list to every computer on the Internet, especially as the Internet grew larger and larger. By the way, this is really common in computer science—complex systems develop from simpler systems, because the simpler systems introduce problems that we haven't thought of before. We end up fixing one problem, which causes another problem, and when we fix that, it might cause additional problems, and so on, until the system becomes quite complex. Often we forget what the original problem was!

DNS

Back to the problem of sending lists of addresses around. The protocol designed to handle this problem is called the Domain Name System, or DNS. It was developed to allow humans to think about Internet addresses in word format, such as eff.org, and not 32-bit binary numbers or dotted decimals like 192.168.12.42. You are familiar with the system, because you use it every day. At college your e-mail address will be someuser@yourcollege.edu; we visit Amazon.com, CNN.com, and other commercial sites; we might read articles from nonprofits on sites that end in .org or .net; and there literally hundreds of others of these so-called top-level domains like .com, .edu, .mil, and so on. Until recently this list was relatively small, just a few dozen plus one for each country, but in 2015 approval was given for hundreds and hundreds of new top-level domains with names like .biz and .city. There are currently 301 country-specific top-level domains (.fr for France, .cn for China, and so on) and 730 generic domains (.auto, .dance, .jobs, and more).

DNS is simple in concept, but there are a lot of moving parts. Let's say that you want to visit www.eff.org. Your computer has no idea what you're talking about; it only deals in 32-bit binary numbers. And so, there needs to be some way for your computer to look up the Internet address of www.eff.org. A special server called a DNS server handles this lookup. Figure 7-11 shows the sequence of events. Your computer first checks a locally stored file, called a cache, to see if it already knows the address. This saves quite a bit of time if the information is already close at hand. Next, your computer asks the closest DNS server, likely one at your ISP or university, if it knows the IP address of www.eff.org. If that server does know the address, it is immediately returned to your computer, and your computer stashes that value away for future use in its cache.

FIGURE 7-11 A series of DNS requests to resolve www.wikipedia.org

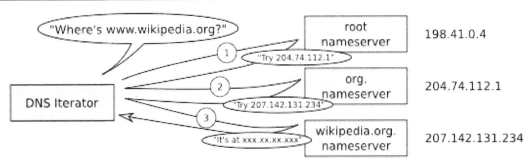

If the local DNS server does not know the address, it communicates with a server called the "dot" server. You might not realize it, but every named Internet address, like www.eff.org, ends in a trailing "." The dot is the root of the Internet domain name system, and there's a server that handles requests for that very top level of the Internet. You can read addresses backward in a hierarchical way, staring with the dot—dot, then org, then eff, then www, with each level down getting closer to a specific computer (eff.org, for example, might have hundreds of machines in the domain).

As you might imagine, these top-level dot servers get a lot of requests. There are only thirteen of them to begin with, and they are scattered all over the world. (Note: While there are thirteen unique addresses for all of the root servers, each of those addresses can access one of several physical computers in a cluster. There are roughly 500 total root servers as of this writing.)

The . server looks at the address that you are looking for, in this case www.eff.org, and notes that it ends in .org. The response from this top-level server is, "Hey, I can't answer your question, but why don't you go ask the .org server if it knows what the address is."

Your local DNS server receives this response from the top-level domain name server, and sees that it needs to talk to the .org DNS server. It sends a request to the .org server and says, "Please give me the IP address for www.eff.org." The DNS servers at this level are also quite busy, and don't have time to answer these questions directly, and so your local DNS server is told to ask the set of servers that handle the E's, since eff.org starts with an E.

In the next step, your local DNS server asks the E DNS server if *it* knows the IP address of www.eff.org. Like all of the others, this server is quite busy, and its response will be the address of a server on the eff.org domain that actually does have the address. Your local server sees this response, notes that it needs to talk to the eff.org DNS server, and makes a request directly to it. The eff.org DNS server, of course, knows the answer to this question, and returns the IP address of www.eff.org. Your local DNS server can now pass this IP address to your computer, which finally makes a connection to the IP address of www.eff.org.

You can see why your local computer will store this information in a cache file for future use, since it can take quite a bit of time to resolve a domain name into an IP address, and we don't want to have to go through that each time you connect to a site on the Internet! The record that is stored in cache by your DNS server on your local computer has a freshness date attached to it, typically 14 to 28 days, to avoid the possibility that an address has expired or changed between the time that your computer cached it and at the time that you're actually going to use it.

Bottom Line

Computer networking seems complex, but when we look at it closely we can see that each layer does a relatively simple task. At the Internet layer the primary responsibility is the routing of messages from one router to the next in a packet-switched network.

Internet addresses are 32-bit binary values which we commonly write in dotted-decimal format, such as 151.101.208.201. We simplify this even more with the Domain Name System, which allows us to work with text-based addresses such as www.eff.org.

Figure Credits

- **Fig. 7.1:** Source: https://publicdomainvectors.org/en/free-clipart/PC-CPU-box-vector-image/13360.html.
- **Fig. 7.2:** Source: https://commons.wikimedia.org/wiki/File:NetworkTopology-FullyConnected.png.
- **Fig. 7.3:** Source: https://commons.wikimedia.org/wiki/File%3AOffutt_Air_Force_Base_operator.jpg.
- **Fig. 7.4:** Copyright © Coderman (CC BY-SA 3.0) at https://en.wikipedia.org/wiki/File:Amiexpress.png.
- **Fig. 7.6a:** Source: https://publicdomainvectors.org/en/free-clipart/PC-CPU-box-vector-image/13360.html.
- **Fig. 7.6b:** Source: https://www.graffletopia.com.
- **Fig. 7.6c:** Source: https://publicdomainvectors.org/en/free-clipart/Simple-router-for-computer-network-vector-illustration/12604.html.
- **Fig. 7.6d:** Source: https://wpclipart.com/weather/clouds/cloud_1.png.html.
- **Fig. 7.7a:** Source: https://www.graffletopia.com.
- **Fig. 7.7b:** Source: https://publicdomainvectors.org/en/free-clipart/Simple-router-for-computer-network-vector-illustration/12604.html.
- **Fig. 7.7c:** Source: https://wpclipart.com/weather/clouds/cloud_1.png.html.
- **Fig. 7.8a:** Source: https://publicdomainvectors.org/en/free-clipart/Simple-router-for-computer-network-vector-illustration/12604.html.
- **Fig. 7.8b:** Source: https://www.graffletopia.com.
- **Fig. 7.8c:** Source: https://wpclipart.com/weather/clouds/cloud_1.png.html.
- **Fig. 7.10:** Source: http://www.cablemap.info.
- **Fig. 7.11:** Source: https://commons.wikimedia.org/wiki/File%3AAn_example_of_theoretical_DNS_recursion.svg.

CHAPTER

Networking

SERVICES AND THE CLOUD

I n Chapter 6 we looked at how to build a local area network (LAN) using switches and
the Ethernet protocol. Then, in Chapter 7 we connected our LAN to the Internet using
routers and the Internet protocols (TCP/IP). Now it's time to take a look at the sorts of
things that we can do on this network.

Nearly all of the activity that takes place on the Internet involves only two computers: a
client and a server. Of course, there are multiple other devices involved, including switches
at the LAN level and routers at the Internet level, but from a computing standpoint there
are just two computers talking with each other. If you are visiting websites, the client is
the web browser running on your computer and the server is a web server in some remote
location. If you are streaming music, the client is an application running on your computer,
and the server is a streaming server sitting somewhere on the Internet.

Generally speaking there are two kinds of computing in this environment: thick client
and thin client. We will look at both and determine which is the most commonly used for
Internet activities. The difference between the two comes down to the question: Where is
the work being done?

Thin Client

In thin client computing, most of the work is done by a remote server. This is the model
that was used by early computer applications, and it persists to this day. In those early
systems, applications ran on large computers that were installed in data centers You would
find these at banks, insurance companies, state departments of motor vehicle registration,
and similar businesses. Think of the stereotypical movie computer—blinking lights, whir-
ring tape reels, and massive size—and you've got a picture of this class of computer. To
work with these applications, a user would log in through a "dumb" terminal, basically a
keyboard and a monitor. The moniker "dumb" comes from the fact that these terminals
have no processing capability; they are merely displays. The monitors on dumb terminals
were often single color, usually green, which gave rise to the term *green-screen* applications.

FIGURE 8-1 A thin-client application used at a library

You can see these green-screen applications even now, as many business segments continue to use applications that run on large systems, accessing them through simple terminals. Typically these applications don't use input devices such as a mouse; instead navigation is done by tabbing through fields on the screen, just as you might have through the fields on a form on a webpage. Function keys like F1, F2, and so on, are also used for navigation in this kind of application. A typical dumb terminal is shown in Figure 8-1.

Incidentally, the reason that green screens are green is quite simple. In Chapter 3 we looked at how monitors are made using three primary colors: red, green, and blue. Using all three creates a color monitor, with the red, green, and blue components being displayed on the screen to create a palette of about 16 million colors. Since the applications in thin-client computing are typically form-based, with no interaction, and are designed not for pleasure but for business use, there's really no reason for color on the screen, and it is less expensive to build terminals that have only one color, in this case green. Other types of monochrome screens were produced, and it wasn't uncommon to see screens of amber text, or gray, and the Wang Corporation even made a beautiful paper-white monitor that mimicked the look of a sheet of paper.

Thin-client applications are typically single purpose, and users spend all day just running that application. Most of us are used to multitasking on our computers, bouncing from one application to another, but in these business situations that just doesn't happen, and users are stuck with one application running on their screen. The result of this is that users learn the application's interface to the point that it becomes muscle memory; you might see a teller at a bank, for example, quickly moving through the screens of an application while barely looking at it. These users know instinctively which buttons to push to go to any screen or form field in their particular application.

Many of these thin-client applications are quite old, written in languages such as COBOL or Fortran in the 1960s and 1970s. You might ask, why would a company hang onto a program that is 30 or 40 or even 50 years old? The answer is that many of these companies invested large amounts of money in these applications, and frankly they do the job just fine. The temptation is always to get the newest and shiniest equipment or program, but from a business standpoint it doesn't make sense to replace something that is working. A program to print "Hello, world.", written in COBOL, is shown in Figure 8-2.

FIGURE 8-2 Printing "Hello, world." in COBOL

```
IDENTIFICATION DIVISION.
   PROGRAM-ID. HELLO-WORLD.
*

 ENVIRONMENT DIVISION.
*

 DATA DIVISION.
*

 PROCEDURE DIVISION.
 PARA-1.
    DISPLAY "Hello, world.".
*

      EXIT PROGRAM.
   END PROGRAM HELLO-WORLD.
```

That isn't to say that there aren't problems. You might recall the scare that many industries went through in 1999 and 2000 called the *Y2K bug*. The problem was that many green-screen applications that were written for large mainframes stored dates using two characters; for example, the date 1972 would be stored as simply 72. This was done because, at the time, memory was extremely expensive, and so by saving two characters on every date that was stored, more memory was available for other parts of the application. This worked just fine until the turn of the century in 1999/2000. At that time, the year 2000 would be stored as 00, which many applications would interpret as being 1900 rather than 2000. When calculating a person's age, for example, the program might subtract the birth year from the current year. If you were born in 1995 your birth year would be stored as 95, and when the year 2000 rolled around, 95 - 00 pegged you as being 95 years old rather than 5.

While it might seem simple to fix, the Y2K bug really did cause some serious issues in many industries. In the insurance industry, for example, mistaking the year 2000 for the year 1900 might mean that someone stopped receiving benefits. There was fear that airplanes would drop out of the sky at the turn of the century, that nuclear reactors would melt down, that the government would grind to a halt, and worse! This was an enormous boon for COBOL programmers; they had written these systems back in the 1960s and 1970s, and now were being called on to comb through millions and millions of lines of COBOL code, looking for possible errors related to the Y2K bug. These programmers, many of them quite old at that point, could name their own price because of the impending doom.

It turned out that the Y2K bug was not as severe as everyone thought. Still, many people took precautions by stocking up on canned goods, withdrawing cash from banks, and avoiding air travel during the last week of 1999 and the first week of the year 2000.

Thick Client

As desktop computers became more more powerful in the 1980s and 1990s, and also less expensive, applications began to be written that took advantage of this new computing power on the desktop. In this model, the server simply provides data to the client, and most of the computing is done on the desktop. The client application requests data from the backend server, does some work on it, displays results, and perhaps stores new data on the server as the application runs. While the trend toward this kind of client-side computing was in progress just prior to the introduction of the personal computer, PCs really accelerated the move.

FIGURE 8-3   A portion of the Wikimedia server farm

Because the client applications require server-side data, the shift toward this style of computing led to the rise of large database companies like Oracle, Sybase, and to some extent IBM. Similar to thin-client applications running on large mainframe servers, these database systems can also be quite large, and typically the value of a company is embodied in its data. Figure 8-3 shows a portion of the Wikimedia server farm, including rack-mounted servers and disk drives.

Because the client applications were being run on ever-more-powerful desktop computers, we started to see an increase in multitasking, which means that the user might access several applications in the course of their job. They might work on a document, access a database to grab some data, open up an image-editing application to drop in a graphic, and so on. This style of computing really changed the way that employees worked, for the most part in a positive way in that it broke up the monotony of using the same program all day long.

It also brought with it large changes for IT departments around the world. In thin-client computing all of the applications and storage live on one, or at most a very few, large machines that are located in a centralized place, the data center. It's relatively simple to maintain these machines, back up their data, manage the applications, and restrict access for security reasons. If the IT department needed to upgrade an application, there was only one copy of it on one machine in the data center.

With the shift to thick-client computing, applications now lived on the desktop, and this became a large systems management problem for IT departments. While the data still lived in the data center, applications were distributed, and if you wanted to upgrade an application you might have to upgrade them individually on hundreds or even thousands of individual machines spread across the entire company. New industries arose providing management services for this kind of computing.

Which Is Better?

Like many topics in computing, the answer to the question, "Which style of computing is better?" is: It depends. Both styles are useful and commonly deployed today, but we tend to to see large business-related applications using thin client, and applications that are geared toward personal productivity using thick client. Cost of maintenance, training for employees, space requirements and cost of data centers, and similar issues are all looked at when deciding on which architecture to use for new applications. Sometimes, it just isn't a choice, when the best application for your business is written in one style or the other. Small- and medium-size businesses often fall into this trap because they don't have IT departments or programmers on staff, and have to buy applications off the shelf. In that case they are stuck with what's offered.

The popularity of thin client versus thick client has switched several times over the past few decades. In the early days of computing, the investment being made was typically in the data center on large mainframe machines, and it made sense to use those machines as much as possible, which led to a thin-client architecture. In the 1980s, minicomputers, which were scaled-back versions of the mainframe, became popular and could be deployed in individuals' workspaces, and while the application style was still more or less thin client, minicomputers provided more capabilities at the desktop, and so we started to see multitasking and larger applications being run by the user rather than on a remote mainframe. In the early 2000s, personal computers started to increase in power and capability, such that every employee had access to a remarkable amount of computing power right on their desktop; now it made sense to write applications that ran on that desktop, taking the load off of the mainframes and minicomputers sitting back in the data center.

What about the Web?

Are the websites that we visit thin-client or thick-client architectures? Once again, the answer is: "It depends." In the early days of the web, web browsers displayed static webpages. This means that the file that was sent by the web server to the browser was simple HTML code, and the page itself had very limited interactivity. This was classic thin client, with all of the computing being done on the back end in the web server. Any data required for the page was held in a database on the server, and the web browser really was just there for display.

In early 2000, JavaScript and other technologies were introduced that allowed programming code to run in the browser itself. This led to a push for web pages that were rich in interactivity, provided by programs written to be run on the browser, or client side. The web server in this kind of architecture simply serves up data and the program itself, but the program is run on the desktop. This is classic thick-client computing.

Around 2010, technologies began to be introduced that pushed more of the computing on websites back to the server side. Today, we're in the middle ground between thick and thin client, with some work being done on the server side, and some work being pushed into the browser. It remains to be seen what the next 10 years will bring, and it's hard to predict whether the pendulum will swing back toward thick client or more toward thin client as time goes by.

FIGURE 8-4 The very first web server; Tim Berners-Lee's machine at CERN

Client/Server

This middle ground between the client and thin client that we see in websites is called *client/server* computing. In the case of the web, the client is a web browser, and the server is a web server at some remote location. This is sometimes also called *request-response* computing; the client sends a request to the server, the server does some work, gathers some data, and sends a response back to the client.

This kind of computing isn't limited to websites. Client/server architecture is used for applications such as streaming music; when you request a song from your favorite site, your app sends a request to a streaming music server, which responds with the stream that you're interested in. When you receive an email, your email program sends a request to an e-mail server, which responds with any new mail that you might have in your mailbox. Many of the applications that we commonly use today that require network access are built using this client/server architecture.

Addressing for Network Applications

As we've seen in our discussions of both local area networks (LANs) and the Internet, each layer of the networking stack (Figure 8-5) uses its own addressing scheme. At the

FIGURE 8-5 The network stack

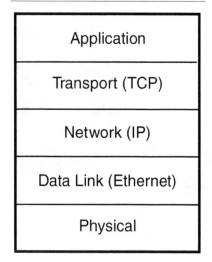

application layer, the layer in which programs such as your e-mail client, your web browser, and your streaming music application live, it is no different.

There is one small detail about networking that we haven't spent much time on. Most computers, like your laptop, or your desktop machine, have only one network connection. It might be an Ethernet cable running to a switch, or maybe a wireless connection to an access point. However, you have many, many applications that want to use the network. At any given time you might be using your e-mail client, your web browser, Skype to make a video call, and you might be streaming music, all at what appears to be the same time. How is it that we can have all of these networked applications use a single network connection?

The answer is that we use yet another address. In this case, we need to give an address to each of the applications that are going to use the network. When a message comes in on the network for, say, your web browser, the network stack needs to be able to figure out which application the message is for. At the application layer, and the layer immediately below it, TCP, the address that we will use is called a *port*. Port numbers range from 1 to 65,536.

To continue the postal analogy, a port is like an apartment number in a large apartment building. An IP address is similar to the street address of the apartment building, and when the postman gets to the apartment building, there might be dozens or even hundreds of apartments at that same street address (analogous to the IP address). To deliver the message, the postman looks at the apartment number on the envelope and places the letter into a slot corresponding to that particular apartment. The apartment number, like a port, uniquely identifies one unit in the apartment. The apartment in this example maps onto an application running on your computer. When a message comes in from the network and it is to be delivered to your web browser, your web browser has a unique port number on your computer, and the messages just delivered to that port. The technical term for this is multiplexing; the use of a single access point to deliver traffic to several different applications.

Fortunately, the port number attached to an application is the last address in this large collection of addresses that we have looked at on the network stack. Let's review what we know about that stack. Figure 8-6 illustrates the network stack and its protocols. At the very bottom of the stack we are encoding the bits as either electrical impulses, or pulses of light, or some other physical way such as a radio signal. Those bits are framed by Ethernet in layer 2 so into a standard format. It's at the Ethernet layer that we first see a To and From address; those addresses uniquely identify a network adapter, or card, on a local area network.

Moving up the stack we see the IP layer, which uses an IP address, similar to 192.168.12.42. That IP address may or may not be unique on the Internet; if we are using network address translation (NAT), it won't be, but will rather be part of a hidden network behind the NAT router. One more layer up is TCP, and the addressing scheme here is the one we just talked about, ports. On top of TCP sit the applications like your browser and e-mail client. Each of those applications has a unique port number associated with it, and that's how messages get delivered all the way up the stack.

Well-Known Port Numbers

In the TCP layer, the message format includes a To and From port number, just like all of the other addressing schemes that we looked at on the stack. It's easy to imagine how the From port number is assigned, since each application will get a port assigned to it, but what about the destination port number, or the To address? Let's say that you want to visit a web site out on the Internet; how do you know what its port number, out of 65,000 possibilities, will be? Fortunately, there is a series of assigned port numbers for standard applications called *well-known port numbers*, published regularly by the Internet Assigned Names Authority, a standards organization, that details all of the port numbers that have been assigned to a multitude of applications. Some of these are more common than others; web servers, for example, are assigned port numbers 80, 8080, 8000, and 433. Most often, a web server will be at port 80 at some particular IP address, so that when you want to connect to that website, you don't have to specify the port number; it is assumed that it will be on port 80. If the web server happens to be on a different port, say 8000, you *do* need to specify the port when you connect to the website; this is done by adding a colon (:) and the port number to the end of the web site address that you want to connect to, for example **https://www.eff.org:8000**.

Each well-known application is given its own permanent port number. E-mail servers sit on port 25; a protocol called telnet that allows us to make a text-based connection to a server, is at port 23. And the shoot-'em-up game Doom, which can be played across the network by many players, sits on port 666. How appropriate!

FIGURE 8-6 Port numbers associated with applications

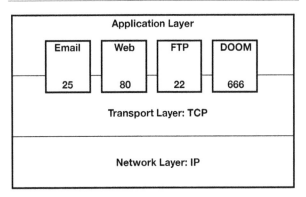

Servers

We now have a complete network stack, from the physical layer at the very bottom, all the way up to the applications at the top of the stack. We've said that a common model for using applications on the network is client/server, and we have thoroughly described the client side of the networking puzzle. But what exactly does it mean that a computer is a server?

There's nothing particularly special about an application or computer that runs as a server. There's no magic code, or special hardware required: all it means to "be a server" is that a program is listening to a particular port for incoming requests, like port 80 for a web server, and responding to those requests as they arrive. A web server, at its heart, really is just returning a file that has been requested; for example, you might visit a page for your course and ask for cs101-schedule.html, which is a file stored on the server. The server hears the request, goes and finds the file for you, and then returns it to the client, which would be in this case your web browser. It then goes back to listening to the port for the next request. Figure 8-7 shows a common rack-mounted web server; in the photo, the computers acting as servers are on the bottom, with disk drives on the top.

FIGURE 8-7   Rack-mounted web servers

One very interesting problem that we often have to solve with a client/server model is that the server sees each request as a new interaction; we say that the server is *stateless*. For web servers, the web protocol, HTTP (Hypertext Transfer Protocol), wasn't designed with the notion of a session, that is, a sequence of requests and responses that are connected together. Imagine you've gone to Amazon.com to shop for shoes. You log on, browse some shoes, throw a couple of pairs into your cart, get distracted by something shiny, and then go back to your cart and pay. Once there, you enter your shipping address, your payment method, and finally authorize the purchase.

For the customer's standpoint this is one long session, spanning maybe half an hour, in which you log on, browse the site, return to where you were, look at your cart, shop some more, and so on. On each page, the site knows who you are, what you were doing, what's in your cart, and even offers suggestions about what you might be interested in. From the server's perspective, though, every time you click on a link it is a brand-new connection. There's nothing inherent in the HTTP protocol to provide a session for sites like this, and so it is entirely left up to the site itself to maintain the session.

The way it works on most sites is that a small text file, called a cookie, is stored on your computer. The cookie is encrypted so that no one can read it, and contains information about you, such as your ID on the site that you are visiting, and anything else that might be useful to maintain what looks like a session on the site. Every time you click on a page, the cookie is sent along with your click to the server, which opens it up to see who you are. If it sees a valid user ID, for example, it will look you up in a database that it keeps just for this purpose. In that database is information about you: your name; your user ID; when the last time you logged on was; and the ID of a shopping cart, if you have one. This happens each time you click on a new link on the page.

Because the cookie is sent with each click, and the server is able to look you up each time, the site can make it appear that you have logged onto one long shopping session with a cart full of shoes.

Cookies caused quite a scare in the early 2000s. An article came out in a popular magazine describing how they were a terrible security risk and advised everyone to delete and disable them. The same thing happened with JavaScript around the same time, and the advice given to everybody was to disable JavaScript in their browsers. The result was that the Internet broke! Sites could no longer use cookies to look up who you were, and so you ended up having to log in multiple times to sites like Amazon, essentially on every page. After a few months of panic, everyone calmed down, turned on cookies again, enabled JavaScript, and the Internet went back to normal.

That's not to say that cookies don't still pose a risk. Many sites use cookies to track your activities online. Ever search Google for a pair of shoes, and then end up seeing ads for shoes on every site you visit for the next month? Thank cookies.

Cloud Computing

The hot new thing in computing now, at least in the marketing departments of the world, is the cloud. Everybody has a cloud, wants a cloud, stores their information in the cloud, runs their business from the cloud, and so on, without actually knowing what exactly this cloud thing is.

Most of us think about "the cloud" as a place to store files, but cloud computing encompasses software running on external machines or being delivered to your local computer; terms such as Software as a Service (SaaS), Platform as a Service (Paas), and Security as a Service (SECaaS) are common. It seems that every quarter a new company launches offering *something* "as a Service." All of these have one thing in common: You are renting either storage space or compute cycles on a third-party's infrastructure. We'll focus on storing files and photos, since that's what most of us have experience with.

The Free Software Foundation Europe notes that, "There is no cloud, it's just other people's computers," and that's exactly the case. When you decide to store your photographs in the cloud, what you're really doing is transferring the digital files containing your photographs from your computer to someone else's computer. The hope is that this someone else has taken great pains to build a system that has multiple copies of your image files, large data centers that are protected against power failures and hacking, and a simple-to-use interface so that you don't even have to think about where your files are going.

From a hardware perspective, this is really just client/server computing. The client is you, and the server contains all of your files. When you want to look at the file, you send a request to the server, the server finds your file, and sends it right back to you. Cloud companies maintain large data centers with thousands and thousands of racks full of disk drives, servers, and networking equipment. Amazon, one of the largest cloud service providers, has over *1 million* servers in data centers scattered all over the world!

So how does the cloud company guarantee that when you want to see your image file it will be there, and not destroyed or lost or misfiled? There are several ways to handle this. The most common approach is to split the files up into pieces and store the pieces across multiple, redundant disk drives, an architecture known as RAID (Redundant Arrays of Identical Disks). Two styles (which can be combined) are shown in Figure 8-8.

RAID0, also called *striping*, splits your files up into small chunks and stores the chunks in alternating fashion on two or more disks. Typically an extra piece of information used to check if a piece is missing or corrupt, called parity, is stored on a separate set of disks. The advantage to striping is that a given file can be retrieved by alternating between the two disks. It takes a non-trivial amount of time to locate a chunk of information on a disk drive, and while one disk is looking for a chunk, the other drive can be sending out data from the previous chunk. Striping is geared toward speed of retrieval.

RAID1, also called *mirroring*, duplicates each chunk of a file across two or more disks. If one disk

FIGURE 8-8   Two forms of RAID

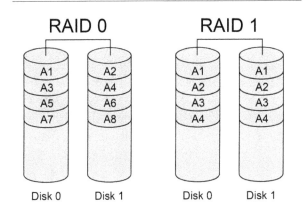

fails, the file can be completely recovered from the redundant disk. Mirroring is geared toward availability—your file will be there when you want it.

It's common to combine striping and mirroring to pick up the advantages of both formats. If a disk drive fails, your file is not lost because the parts are stored in multiple places; and the time it takes to read a particular file is reduced because a read instruction can be issued simultaneously to several disks instead of having to wait for each in turn.

RAID storage is not limited to companies with large data centers; you can buy RAID storage appliances for home use. In fact, I strongly encourage home users to take this approach to secure their files from loss.

De-duplication

For files that contain personal photos, documents, letters, and so on, it's a requirement that when you ask for your file you get the original back. One exception is music. Let's say that you have a copy of the Beatles' White Album on your computer. You want to store this music on the cloud. It doesn't make sense for a company such as Amazon or Google or Microsoft, who might have millions of customers who want to do the same, to store millions of identical copies of the same album. Instead, they go through a process called de-duplication in which they run mathematical algorithms on the file to create something called a *hash value*. This kind of hash value is a number generated by mathematical equation that is guaranteed to be unique to a particular file. When you upload a file, the hash is computed, compared with files that already exist on the system, and if there's a match, your file is not stored directly, but rather a reference to an existing file is stored. Because of the way hashes work, the file will be identical to the one that you were trying to upload, and so there's no missed information when you download your file later on. In this way cloud storage companies can save significant amounts of space by not having to store hundreds or thousands or even millions of copies of the same file.

Synchronization

There are at least two ways to handle synchronizing information that is stored in the cloud. One way is to store all of the files on the cloud server, and only download them to your computer when you want to work on them. For example, if you're working on a document, it will permanently live on the cloud server until you open it up to edit. At that point the file is transmitted over the network to your computer, and you can do some work on it. When you save the file, it is uploaded to the cloud server and removed from your computer. A reference to the file is left on your computer so that you can still see the file in a folder, but the actual file itself has been moved. This is the way that netbooks like Samsung's Chromebook, shown in Figure 8-9, work. These devices are very inexpensive and designed to work exclusively with files that are stored on the cloud. Because the cloud is used as a giant disk drive in the sky, there's no need to put one in the notebook itself, and so significant money can be saved by reducing the hardware requirements for the laptop. These devices often have just a few gigabytes of internal memory, enough to store any files that you're working on prior to them being sent back to the cloud.

In systems like this, there's one master copy of the file, stored on the cloud server, and when you modify the file you are modifying the original. The obvious advantage is that it is very easy to manage the file since it only exists in one place. The only time you really get into trouble is if you simultaneously open the file on two different devices and try to make changes to your document. This is typically handled by storing two copies of the file on the cloud, each with edits from one of the devices. They are marked as being conflicted, and it's up to you to decide which one is the actual copy, or to merge the changes together into a single file.

A second way to approach cloud storage is to have multiple copies of a file, one on each device that is using it, plus one master copy on the cloud server. These multiple copies are kept in sync by a small piece of software that monitors the changes made to each file. When a change is detected, they are pushed to the cloud server, which then notifies all of the devices that have copies of that file. Those devices then can synchronize their own local copy with the master copy that is stored on the cloud. It's complicated, but there are many advantages to this approach; for example, you don't need to be connected to a network to work on your files. The files are stored locally, and the next time you're on a network, any changes will be sent to all of the other devices through the cloud server.

FIGURE 8-9 A Samsung Chromebook

Bottom Line

Two kinds of computing, thin client and thick client, are prevalent on the Internet. The difference between the two has to do with where most of the work is being done, either on a remote server (thin client) or locally on a PC or workstation, with data being supplied by a remote server (thick client). The web is in the middle ground; client-side programs running in web browsers have moved much of the traditional work of a web server to the desktop.

Cloud computing is a third style of using the network. In it, files are stored, or programs are loaded from, a remote server. We often don't know physically where our files are in this sort of arrangement! Cloud services typically employ large disk farms arranged in RAID arrays to protect the integrity of the files that they are storing.

In the network stack, TCP ports provide a way to multiplex a single network connection into multiple networked applications. They allow us to use several applications at once on the network even though only one wire or wireless connection may be attached to a computer.

Figure Credits

CHAPTER 9

FOSS and Web Servers

I t isn't something that we think about all the time, but every day we interact with dozens of servers on the network. Every time you send an e-mail, an instant message, stream a movie or music, or even make a purchase at your local store, information is being sent from a server on the Internet to a local device. For most of us, the vast majority of servers that we interact with on a daily basis are web servers.

There is a surprisingly large number of web servers on the Internet at any given time; the number passed 1 billion servers in 2014 and continues to grow at a rapid pace. One reason for the explosive growth of the World Wide Web is that the barrier to entry is relatively low. Most of those billion or so websites are running on servers that are essentially free. The physical hardware that the server is running on isn't free, nor is the network connection, but the server software itself most likely is one of several free and open-source software (FOSS) packages.

You would think that a potential market of 1 billion would attract several commercial entities to this space, and that server software would be a large moneymaker for several competing companies. However, in the late 1970s and early 1980s a movement began to provide high-quality software at no cost to developers, companies, and other organizations. It was the introduction of this free and open-source software that really drove the kind of growth that we see today in the World Wide Web.

But what does it mean to be "free?" And what do we mean when we say that software is open-source?

Richard Stallman and the Open-Source Movement

One would think that a simple word such as *free* would be equally simple to understand, but in the context of software there are many nuances to the idea of freedom. The free and open-source software movement owes much of its existence to Richard Stallman, who in turn built on ideas proposed by Stewart Brand, who in the 1960s and 1970s ran a magazine/ catalog called the *Whole Earth Catalog* (Figure 9-1). The catalog was a treasure trove for

FIGURE 9-1   The first Whole Earth Catalog

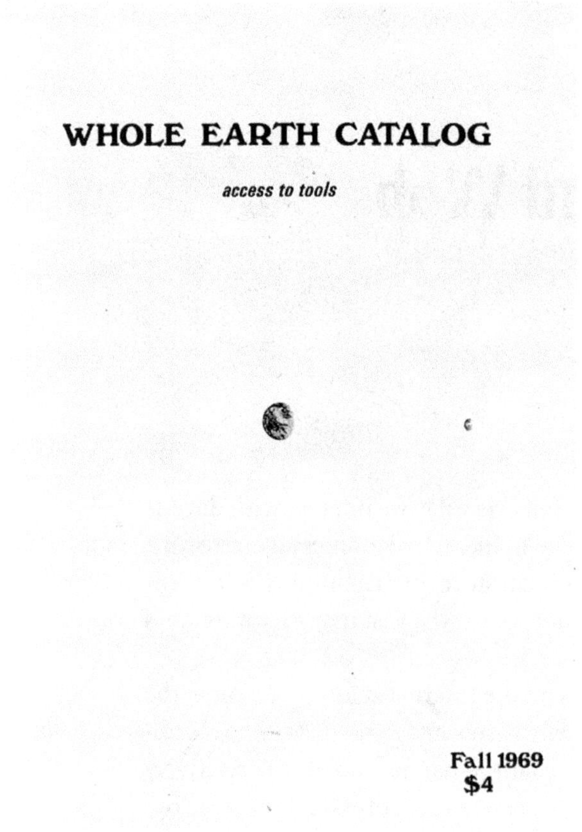

WHOLE EARTH CATALOG

access to tools

Fall 1969
$4

the free-thinker and hippie movements of the time and offered just about everything you needed to live an alternative lifestyle, including cooking utensils, clothing, tools; just the sorts of things that free thinkers might need.

Stewart Brand had an idea that was condensed into the short phrase "information wants to be free," but the difficulty came in the definition of the word "free." At a conference in 1984, Brand was speaking to Steve Wozniak, one of the founders of Apple Computer, and said:

> On the one hand, information wants to be expensive, because it's so valuable. The right information in the right place just changes your life. On the other hand, information wants to be free, because the cost of getting it out is getting a 'little', lower all the time. So you have these two fighting against each other.

1984 was a bit of a pivot point in computing history; it was the year the Macintosh computer would be introduced to the market, with its famous Orwellian television ad, and more and more Americans were beginning to get online and communicate in ways that they had never done before. It was a time when shareware became increasingly popular as a way to distribute software, and it wouldn't be long, just six or seven years, before the beginnings of what we now know as the World Wide Web would emerge.

Once people began to go online, onto bulletin boards, email, and file services, information became easier and easier to disseminate. It took only one post on a single bulletin board site for a document to be readable by anyone in the world. In fact, that was the US federal government's argument against Phil Zimmerman in 1991 when he was investigated for export violations for spreading his encryption software, Pretty Good Privacy (PGP), by placing a copy of it on a file server accessible to the Internet. The government claimed that by placing the file on the server, it became available for anyone in the world to download and read, and the particular software that Phil had posted included details of an extremely strong encryption algorithm that at the time was on a list of restricted exports; it was a federal crime to distribute that information to any country that was on the list. The file was on the Internet, and so anyone in the world including those in those restricted countries could download and use the information. The investigation ended in 1996 without an indictment.

It was against this backdrop that Stewart Brand began thinking about information and how it would be distributed in a new world that included ubiquitous networks. That was the "information wants to be free" part of of his musing, and it wasn't that he was advocating that information be completely free of charge, but rather acknowledging that once information gets out, there's really very little hope of putting the genie back into the bottle. Brand recognized that information is powerful, and therefore valuable, and tried to strike a balance between that intrinsic value and acceptance of information sharing in the new computing age.

FIGURE 9-2 Richard Stallman

Another person who had given a lot of thought to this problem was Richard Stallman, often known by his initials, rms, who in the 1980s was working at the MIT Media Lab after finishing his degree in physics at Harvard in the mid-1970s (Figure 9-2). Stallman was interested in the distribution of computer programs, which to this point were typically sold in executable formats, unreadable by humans, and saddled with very restrictive licenses with teams of lawyers at the ready if somebody tried to violate the terms of the license. To some extent software was treated as a physical product, much like a book, and in fact the same arguments that surrounded books, and still do, with regard to things like copyrights and fair-use rights, applied to software.

Stallman envisioned a world in which software could be freely distributable as a way to improve the human condition; he believed that while software was intrinsically valuable, its benefit to humankind was also valuable, and he wanted to encourage a system in which useful software could be shared by individuals or even organizations without the fear of being prosecuted because of licensing restrictions, copyright violations, or other legal issues.

What he came up with was something called the GNU General Public License (GPL) which was published in 1989. GNU stands for, in typical computer nerd recursive fashion, "GNU is not UNIX." GNU as an organization was not only interested in the free software movement, but also wanted to create and distribute a free operating system which Stallman called HURD. After almost 30 years in development, HURD is still not released, but it and other GNU projects paved the way for a significant portion of the software

we use today, and the GPL became an important foundation for the distribution of software under free and open-source agreements.

The GPL states that the recipient of a software program is free to use that software in any way that they deem fit, whether they paid for the software or not, with a significant provision: If any changes are made to the software, the GPL requires those changes to be released back to the community of users of that software. If, for example, you downloaded a piece of software that manipulated images, such as GIMP (GNU Image Manipulation Program, Figure 9-3), you could use

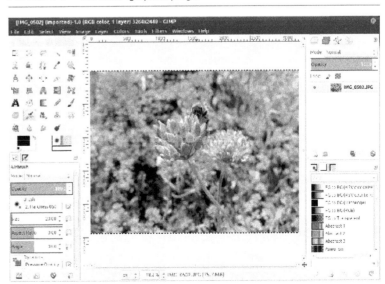

FIGURE 9-3 The GIMP graphics program

the software to create and sell posters, run a photofinishing business, make illustrations for books you sold, and so on. However, if you change the software in any way, such as improving how it resized photos, you would have to release those changes to the world or be in violation of the GPL.

The idea that you can modify and release changes to software in this way implies that you actually have the source code for that software. Computer programs that are purchased commercially often don't include the original source code, and instead what you purchase is a license to use the executable program. For example, if you have a copy of Microsoft Office that you use for spreadsheets and word processing, what you have on your computer is an executable program; you can't open it up and read the original code that was used to create the program. GPL software, on the other hand, has a provision that anyone who releases software under the GPL license must also provide the source code for that software. If you purchased a copy of an image manipulation program, and it was released under the GPL, you would also get the full source code that was used to create that program.

This brings up some really interesting issues around the creation and distribution of software. If you are Microsoft, or Adobe, selling software for relatively large amounts of money, you don't want your customers to have access to what essentially is your proprietary code. And it's not just that you don't want your customers to be able to modify or share that code, the program might also contain proprietary algorithms, your secret sauce if you will, that differentiates your product from others in the market. And so we don't often see large commercial software products being released under the GPL.

Stallman's take on *free* software is the difference between the words *gratis* and *libre*. *Gratis* means absolutely, completely free, as in somebody giving you a free beer. Usually there are no strings attached to that, you just enjoy the beer, say thank you, and go on your way. The other kind of free is in the sense of *libre*, which means that while the software or information is free of charge, it comes with responsibilities; we often say that this is free as in "a free puppy." Stallman himself said:

> I believe that all generally useful information should be free. By "free" I'm not referring to price, but rather to the freedom to copy the information and to adapt it to one's own uses. When information is generally useful, redistributing it makes humanity wealthier no matter who is just distributing and no matter who is receiving.

It is because of this difference between *gratis* and *libre* that we can sell open-source software. In many cases it is not the software itself that is being sold, but rather a license for its use, which includes a copy of the source code. You would think that free software would imply that it wasn't possible to make money off of that kind of product, but in fact the free and open-source software movement has spawned some really large companies that are focused entirely on selling and servicing this kind of software. For example, Red Hat, a distributor of the free operating system Linux, has many large corporate customers; generally speaking they make most of their money on service contracts. If you're a Red Hat Linux customer, and are a large organization, you probably also have purchased a maintenance and service contract from Red Hat, and perhaps some training, some documentation, and consulting services, all of which make up the bulk of Red Hat's revenue.

There's one other interesting provision of the GPL that prevents individuals or companies from taking free and open-source software, modifying the software, and then releasing a non-free version of the software. The idea is called *copyleft*, in opposition to copyright, and it requires that any new software that has been developed with any portion of software that is under the GPL, even if it is just a few lines, is itself subject to the GPL. If I have a million lines of code in my shiny new program that I want to sell commercially, and it contains even one line of code that I took from a project that was licensed under the GPL, my entire million-and-one lines of code then become subject to the GPL. This has been a bit contentious in the software community, because it really does limit the way that commercial entities can use software licensed under the GPL, but to this point, while there is tension between the two camps, it has not been the case that any significant litigation has risen out of a company using GPL code and then releasing software under a more restrictive or proprietary license.

The Open-Source Community

Stallman's GPL and the notion of copyleft sparked a movement in the software world. Combined with more ubiquitous computing platforms and the rise of the usable Internet, it encouraged programmers to come together to help one another create software together that was then released under the GPL for anyone to use. Probably one of the most famous projects of this time was the operating system Linux, which was created by Linus Torvalds (Figure 9-4), first released in 1992; today it runs the vast majority of web servers on the internet. Thousands of volunteers devote their personal time to working on the operating system, releasing updates and new versions. Some large companies, like IBM and HP, devote some of their staff to working on Linux, with the understanding that, since it is released under the GPL, they are allowed to use it in their own businesses, and that any changes they make to improve the operating system are then released back to the community for the good of everyone.

FIGURE 9-4 Linus Torvalds

While Linux is probably the largest open-source project that people can name when asked, there are hundreds of thousands of smaller projects, staffed mainly by volunteers, that produce software for just about anything you might want to do on a computer. There are entire replacements for Microsoft Office, for example, such as Libre Office (https://www.libreoffice.org).

For every commercial software product there typically is an open-source version that is if not the equal of the commercial product, very close to it in terms of functionality, performance, and interoperability. Many artists prefer using the open-source product GIMP instead of Adobe Photoshop, for example. Software developers devote their own time and resources to these projects just for the pleasure of coding, and for the satisfaction of knowing that they are helping individuals all around the world who need high-quality software and prefer to use something that is both free as in a free beer *and* free as in a free puppy.

The vast majority of open-source projects are housed in a single spot on the Internet called GitHub (https://www.github.com), and if you're interested in seeing what the open-source community is up to, and maybe even joining a project yourself, you can browse through the 4,000 new projects started every day, some big, some small, and join the 10 million users around the world all actively working on projects together. The name GitHub derives from a program called git, which is a software repository and tracking system that provides collaboration and other tools for programmers. Git was originally conceived by Linus Torvalds as part of the Linux development efforts, because he didn't like existing revision control systems; he launched git as an open-source project to support his team's work on the operating system. Today git is one of the most widely used version-control systems for both open-source and commercial projects.

Open-Source and Security

There are two related advantages to open-source software beyond the financial savings. We often say that open-source software benefits from many eyes, and by that we mean that because the source code for each program is freely available for anyone to see, there are many people working their way through the code looking for bugs. Usually security, or the lack of security, of a program is related to bugs, or mistakes, in the code that are exploited by hackers. If I am the producer of a piece of commercial software and I have five people in my company who are experts in software security, I expect them to find every single bug, and every single security vulnerability, so that they can be fixed before the product is shipped.

In the open-source world, there literally are hundreds or thousands of individuals, many or most just as skilled as those employed by commercial firms, doing the same thing; looking through the code, identifying and reporting bugs and errors, and often providing the fix at the same time. The result is that open-source software tends to be more secure because it benefits from these extra eyes looking through the code. That's not to say that every open-source program is rock-solid secure, and we see vulnerabilities exploited almost weekly in both open-source and non-open-source projects. However, if you are an individual or company who is depending on the security of your software, it helps to be able to read through the source code that is provided by open-source projects in order to evaluate yourself and satisfy yourself that the code is secure.

The Apache Web Server

One of the most widely distributed open-source software projects is one that you probably use every single day without realizing it: the Apache web server. Whenever you connect to a website on the Internet, there's about an 80% chance that the site you are accessing is using the Apache web server to process your request and send you back to a web page. The Apache project was launched in the mid-1990s in response to a web server and web browser called Mosaic, originally developed by a company of the same name; the company was later renamed Netscape. Mosaic was the first web browser available on the new World Wide Web, and almost immediately after its initial release was met by a host of competitors, including the Mozilla project. Mozilla stood for "Mosaic Killer" and the goal of the project was to create an entirely open-source web browser; Netscape insisted on releasing its products under a modified open-source license that allowed Netscape to retain proprietary and intellectual property rights on much of the core of the browser and server.

In the mid-to-late 1990s a small team of volunteer programmers would periodically release patches, or corrections, to Mozilla's source code; internet lore has it that this "patchy" server became the core of the Apache project itself ("a patchy server"). The project grew rapidly and today is by far the most popular software being used to host websites on the World Wide Web; in 2015 it held about 60% of the market of the top million websites.

Apache is released under an open-source license, which means that it is free as in free beer. It is extremely robust because it's open-source and benefits from the many eyes that scrutinize the source code. It's easy to maintain, does not require the Windows operating system, which for some opponents of Microsoft is a win, and it runs on a wide variety of platforms. You are most likely to see an Apache server running on the Linux operating system, which results in a completely free and open-source server platform.

The Apache web server has been extended and enhanced over the past 20 years to encompass just about every technology that is available on the Internet that relates to the World Wide Web.

Server Operations

So what does a web server actually do? You can probably think of some extremely complex web pages that you might visit on the World Wide Web, and you might think that the way those pages are created and delivered to you might also be incredibly complex, but the reality is that in operation, the server is incredibly simple. It really has to be, if you think about it; popular websites might receive millions of visits per day, and if complicated software were used to create and deliver those web pages, there would be a high likelihood that the server would break frequently. Instead, the server and its operations are kept as simple as possible so that they can keep up with demand and remain functional in a variety of conditions and traffic loads.

The web server is connected to a network, typically the Internet, and listens for incoming requests for web pages. The request is probably coming from a web browser, though that is not always the case. When a request is received it includes information about the web page that the user wants to look at. You might want to see `contact-us.html`, for example, which might be a page with contact information for the owners of the website. That file is located on a hard drive on the server, and when you request it with a URL such as `http://big company.com/contact-us.html`, all the server does is find the file `contact-us.html`, and send it back to your browser.

That's it!

This is not to say that all web pages have to be so simple. The page itself might have information that is looked up in a database that relates to you or what you happen to be doing on the site; for example if you are visiting a shopping site, and have a shopping cart, every time you visit a page on that site a lookup is made in a database with your user ID to see if there's anything in your shopping cart, and if there is, that information is included in the page that the server returns to you. Some pages contain programming code, which is either executed on the server side, as in the case of languages such as PHP, or executed in the browser, as is JavaScript code. Even in cases where a web page is very complex in terms of its content, with information coming from several different sources included in the page, individual operations used to assemble that page and send it back to your browser are done quickly and efficiently, so that the server can be ready for the next request.

The Universal Resource Locator (URL)

When we visit a website, we type the address of the site into our browser search bar. The address is called a Universal Resource Locater, or URL, and takes the form `http://www.somecompany.com/somepage.html`. There are several parts to this URL. The HTTP portion just specifies that the network request is being made with the Hypertext Transfer Protocol, or HTTP. The protocol has rules for how requests are sent and results received between a web browser and a web server. The next part of the URL is the name of the computer on the Internet; `www.somecompany.com` would be a computer named www at a company called somecompany, and that company has registered its domain in the commercial web space which is indicated by the .com at the end of the address. Domain names are discussed in Chapter 8.

After the host name comes a /, followed by the name of the resource we are interested in. In the case of a URL like `http://www.somecompany.com/contact-us.html`, the single file `contact-us.html` contains the content of the web page in a format called the Hypertext Markup Language (HTML), and the file is returned to the browser once the server locates it. Just like our own computers, on which we store files in folders, web servers also have folders, and you can infer the structure of those folders from the URL. For example, when we see the URL `https:// www.somecompany.com/catalog/dishes/French/plates.html`, we know that on the web server is a folder called `catalog` and in that folder is another folder called `dinnerware`, and in *that* folder is still another folder called `French`. Inside this final folder is a file called `plates.html`.

There is nothing magical about how the server stores these files; it looks for the most part just like the way that we would store files on our own computer; the URL is just a way of telling the server where the file happens to live on the server. In fact, another kind of URL can point to a file stored locally; if you have a file called mycontacts.html on your computer, it could be retrieved by your browser through the URL `file:///Users/pd/mycontacts.html`. Your web browser understands several protocols in addition to http and file, each of which can be used in a URL.

There are two special cases that the server takes care of for us. If the server receives a request for a file that does not exist, it needs to indicate this in some way to the browser so that the browser knows that there was a problem. The error code that is returned by the server is `404`, and you probably have seen several 404 error pages as you browse the web on a day-to-day basis. This just means that for some reason the server couldn't find the file and instead returns this error number. Sometimes it returns a special custom `404.html` page, some of which can be quite artistic, and other times it just returns the error code and lets the browser figure out what to do next.

The second special case is what we don't know the name of the file on the server side that we are interested in, or we just want to visit the "front page" of a particular website. Using our example from above, we might type into our browser `http://www.somecompany.com` and then hit the Enter key. On the server side, the server software examines this request, and notices that we haven't specified either a folder or a file such as `contact-us.html`, and so it returns a default file. The default is typically called `index.html`, and it's the page that is displayed when a specific page is not requested. This is usually the "front door," often called the *landing page,* to most sites.

What Is in the Returned File?

Typically, when you visit a website, the file that the server returns to you is in HTML format. HTML stands for the Hypertext Markup Language, and it is a way for developers and designers to indicate within a file how it should be displayed on a web page. HTML allows us to make text bold, position it in a specific spot on the page, create tables, include images, and so on. Anything that you might expect a web page to do is covered in the HTML language. We'll take a closer look at HTML in Chapter 10.

There might also be programming code included in the page that is returned, and this is usually in the JavaScript programming language. You can see examples of this in your own browser; in your browser, right-click within a web page and select the option from the pop-up menu which will display the HTML code returned to your browser by the server. The option is typically called "display page source" or something similar.

The browser's role in all of this is to read and interpret the HTML tags that are included in the file such as paragraphs, headers, or bolded text and then display the information in the appropriate way on your screen. The web browser is really an HTML rendering engine. An unfortunate side effect of this is that each browser maker, such as Microsoft, Apple, and Google, have the responsibility to read and interpret the HTML code that is being sent back to their particular browser. It's that interpret word that causes problems—one browser maker might interpret text that is marked to be displayed in bold as being just that, **bold**. Another browser from another manufacturer maker might interpret a bold marking as being *italic and bold* or ALL CAPITALS.

The HTML in the file returned by the server really is just a set of hints describing at a high level what the information on the page *is*: emphasized, a list, a table, and so on. It's up to the browser to figure out what that actually means and to display it in the correct way. This makes life tough on web developers, because they have to take into account minor variations in how browsers display information given an identical file. If you look at the top of the HTML source code of many web pages you will see a lot of conditional statements that test the capabilities of the specific version of the browser being used; since IE6 displays elements of the page one way, IE7 another, and so on. These conditional statements allow web developers to create a page that can be displayed under a variety of browsers, or how they interpret the information sent to them by the server.

Bottom Line

Web servers are the central mechanism used to distribute information on the World Wide Web, and the majority of web servers on the Internet run the Apache web server, which is a free and open-source software project distributed by the Apache foundation. It's also quite likely that the web server itself, Apache, is running on another piece of free and open-source software, the operating system clinics. In each case, the operating system and the web server really are free; however, they are released under licenses that require any improvements to the code to be redistributed back to the community of users; usually the license is the Apache license, or they could do public license GPL.

The server itself listens for requests coming across the Internet from a web browser, locates a file in the server's file system, perhaps includes information in the file that is pulled from a database or other source of information, and returns the page to my browser. The web browser looks inside the file, interprets the HTML code that it finds there, and displays the page on your screen. These pages are designated by a URL, or universal resource locator, that takes the form `http://www.somecompany.com/about.html`.

The programs that make up both the server and the browser are kept as simple as possible, because complex programs faced with a large load of requests are highly likely to fail at critical times.

Figure Credits

Introduction to HTML

H TML, the Hypertext Markup Language, is the *lingua franca* of the World Wide Web. Every website that you visit is built with it. While we refer to it as a language, it would be more appropriately called a system or a structure—HTML is not the text that we see, but a way of describing the structure of the content. It's important to understand not only the technical details of how to use HTML on a web page, but also the underlying approach to how that information is presented.

A Brief History of HTML

In 1990 Sir Tim Berners-Lee, a physicist working at the European Center for Nuclear Research, or CERN, had a problem to solve. CERN is a large institution, and the research that was taking place there generated a lot of documents and data which needed to be shared among the various researchers and coworkers. The traditional methods of making and distributing paper copies, or placing files on a central server for people to download and read, worked to a point, but Berners-Lee was interested in something a little more efficient and that would allow individuals to collaborate more easily on information using their computers.

Early in that year Berners-Lee had written a memo that described a simple system for sharing documents online and that provided a way to link those documents together. As the year progressed he fleshed out the details of his idea, and created both a simple server and a protocol that could be used to share documents across the network, marked up with a simple tag-based structural language.

The language would become the hypertext markup language or HTML, and his simple server, which ran on a NeXT cube (Figure 10-1), was what we now recognize as the first web server. In fact, it was Berners-Lee who came up with the name World Wide Web.

HTML and the web were not the first information-sharing services available on the Internet; around the same time as HTML was introduced a system called *gopher* was gaining in popularity. Gopher used a menu-based system for information retrieval. Documents were

FIGURE 10-1   The world's first web server

FIGURE 10-2   The first image on the world wide web

stored on a server, and users would navigate a series of hierarchical menus to find the information that they were looking for. In the early 1990s a search-based service called *archie* was also making waves. Archie allowed users to quickly search for information stored on FTP (file transfer protocol) servers and remained popular into the mid-1990s. There were several spin-offs of archie including *veronica* and *jughead*, both search engines specifically for gopher sites.

Around the end of 1990, Berners-Lee had developed the three tools that we now use every single day: the web server, a web browser, and a markup language used to display information in the browser. Of course, the first image posted on the brand-new World Wide Web was of young women in scanty clothing (Figure 10-2). Some things never change!

This idea of linking documents together was not new. Ted Nelson, a researcher at Harvard and Keio University developed in the 1960s and 1970s a system that he called Xanadu, which featured many of the same architectures and structures as the World Wide Web. It was Nelson who, in a paper in 1965, coined the term *hypertext*. In the mid-1980s, Apple Computer, under the direction of Steve Jobs (who, incidentally, had just been rehired after a stint running NeXT) developed an information system called HyperCard that presented documents, images, spreadsheets, and other material on individual cards that could be stacked into decks and linked together. Hyper-Card was extremely popular on the then-new Apple Macintosh.

HTML itself is based on earlier structural languages such as SGML, the Standard Generalized Markup Language, and is similar to XML, the eXtensible Markup Language that derived from it. Both are "-ML" systems—the ML stands for Markup Language, indicative of its use as a way to provide information *about* content. SGML, XML, and HTML have nothing to do with the actual content of the page; instead they focus on the *structure* of that content.

Structure versus Content

The structure of a document is incredibly important when we are trying to store and retrieve information on a computing system. It's easy for humans to scan a document and quickly determine what the subject is, who wrote it, how long it is, and so on, but a computer only understands what we have told it about a document. If we store the text of a research report on the computer, there's not really any way for the computer to know that the document is about research, and not a poem about dogs running through the green grass. To bridge this gap, we provide information *about* the information, called *meta-information*. Meta-information describes the document and includes standardized fields of information such as who wrote the document, the subject of the document, its title, associated documents, revisions to the document, and basically anything else that might be necessary to find, index, retrieve, and share the information that's being stored.

XML

To illustrate this, let's look at an XML document that describes an employee:

```
<xml>
    <employee>
        <name> </name>
        <id> </id>
        <salary> </salary>
        <department> </department>
    </employee>
</xml>
```

EXAMPLE 10-1

Note that there is nothing in this text that actually mentions a specific employee; instead it is meta-information *about* an employee. All of the pieces of information necessary to identify a particular employee is included: We see fields for the employee's name, his or her ID, salary, and department. You can think of this as a template for an employee, and we can fill in the details of specific employees later. Essentially the metadata tells us structural information about all employee records. It is not the actual data.

Next, let's take a look at the template being used to describe individual employees:

```
<xml>
    <employee>
        <name>Bob</name>
        <id>12345</id>
        <salary>50000</salary>
        <department>PSY</department>
    </employee>
    <employee>
        <name>Sara</name>
        <id>21245</id>
        <salary>80000</salary>
        <department>CS</department>
    </employee>
</xml>
```

EXAMPLE 10-2

One thing about a structure like this is that we can enforce it; the computer program that processes this information can look to make sure that when we store information about a specific employee it includes the employee's name and ID, and will generate an error if either of these fields are missing. Again, it isn't the *specific* employee that's the issue, it's that the information we provided doesn't match what we said is needed to fully describe an employee. This kind of structure also allows us to easily index and search information, so that if we needed to generate a report that listed all of the employees in a company, we could simply work our way through the list of XML documents for each, and pull out the `<name>` field to place on our report.

In the context of XML and HTML, we call this kind of meta-information *markup*, the M in these systems' names. Both XML and SGML can be very "strict" markup languages in that the structure can be very tightly enforced. HTML is quite a bit looser, in that if a piece of information is missing, or doesn't appear in the correct spot, most browsers will make note of the issue but will still display all of the information on a page. HTML is not generally used to *enforce* structure, but rather to *describe* structure.

Structure and Style

One way to envision this idea of meta-information or structure around a document is to think of the way that most people write term papers. Let's say that you have a paper that is 50 pages long and you've broken it up into sections marked by headers. Most people, when they need to create a top-level header, say, a chapter title or section title, will increase the size of the font that they're using, perhaps make it bold, and maybe even right-justify it so that it stands out. This is not a bad approach, especially if you are consistent, and it can be applied to things like lists and any other textual element on the page. For lists, for example, you might just tab over or place a bullet in front of the list item, and smaller heads like subsection headers might also be bold but justified left.

Even though this document would look fine on a printed page, what if you decided later that those right-justified top-level heads really needed to be left-justified? To change them, you have to find them first, and that would involve searching for all text of a particular font size in a particular font face and that is right-justified. As you found each one you could left-justify it to make the change. What if you missed one? What if one of the headers was bolded but had not been right-justified? You essentially have to read through the entire document looking for all of the instances of something that is bold and right-justified in order to identify the heads in the document.

To make this simpler, most word processors such as Apple Pages or Microsoft Word allow you to mark a piece of text as being a Head Level 1. If you're consistent with this, it becomes trivial to find and change all the Head Level 1 text in a document. In fact, if you want to change the justification of your heads, you can apply that change directly to just the style definition, and all of them would change automatically. Similarly, if you wanted to create a table of contents or index, looking for text that has been styled as header levels, or index terms, or figures is simplified because you just look for the styles rather than the text, and for each style pull the information that you need for your table of contents.

What we're doing here is separating the structure of the document from its presentation or content. From a processing standpoint, we don't actually care what the text is—the content is irrelevant. We truly are only interested in the structure. We want to find all of the figures, or we want to change the way lists are presented on the page. This has nothing at all to do with the actual content of these items, but rather their structural definition in the document.

HTML and Structure

Like styles in a word processor, HTML has nothing at all to do with the content of the web page. Rather, HTML identifies the structural components of the page and provides information to the web browser about that structure, so that the browser can decide how to display a given element. Let's say that we have marked up a document and used the HTML `<em>` (emphasis) tag to identify a piece of information that should be emphasized. There's nothing in HTML itself that tells the browser what to do with that text. Some browsers might see the emphasis markup and decide that an italic font is appropriate; another browser might decide that bolding the text makes more sense in order to emphasize it. The point is that the HTML document itself does not provide any information about *how* the text is displayed. It is up to the browser to determine how it will display elements on a page based on their structural definition.

In the early days of the World Wide Web, it was not uncommon for an HTML page to look quite different depending on which browser it was being viewed in. This led to some really awkward development decisions for those who were building the first websites, because it meant that they had to essentially write several versions of each web page based on the browser that would be displaying it. Microsoft was particularly egregious about this, inventing new tags for HTML, redefining how other tags would display information, and generally trying to differentiate themselves in the market by providing a "different" browsing experience in their own web browser.

In the 20 years since those early browsers, the industry has settled on, if not standards, a consensus on how information marked as emphasis, or header, will be displayed on the page, so that now there's at least some consistency from browser to browser and developers no longer have to develop or write multiple versions of their web pages. That's not to say that there are not inconsistencies among most browsers, because there still are, but for the most part when you design a web page you can be relatively certain that it will look the same for every reader of that page across the major browsers.

HTML Tags

HTML is a *tagged* language. Its format is very similar to XML and SGML; structural information about a page is defined by tags that start and end with an angle bracket (< and >). For example, a top-level header on a web page is identified by the tag as `<h1>`. Most browsers will render an `<h1>` tag as text that is larger than the body of the page, and usually bold. In some cases the font family might change from serif to sans-serif, and the header might be justified to the left, right, or center; for the most part, though, an `<h1>`

looks the same across browsers. Likewise, paragraphs are delineated with a paragraph tag: `<p>`. Paragraph tags mark the body text of a page.

Every page that you read on the World Wide Web is written this way. We don't see the tags, because the browser is interpreting them and then displaying the text on the page based on its interpretation. It is easy to see the HTML tags on any particular page. In most browsers, right-click on the page and select the menu pick similar to "Show Page Source," which will display all of the HTML that was used to create that particular web page. This can be really instructive if you happen to see a page that uses techniques that you like, and you want to learn how they were done. Just look at the source of the page, and you can see all of the tags the developer used.

HTML Tag Format

Every tag in HTML has a beginning and an end. For example, if you wanted to define a top-level header, you would write an `<h1>` tag, the header text, and then an ending tag, `</h1>`. End tags are marked with a forward slash, as in `</h1>`. Technically, every HTML tag is supposed to end with a matching tag, but as mentioned before, HTML is much less picky about the structure of a page than, say XML, and so if you write a paragraph that starts with the `<p>` (paragraph) tag but forget to include the `</p>` at the end, the browser will forgive you this small infraction, and simply display the next paragraph when it sees a new `<p>`.

HTML Page Format

HTML is a structural language, and the page itself has a structure. Each HTML page begins with an `<html>` tag and ends with an `</html>`. In between the opening and closing `<html>` tags, there are three large sections of organization. First is the head of the document, marked with the `<head>` tag. The head includes information that is not necessarily displayed on the page; the title of the page which will appear in a tab or the top of a browser window, for example, or JavaScript functions that will run in the context of the page, but not be displayed. Here we also place things like meta information about the page itself for search engines such as Google to read and index, as well as links to style sheets, graphics, and any other items that might be necessary for the display of the page.

Following the head of the document is the body of the document, delineated by the `<body>` and `</body>` tags. As you might expect, the body of the document holds all of the text that will be displayed on the page. This is the place for all of your content, images, hyperlinks, and so on.

At the bottom of each document, just before the `</html>` tag, is an area traditionally reserved for copyright information, contact-us links, and the like; it is called the footer of the document and text and it is delineated by `<footer>` and `</footer>`. Most browsers render text in the footer section in a smaller font than the body of the document, and many will also center this information.

The complete structure of an HTML document is shown here:

```
<html>
    <head>
    <title>The title is displayed in the browser title bar</title>
    </head>
    <body>
        <h1>Chapter 1</h1>
        <p>
        It was a dark and stormy night, and the Citgo sign
        flickered ominously in the misty wind.
        </p>
        <p>
        Little did we know that life was about to
        change...<i>for the worse</i>.
        </p>
    </body>
    <footer>Copyright © 2017</footer>
</html>
```

EXAMPLE 10-3

Since HTML is relatively unforgiving of mistakes in tagging, you can leave entire sections out, and the page will still display. For example, if you leave the `<head>` section out, the page will display just fine. Many designers no longer use the `<footer>` tag, preferring to mark up that text more stylistically than the browser defaults. Still, some browsers will complain if they run across a document where the `<title>` tag, normally embedded inside the `<head>` of the document, appears in the text, and warn about similar infractions, but again most of the time the page will display just fine.

Simple HTML Tags

You've seen a few simple HTML tags already. The following table includes the most common tags that you will use when writing web pages.

Tag	Purpose	Example
<h1>, <h2> ... <h6>	Top-level document tags (header levels)	<h1>Summary</h1>
<p>	Paragraph	<p>A little night music!</p>

Tag	Purpose	Example
<li>	An item in a list	<ol>
<ul>	Unordered (unnumbered) list	<li>Item 1</li> <li>Item 2</li>
<ol>	Ordered (numbered) list	</ol>
<img>	An image and its source	<img src="maggie.jpg">
<a>	Anchor (hyperlink) and destination	<a href="http://bu.edu">Boston University</a>

Bottom Line

The hypertext markup language, HTML, is the fundamental building block of the web. It is used to provide information about the structure of a web page, rather than the content.

Each HTML tag is really a pair of tags: an opening tag, such as <p>, and a closing tag, such as </p>. An HTML document also combines tag pairs to establish the major parts of the page: <head>, <body>, and <footer>.

Figure Credits

- **Fig. 10.1:** Copyright © Coolcaesar (CC BY-SA 3.0) at https://commons.wikimedia.org/wiki/File:First_Web_Server.jpg.
- **Fig. 10.2:** Source: https://en.wikipedia.org/wiki/File:Les_Horribles_Cernettes_in_1992.jpg.

CHAPTER

11

Programming Languages

Computers are nothing more than simple machines. We say that they are deterministic; that is, for a given set of inputs, they will always produce the same output. Another way to put this is that computers can only do what they've been told to do. Even systems that we consider to be "smart" such as IBM's Deep Blue or Watson, computers that beat humans in games of chess or Go and diagnose disease, are only doing what they've been programmed to do.

There are two kinds of programs, those that are written to perform a very specific set of tasks, and those that are created to handle general inputs. An example of the former might be a program that controls a device that fills the jelly jars in a manufacturing plant. When it sees an empty jelly jar, it fills it to a very specific level, and places the cap on. An operating system, on the other hand, such as Microsoft Windows or MacOS, must respond to unpredictable events, since we never really know what a user intends to do. Even in those cases though, the tasks can be broken down into very specific steps that respond to events. We don't know when somebody is going to launch a program, or even what program they will launch, but the task can be broken down into a set of generic steps that involve loading a program from disk into memory, reading a preferences file, and launching any arbitrary program in response to the event.

This might seem like a subtle difference, but one that could make a big difference in how you approach writing a particular program. The general case is always much more difficult to solve than the specific case. When you are solving a specific problem, it can be completely characterized, you can optimize that process, and the bounds of the computation are very well-defined. For general cases, we have to take into account many more variables, because we just don't know sometimes what's going to happen next.

Living Switches

Early computers such as ENIAC were very difficult programs. Even though the programs themselves were typically quite short, sometimes just a single algorithm, the program had

FIGURE 11-1 Grace Hopper at the console of the UNIVAC computer, 1960

FIGURE 11-2 Front panel of the MITS Altair 8800

FIGURE 11-3 A single punch card

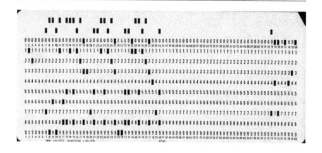

to be loaded by arranging patch cables, which were just links to the wire with the plug on each hand, in patterns that would wire together the circuits, backing tubes, and relays that made up the machine. Changing the program on such a machine might be a multi-day task, as the old program was removed, the new one loaded up with patch cables, and then tested to be sure that all of the patch cables had been placed in the correct spots.

There weren't that many innovations in this "user interface" in the early years of computing. Patch cords gave way to individual toggle switches on the front panel of the computer, and some machines featured input driven by punch cards similar to those used by Jacquard in his loom. You have probably seen the classic "computer" of science fiction movies from the 1960s and 1970s; whirling tape drives, and lines of flashing lights alongside banks of toggle switches. Figure 11-1 is an image of Grace Hopper at the console of the UNIVAC computer around 1960; by this time we were starting to see a trend toward what we would now consider a more "modern" computer.

Toggle switches allowed the computer programmer to load individual instructions and data into the computer's memory. Figure 11-2 shows the switches on an MITS Altair 8800. In the photo, switches that begin with **A** are used to set up an address in the computer's memory, and those that start with **D** are used to input data to store at the chosen address. The technique was to set up the value to be input with toggle switches, using binary numbers, and then hit the **Deposit/Next** switch to load the value into the computer's memory and move to the next location. All this was certainly faster than stringing patch cords all over the front of the computer, but it still was pretty tedious, and prone to error. Programs were translated by hand from a human-readable format into binary, and then loaded manually one instruction at a time.

Punch cards, which were a huge innovation in terms of programming, had their flaws. Punch cards are thin pieces of paper, or card stock, punched by a special machine and read by a second machine (Figure 11-3).

The punch cards had to be "typed" by hand, and anytime you have a human involved, you've introduced a way for errors to creep in. It wasn't uncommon for a programmer to spend the afternoon typing up a set of cards, and then hand those cards to a computer operator, only to be told the next day that there was an error on card number 479. Even worse was that day when the programmer tripped going down the hall with a box full of cards and scattered them all over the floor; this has happened at least once to any programmer over the age of 50. Those of us experienced in such things got in the habit of taking a deck of these cards and painting a diagonal stripe across the top of them with a marker to make it simpler to put them back together when the inevitable happened.

The Language of Ones and Zeros

Most of the time, early programmers were inputting their programs in binary format. Each computer, whether it be a one-off such as ENIAC, or a commercial computer such as the Altair, implemented a set of instructions in its central processing unit (CPU). For example, to add two numbers together, you might input the binary value 01000001, which indicated addition, and then the two numbers to add, also in binary. This kind of language is known as "machine language," and it is the language native to binary computers. To program these kinds of computers, a programmer would write out the lines of the program in some human readable fashion, such as the word "add" and then go through a process called *assembling*, which is the translation of the human readable code into the ones and zeros of machine language that the computer understands.

Even as late as the mid-to-late 1970s it was not uncommon for programmers to work in this fashion. It took a lot of time, was very tedious, very error-prone, and was just the sort of task that a computer would be very good at doing.

Around the same time that innovations were being made in the input and output mechanisms of computers, new programming languages were being developed to assist programmers in writing code in a way that made more sense to humans. In the 1950s we saw languages such as Fortran (1957) and COBOL (1959), and in the 1960s languages such as C and PL/1 were developed along the same lines. The goal of all of these languages was the same: to abstract the general idea of "programming" in such a way that a human could read the program, understand the logic, and develop new programs in a way that was faster and less error-prone.

These high-level languages required an additional step, the assembly of the human-readable code into machine language. Languages such as COBOL and Fortran and C introduced abstract concepts such as PRINT, which really was a long sequence of machine language steps. Programs had to be written that would read the source code in human-readable language and output machine code in computer-readable language.

BASIC

One of these early languages was developed at Dartmouth College in the early 1960s by John Kemeny and Thomas Kurtz. They called it BASIC: Beginner's All-purpose Symbolic Instruction Code. It was designed to be a high-level language that was easy to write, easy to read, and easy to learn, and it was used in many educational institutions to teach basic programming techniques. BASIC became extremely popular when several manufacturers, including IBM, made the decision to ship it with their early personal computers. This provided every home computer user with a way to create their own programs, even if they were simple, and it introduced them to the world of computer programming. It also put a general-purpose programming language into the hands of all of the users of these new machines, which meant that an entire community of computer enthusiasts began to write programs for these computers, which in turn increased the popularity of those machines.

One of those early machines was the Altair 8800 (Figure 11-2). The Altair was manufactured by a company called MITS and was sold as a kit, advertised in electronics magazines such as *Popular Electronics*. One of the readers of that magazine, a young man named Bill Gates, wanted one of these machines, but they were relatively expensive at the time. Bill called up the manufacturer and basically lied, explaining that he and his "team" were working on a BASIC interpreter for the Altair 8800, and could they possibly get a unit to do testing on? Bill's partner in this little venture was Paul Allen. The two had never seen Altair 8800, and they certainly weren't working on a BASIC interpreter for it.

It worked out in the end, though, as Bill and Paul received units to develop the interpreter on, and one of the first meetings between Bill, Paul, and MITS went so well that Paul Allen was hired by the company. Gates took a leave of absence from Harvard to go work on the new program. Shrewdly, Gates and Allen retained the rights to the software that they were developing, and instead of selling it outright to MITS, licensed it to them. They did the same thing with a small company called IBM, who needed an operating system for their soon-to-be-announced IBM PC, setting the stage for what would become Microsoft.

Was BASIC the First Language?

Due to the popularity of the IBM PC and subsequent clones of it, the Basic language became very well-known. It was taught in schools, in magazines, hundreds of books were written about it such as *Learn BASIC in 10 Days!* And tens of thousands of aspiring teenagers stayed up late at night poring over these manuals, learning the intricate secrets of the language.

But BASIC was by no means the first programming language. During the 1950s and 1960s there was an explosion of work on new languages for specific purposes. Fortran (FORmula TRANslation) was written in 1957 and was designed for mathematicians and scientists who needed to do complex calculations in the laboratory. Another language, COBOL (COmmon Business Oriented Language) was developed by the Department of Defense by a team led by Grace Hopper in 1959. COBOL was extremely popular in business, and IBM featured it as the language of choice for its early mainframes that were being marketed to businesses at the time.

COBOL and Fortran are extremely different languages; if you put them side-by-side you would be surprised to learn that the two languages, when compiled and assembled, resulted in very similar machine language. It was after all machine language that was the real language running on the computer, just a series of binary digits that were being interpreted by the hardware of the computer units, central processing unit CPU.

The First Computer Program

Credit for the very first program ever written is given to a woman, Ada Lovelace (Figure 11-4), who was fascinated by Charles Babbage and his analytical engine.

Though Babbage never produced a working example of his computer, in academic circles it was well-known and seminars were given discussing its theoretical workings. In 1842 Ada, who was a polymath and the daughter of the poet Lord Byron, wrote out these steps necessary to compute Bernoulli numbers using Babbage's analytical engine (Figure 11-5). In honor of Lovelace's accomplishments, the programming language Ada, first deployed in 1983, was named for her. For many years, if you wanted to sell computer software to the US government, it had to be written in Ada, which had been established as the "standard" language for government computing.

FIGURE 11-4 Ada King-Noel, Countess Lovelace, c. 1840

Two Approaches to Programming

Like most things in computer science, there are multiple ways to accomplish this translation of human readable text into machine language. The end goal is the same: we want to provide the CPU machine with instructions that it can execute. One way of doing this is to write the program, and then do all of the translation ahead of time; all of the things that are necessary for the program to run are created prior to the program actually being loaded into the CPU, sometimes weeks or months ahead of time. This approach is called

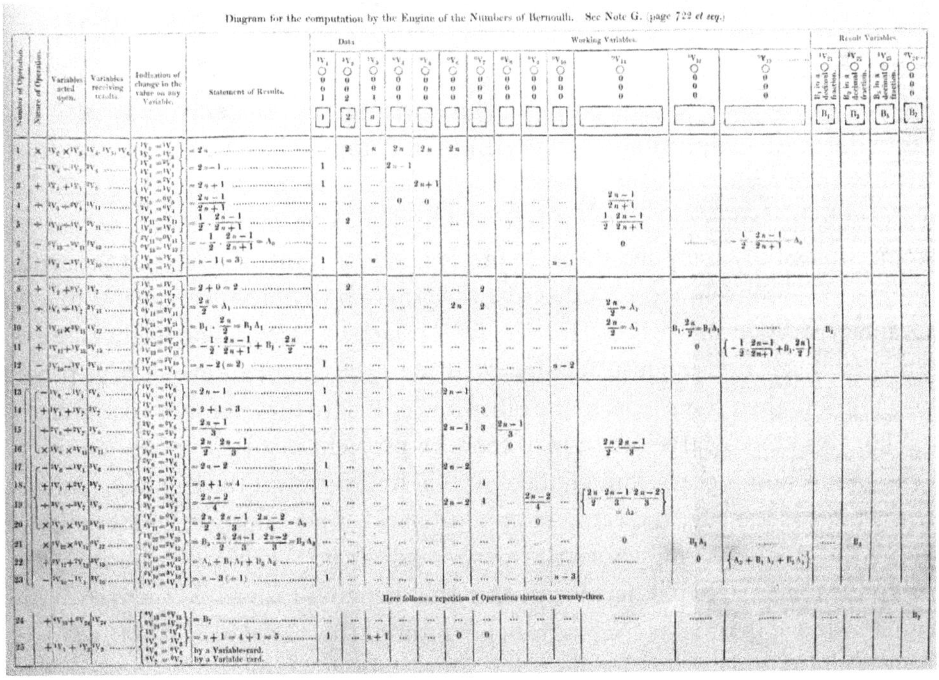

FIGURE 11-5 A computer algorithm for computing Bernoulli numbers by Ada Lovelace, 1842

compilation, and the languages that use this approach, such as C++, Fortran, COBOL, PL/1, and others, are known as compiled languages.

Another way to approach this is to wait until the very last moment to translate the human readable text into something the computer understands. When a program is loaded from disk, it is processed by an intermediate program called an *interpreter*; which converts each line of code in turn into machine code. This line-by-line approach is called *interpreting*, and interpreted languages that use this method include Python, BASIC, and JavaScript.

A third approach, a hybrid of the two previous approaches, is used by languages such as Java. Java code is compiled ahead of time into an intermediate format called byte code; this code is what we store and transfer from one machine to another. When it comes time to run the program, the byte code is executed in a small program called a Java Virtual Machine (JVM), which compiles the byte code into specific machine instructions that can run on the CPU.

The advantage of doing this is that each CPU chip has its own instruction set; that is, the actual instructions that have been wired into the CPU's logic circuits. Each CPU family, such as the Pentium, the Core family of CPUs from Intel, AMD, and so on, have a slightly different instruction set from one another, especially CPUs manufactured by different companies. Compiled languages such as C++ must be compiled to target a specific CPU or CPU instruction set. This means that if a new CPU comes out that has a different instruction set, the program has to be recompiled to take advantage of its new features.

Java gets around this by using its byte code as an intermediate language; since the JVM is responsible for compiling byte code and translating it into instructions that a specific CPU can understand, if a new CPU comes out all that is necessary is to update the Java Virtual Machine for that specific CPU. The Java code itself does not need to change. This is another form of abstraction, similar to what we have seen in other areas of our discussion such as the network and the hardware abstraction layer in computer hardware.

Which Is Better?

Given these two approaches, compiling and interpreting, you might naturally ask, "Which one is better?" As with just about everything in computer science, there are no clear advantages to one over the other; there are advantages and disadvantages to each.

With compiled languages all of the error checking is done ahead of time, so that once a program successfully compiles, there is a pretty good assurance that at least the syntax of the program is absolutely correct, otherwise the program would not compile. While this is an advantage, a disadvantage is that for very large programs compilation might take a really long time; it wasn't unusual just 10 years ago to start the compilation of a large program, go to lunch, and then come back to the office and still have to wait for the compilation to finish. For this kind of large program, if there's a problem that isn't uncovered until late into the completion process, it might take several hours to start the compile, realize that there is a bug, fix the bug, and then recompile. On the other hand, we can be pretty sure that once the program compiles it will run successfully on the target hardware.

Interpreted languages like JavaScript skip this step and instead do the translation to machine code just in time, as the program is running. This can save a lot of time in development, since we are not waiting for hours on end for our program to compile. On the other hand, if there is a bug we might not realize it until it comes time to actually run the program, which might happen when your customer fires the program up for the first time.

Most of the time the choice of language to use for a particular application is pretty limited; you might work in an environment where one language is preferred over another, or it might be that some aspect of your program only works with a very specific language, or maybe you are writing programs to be run in a browser on a web page, and in that case that your only choice is JavaScript or one of its derivatives.

Some languages are better for certain tasks than others. For example, you probably would not use a language such as C++ to do a simple sort of a text file; it would take some time to write and debug the code and compile the executable. Instead, you might choose a script-like language such as Python in which you could write four or five lines of code quickly and then immediately run it against the file that you wanted to sort.

Likewise, if you are writing a complex stock trading application, you probably would not choose a language such as JavaScript for the task, because in such an application performance is paramount, and interpreted languages tend to be somewhat slower than compiled languages. So, choosing a language for your application means asking yourself a lot of questions, and the answers to those questions will tend to push you in one direction or another.

Libraries

One thing that we try to avoid when writing programs is reinventing the wheel. It just doesn't make sense to write code for a problem that has already been solved. Especially if it is a complex problem, we want to use code that has been tested thoroughly, is well understood, and, we hope, well documented. Code like this might be an encryption algorithm, ways of managing data in a database, routines to move the mouse across the screen, and so on. Most languages include a set of *libraries* that cover most of the common scenarios that we might run into. These specialized libraries can be large or small, and they consist of code that has been thoroughly vetted. Using them makes our programs more robust, the idea being that with so many people using the same code, any bugs in it have probably already been found and fixed.

Entire companies have sprung up offering just libraries for various programming languages, and other companies who sell products used in computing usually offer their own company-built libraries for programmers to access. For example, if you're using an Oracle database, you will likely use Oracle's libraries to access and manipulate data in the database.

Hello, World

The very first program that a programmer writes in a new language is typically one that prints the phrase **hello, world** on a console, screen, or on paper. Figure 11-6 shows Hello World programs in a variety of languages, including C++, JavaScript, Python, Java, and a portion of one written in assembly code, which is a very low-level language, just one step above machine code. As you can see, the languages have a lot in common, but also

FIGURE 11-6 Hello, World in several languages

```
C++:
#include <stdio>
int main () {
cout << "HELLO WORLD" << endl;
}
                                    Javascript:
                                    console.log ("HELLO WORLD");

Java:
public class HelloWorld {

    public static void main(String[] args) {

        System.out.println("Hello, World");
    }
                                    Python:
}                                   print ('HELLO WORLD')

Assembly:
; Set VDP write address to #808 so, that we can write
; character set to memory
; (No need to write SPACE it is clear char already)
LD A,8
OUT (C),A
LD A,#48
OUT (C),A
; Select 40 column mode, enable screen and disable vertical interrupt

LD A,#50
INC E
OUT (C),A
OUT (C),E
```

differ significantly from one another. There are entire books dedicated to just showcasing Hello World programs in many of the thousands of programming languages that are in common use today!

One of my favorite sightings of Hello World came at a commencement ceremony a few years ago, where a student had written on top of her mortarboard *Hello, World!* It was particularly poignant, because Hello World is, as we've noted, usually the first program that a programmer writes, and now at graduation, all done with her studies, she was ready to face the world. Hello, world!

Common Language Features

Even though the myriad of programming languages differ greatly from one another in terms of how they're written, they'll typically share four features, which we will look at in this section:

- Variables
- Logic
- Input/output
- Math

Variables

A variable is a symbol that represents a value. You've used variables in the past, maybe without even knowing it. When we see problems expressed like, "Maggie has two apples, and Billy has three apples. If Billy gives Maggie his three apples, how many apples does Maggie have?"

To solve problems like this we write equations with symbols to represent the number of apples that Maggie and Billy have. So, we might say

let x = 2   (number of Maggie's apples)

let y = 3   (number of Billy's apples)

To discover how many apples Maggie has after Billy's generous gift, we would say:

$$x = x + y$$

In this example, X and Y are variables, they represent the numbers that we are working with. Note that the variable X had two values; initially it was set to 2, because that's how many apples Maggie originally had, and then later it was assigned the value 5, which was the result of adding Maggie's apples and Billy's apples, or X + Y. That's why these are called variables; the value that they contain can change.

Variable Types

Variables and their values are stored in a computer's memory as a program runs. Depending on the language that you are using to write your program, you might have to specify ahead of time what kind of information you are storing in a variable. Languages like this are called *strongly typed*, and if you tell the program that a variable is going to hold a numeric value such as an integer (a counting number like 1, 2, 3 ...) and then later try to store a different kind of value, such as a number with a decimal point (called a floating point number, as 123.456), the program will flag this as an error.

The reason is that in languages such as C++ the amount of memory a variable takes up is different depending on what kind of information is being stored. For example, an integer might take up two bytes of memory, while a floating point number might take four bytes. If we define a variable to be an integer, and two bytes of memory are set aside for it, and then later on try to store a four-byte value in that two bytes, clearly this is a problem.

Other programming languages, such as JavaScript, are *weakly typed*; that is, they figure out on the fly what kind of information is being stored and then set aside the appropriate chunk of memory to store that value. In these languages, we don't have to specify what type of value it is going to be, the language just figures it out. Sometimes this is called *duck typing*, the idea being that if it walks like a duck, and quacks like a duck it must be a duck. Similarly, if it looks like an integer and is being used like an integer, it must be an integer.

Duck typing of this sort is a point of contention among programmers. One camp feels that *everything* should be strongly typed, and that programmers should be very explicit about their intent when they write programs. After all, they say, the program is a textual representation of logic that is in the programmer's head, and while the programmer might be able to handle some ambiguity in the logic, the computer itself cannot. There is no "gray" in an executing program, it is all black-and-white from the computer's standpoint. The duck-typing camp feels that the computer and its compilers and interpreters are smart enough to figure out what is being meant, and so why not use those facilities to ease the burden somewhat on the programmer?

There is no right or wrong answer when it comes to strong versus weak typing. However, weakly typed languages like JavaScript do have a few gotchas that can creep up if you were unaware of how it is interpreting the values that you're providing. For example, perhaps we want to know whether two things are equal:

```
is 5 equal to "5"?
```

While this doesn't appear to be the case, JavaScript will do its best to convert one of the values into the type of the other so that they can do the comparison. It will convert the character "5" into the number 5, and then try the comparison. C++ would throw an error on the statement, or return a different result. Really, whether language is strongly or weakly typed just means that the programmer has to keep that in mind as they are writing their code.

Assigning a Value to a Variable

We use the equal sign (=) to assign a value to a variable. For example, we might say:

```
a = 5
```

This associates the number five with the variable **a**. Variables can also hold the value of another variable. We might say:

```
a = 5
b = 37
c = b
```

The variable **c** would have the value that the variable **b** holds, or 37. You can use variables in expressions, too, so that if we wanted to add 37 and 5 together, we could say:

```
c = a + b
```

C now holds the value 42.

Strings

A special kind of variable, called a string variable, is used to hold a sequence of characters, like a sentence. Strings are normally stored in memory in contiguous memory locations, with each character being stored as one or two bytes, depending on its encoding scheme. We use quotation marks to identify strings, so we might say:

```
a = "this is my lovely string!"
```

In addition, most languages have built-in functions, sometimes through libraries, to let us manipulate strings. We can get the length of the string, search for substrings inside the string, do substitutions of text, and so on, right from our program.

Logical Operations

Consider this problem:

```
    x = 5
is x > 42?
```

EXAMPLE 11-1

Obviously the answer is no, because 5 is not greater than 42. Constructs like this, called *comparisons*, are used to build logic into our programs. For example, the **if** statement allows us to conditionally execute code based on the results of a comparison operator: If the statement is true, do a series of steps, otherwise do a different series of steps. Comparison operators include greater than (>), less than (<), equal to (==), and so on. An example might be:

```
    x = 42
if x > 50
      print "This is big!"
else
      print "Hmm, a little small"
```

EXAMPLE 11-2

We also can use operators that are similar to the logic gates that we examined earlier. These logical operators, AND (&&), OR (||), and NOT(!) allow us to combine comparisons and make a decision based on that result. Consider this, which prints a success message only if both conditions are true:

```
x = 42
y = 7
if (x < 40) && (x > 5)
print "That works!"
else
print "Missed again ..."
```

EXAMPLE 11-3

Loops

Often we need to repeat a series of steps over and over until some condition is true. In programming, we call these *loops*, and there are two ways to write them.

While Loop

When we don't know how many times a loop should run, we can keep it running until some external condition is satisfied. For example, we might be interested in reading the contents of a text file one line at a time, but we don't know ahead of time how many lines of text are in the file. Using a *while* loop, we can write a portion of our program that opens the file up, reads a line, and then continues to read until it reaches the end of the file. This will work with a file of any length, because the condition that is being tested is whether or not the file is empty.

For Loop

In the cases where we *do* know how many times we want to run a loop, we could use a *for* loop instead of a while loop. A for loop executes the body of the loop a specific number of times. If, for example, we wanted to print out the counting numbers from 1 to 10, one at a time, we know ahead of time how many times this should run, then, and so it would not make sense to use a while loop; instead the for loop is more appropriate.

Input and Output (I/O)

Another feature that programming languages share is the ability to accept input from external sources and to provide output from the program. Input sources might include a keyboard a file, a mouse click, a sensor, or a microphone. Output destinations might include a screen, a printer, a bell, or a light. I/O syntax varies from language to language, but nearly every language provides these features.

Math

The final area to look at is mathematics. Programming languages for the most part adhere to the standard mathematical operators, the same as you might see on a calculator: +, -, x, and /, and so on. We also find features such as a modulus operator (%), which returns the remainder of a division, and any specialized functions that the programming language has been designed to handle. For example, a programming language called APL is designed to make matrix multiplication simple, and it uses a special mathematical symbol to multiply two matrices together in one step, something that requires several steps in other languages.

Bottom Line

There are literally thousands of programming languages, each designed to solve some specific problem. Practically speaking, most programmers work with a subset of a dozen or so languages, and it is not uncommon for a programmer to use only one or two languages throughout their entire career. Even though there are so many languages, they all share similar characteristics and fall into one of two camps: compiled languages and interpreted languages. Whether it is compiled or interpreted, the result is that the human-readable programming language is transformed into binary values, called machine language, that the CPU in the computer can execute.

Some languages were designed to be very simple, like BASIC; some are very complex, like Objective-C; but it's true that once you have learned one language, it's easy to pick up another, because they share so many aspects.

Figure Credits

CHAPTER 12

An Introduction to JavaScript

I'm often asked by students new to computing, "Which programming language should I learn?" This is a surprisingly difficult question to answer, because it really depends on what a particular student intends to do with their programming. Traditionally, computer science departments built their offerings with languages such as C or C++, which are relatively complex, or Java, which can be difficult for beginners. A recent trend is to start new programmers out with the Python language; it is much less complex than C/C++ or Java but no less powerful.

The trouble is that there are literally thousands of languages to choose from, each with its own strengths and weaknesses, and some are specific to particular fields of study. If you are an engineering student, Matlab is a good choice; statistics majors will want to learn Stata, and those interested in artificial intelligence and machine learning will be well-served by Lisp.

Over the past few years my answer to students' questions about a first programming language has been JavaScript. It has grown from a browser-only scripting language used to animate buttons on web pages into a full-blown, powerful language suitable for general computing in any field. It also is relatively simple to learn, unlike traditional languages such as C or Java. The big win, though, is that JavaScript retains its deep ties to the web browser and is the only language suitable for writing programs that will run in the context of a web page. For these reasons it is an ideal platform to learn programming concepts and also how to do some creative things on the web.

It's important to note that the discussion of JavaScript in this and the next few chapters covers just the basics of the language and completely ignores some more advanced aspects. It is enough to introduce you to JavaScript and to explain how to write simple programs that will run in the context of a web page, but these are just a few ways that the language can be used. JavaScript is a full-blown, powerful language with many facets, and my hope is that once you get a taste of what it can do, your interest in learning more about it will be sparked.

Some History

JavaScript was not always thus called. Soon after the introduction of what would become the World Wide Web in 1993, web browsers were developed to give users access to this new resource. For a short period there was only a single browser available, NCSA Mosaic. In 1994 a team including Marc Andreessen formed a new company, Netscape Communications, with the goal of developing a browser to compete in the growing market.

In the first year or so of the web, pages were more or less simple text and a few links, with maybe a picture thrown in for appeal. Microsoft, Netscape, and other companies were all busy working on ways to add programming functionality to their browsers, and in 1995 Netscape partnered with Sun Microsystem on a way to embed Java programs into web pages. These programs were slow and awkward, but they proved that interactivity in a page could be provided by code running in the browser itself.

In that same year, 1995, Netscape hired Brendan Eich and asked him to work on a new embedded language. At first he worked on support for a language called Scheme, but Java was becoming popular among developers and it made sense to provide a lighter-weight language with similarities to Java. Originally called Mocha, the new language shipped with the Netscape Navigator web browser as Livescript, and at the end of 1995 went through another name change to JavaScript as a way to capture some of Java's popularity.

Unfortunately the name, JavaScript, implies that the language is a scripted version of Java. In fact, the two are completely unrelated and share only the most basic features. In 1996 Microsoft reverse-engineered the language and released their own similar but not quite identical flavor, which they called JScript. The two were incompatible and many developers were forced to decide whether their web sites would support either Netscape Navigator or Microsoft Internet Explorer, since developing sites for both was often impractical.

In late 1996 JavaScript was submitted to Ecma International, a worldwide standards organization, with the hope of creating a single standard version of the language. Such a standard was released and revised in 1998, and began following a periodic review, revision, and release cycle. One would think that at this point everyone would agree to use the standard version of JavaScript, but as late as 2005 the various players, especially Microsoft, were still sparring, and developers still had to support multiple incompatible versions of their programs.

Finally, in 2008, agreement was reached on a single standard. JavaScript continues to be improved and released in new versions, coordinated by Ecma. The standard itself is a specification, really just a description of how each feature of the language should operate. It is up to individual organizations to implement the standard in their own JavaScript engines, and so there are still minor variations in the language depending on where it is being run.

The current version of ECMAScript, as the standard is called, is ECMAScript-2016, also called ES6. The previous version, ES5, was released in 2011. ES6 makes significant changes to the language; the examples in this book are based on it. A large number of web sites still rely on programs written in ES5 but are slowly migrating to the new version. An even newer release, ES7, is beginning to be deployed in small waves.

Front End versus Back End JavaScript

JavaScript has traditionally been seen as a programming language built for web browsers. JavaScript programs are embedded in web pages and executed by an engine within the browser. This kind of embedded-in-a-web-page programming is called *front end* programming, distinguishing it from programs that run on a server, or *back end* programming. The majority of web sites that you visit daily use JavaScript to enhance their pages with interactive features, fancy menus, image manipulation, and more. If something on the page isn't text or a link, it's probably a small JavaScript program.

Front end JavaScript has been common since the language was introduced in 1995, but the past several years have seen an explosion in the amount of JavaScript deployed for back end work. The primary reason for this shift is the introduction, in 2010, of a new JavaScript engine by Ryan Dahl called Node.js. While it had been possible in the past to write server-side JavaScript programs (in fact, the very first versions of the Netscape browser were paired with a server-side component), the timing of Node.js was perfect, capturing the imagination of a new wave of entrepreneurial programmers eager to launch new products quickly.

Around the same time that Node.js was released, several database products appeared that used JavaScript, at a high level, as a storage and query language. These databases, such as MongoDB, integrate seamlessly with back end JavaScript, and their rise in popularity gave birth to the full-stack JavaScript developer. For the first time, JavaScript could be run on the front end in a browser, communicating with JavaScript code running on a back end server that managed data using a JavaScript-friendly database such as MongoDB. Full-stack developers are in high demand, and the growth of that sector seems to be increasing.

One additional feature helped propel JavaScript to the top of the list of popular programming languages—the establishment of a central repository for contributed code and a mechanism, called a package manager, to find, load, and improve on code from the repository. Today there are nearly half a million packages available at npmjs.com (NPM is the Node Package Manager) that can be freely used for just about any computing task you can imagine. In some ways the package managers have shifted software development away from unique solutions toward an economy where programs are wired together using existing snippets found in the repositories. This shift has also brought the advantages of open source software to JavaScript programming, especially that hundreds or thousands of developers can read and improve the packages that they use in their own code.

In a typical deployment, Node.js is run as a server, responding to requests from web browsers. However, it is also a simple task to use Node.js to run JavaScript programs from a command line, and that is how we will interact with it as a platform for learning how to write our own JavaScript programs.

Running Programs from the Command Line with Node.js

Even though JavaScript was designed to be run inside of a web browser, it is also possible to run it from the command line using a program called Node, a JavaScript interpreter.

While it would be cumbersome to work on large programs using this method, it's perfectly suited to exploring features of the language a few lines at a time. In the next chapter we'll see how to build more significant programs and connect them with a web page.

Download Node.js

Node.js is a program that you will install on your computer. While the instructions here are illustrated on a Mac, the process is roughly the same for a Windows PC.

Open a web browser and navigate to `https://nodejs.org`.

There are typically two choices available for download; an LTS (Long Term Support) version and a "Current" version of the program. Either is fine, though you will gain more advanced features by clicking on the current version.

Once the file has finished downloading, click it to open the Node.js installer. You can safely choose the default for any option offered.

Once Node has been installed on your computer, open a terminal window (Applications | Utilities | Terminal on MacOS, Command Prompt on Windows) and type the command `node` at the prompt as shown in Example 12-1. You can get help on basic operations with the `.help` command.

FIGURE 12-1 Installing Node.js (MacOS)

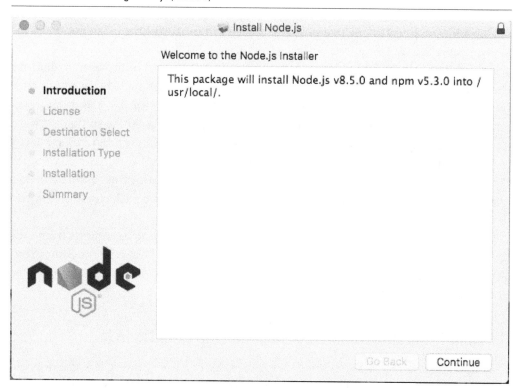

```
$ node
> .help
.break    Sometimes you get stuck, this gets you out
.clear    Alias for .break
.editor   Enter editor mode
.exit     Exit the repl
.help     Print this help message
.load     Load JS from a file into the REPL session
.save     Save all evaluated commands in this REPL session to
          a file
>
```

EXAMPLE 12-1   Getting to the Node prompt and getting help

In this chapter you will use the command-line interface to Node to enter and run short JavaScript programs and statements; the result will be displayed directly in the terminal window. For example, to display the result of the statement 10 + 32, type the statement at the prompt and hit the Return key, as shown in Example 12-2.

```
> 10 + 32
42
>
```

EXAMPLE 12-2   Adding two numbers together in the Node window

To exit the Node program, type `.exit` at the prompt. You can save your work at any time with the `.save` command, followed by the name of a file. For example, `.save myProgram.js` will save the JavaScript that you have entered to that point in the terminal to a file named `myProgram.js` in your home directory. The `.load` command reads a saved file into the terminal and runs it.

In the examples in this book that show working with Node from the command line, the Node prompt, >, is the spot where you will type JavaScript statements followed by the return key. The result of a statement is typically displayed below it.

Variables

Fundamental to most programming languages is the idea that we can temporarily store a value in the computer's memory. Sometimes the value is something that a user has input into the program, or it might be an intermediate result, or even a constant such as pi that will be used in a calculation. All of these are stored in memory by using a *variable* in our program.

You have quite likely used variables many times in your studies. Remember working on problems of the form "If Johnny has two apples and Sally has three, how many apples does Sally have after Johnny gives her his?" The solution takes the form:

```
let X = Johnny's apples
let Y = Sally's apples
Y = X + Y
```

EXAMPLE 12-3

In this example, X and Y are *variables*; they stand in place of the actual numbers 2 and 3. By expressing a solution this way, we have created a template that can be used for any values of X and Y. If Johnny finds a few more apples in his pocket, it's simple to change the value of X and get an updated count of Sally's apples—we'd set X to 2 originally, but change its value to 4 when Johnny comes clean with two more pieces of fruit.

Variables in JavaScript work just the same way. We first give the variable a name, and then assign a value to it. The value can change as the program runs, and we use the variable rather than the actual numeric value to make our program able to handle more than just one combination of values.

Defining a Variable

To create a variable, use the word `let` followed by the variable's name:

```
let johnnysApples
```

EXAMPLE 12-4

Rather than X or Y, this variable's name is more descriptive—it's easy to figure out what the variable holds just by its name. Generally speaking, we try to be as descriptive as possible when naming variables so that the intent is obvious. Compare these two statements:

```
Y = Y + X
sallysApples = sallysApples + johnnysApples
```

EXAMPLE 12-5

In the first line, there's no way to tell what the variables X and Y are referring to. The second line is much more obvious. When you are working on a non-trivial program of hundreds or thousands of lines of code, naming your variables in a descriptive way helps both you and anyone else who must read your code understand the program's logic.

The variables `johnnysApples` and `sallysApples` are written in a style called *camel case*. In this style, the first letter of the variable name is written in lower case, and upper case is used at the start of each succeeding word. The following table shows how the variable johnnysApples would look in several different styles. Which style you use is up to you, but try to be consistent, using the same style throughout your programs.

Style / Case	Variable
Camel	johnnysApples
Pascal	JohnnysApples
Snake	johnnys_apples
Screaming snake	JOHNNYS_APPLES

Another common naming convention is to use all capital letters (aka screaming snake style) to name variables that hold constant values. For example, if you use a tax rate of 6% in your calculations, you might assign it in this way:

```
let TAX_RATE = 0.06
```

EXAMPLE 12-6

Assigning a constant value to a variable might seem like a contradiction, and in fact most languages provide a way to mark a variable as being a constant value; if you later try to change the value, the program will display an error. In JavaScript, the `const` keyword provides this functionality. It takes the place of the `var` keyword:

```
const TAX_RATE = 0.06
```

EXAMPLE 12-7

Assigning Values to a Variable

In the `TAX_RATE` example above, the equal sign (=) is used to set the value of a variable. Providing a value at the same time a variable is introduced is called *initialization*. It isn't necessary to initialize variables in this way except in the case of a constant value. If, for example, we knew that we would need a variable to store a user's first name at some point in our program, we could create the variable with:

```
let firstName
```

EXAMPLE 12-8

One potential issue with this sort of statement is that the variable remains uninitialized; it has not been assigned any value. JavaScript supplies the default value *undefined* in such a case. More typical is to assign a value to a variable when it is created so that you know exactly what is stored in it. For variables that will hold a number, the value 0 (zero) is usually a good choice. For text, a blank would be appropriate:

```
let firstName = " "
let quizGrade = 0
```

EXAMPLE 12-9

Once a value has been assigned to a variable, another value can be stored in it, as long as the variable was not marked as constant. For example, the first line in the example below creates a variable and initializes its value to 0, and a different value is stored in the variable in the second line:

```
let theAnswer = 0
theAnswer = 42
```

EXAMPLE 12-10

Notice that we didn't use the keyword `let` in the second line; it is used only when creating a variable for the first time.

Attempting to change the value of a constant will result in an error:

```
const stateCount = 50
stateCount = 51

TypeError: Assignment to constant variable.
```

EXAMPLE 12-11

Comments

Programming languages provide a way to include explanatory comments in a program. In JavaScript, comments are marked in one of two ways:

```
    //This is a comment
  //that spans two lines
```

or

```
    /* This
  comment
  spans
  several
  lines */
```

EXAMPLE 12-12

The first style, using // in front of a line of text, is typically used for short notes, especially those that are only a single line long. Often this kind of comment is used at the end of a line of code, for example:

```
  const TAX _ RATE = 0.06 //Rate is for Massachusetts
```

EXAMPLE 12-13

The second style, in which /* and */ surround the comment, is useful for longer text:

```
  /* Tax rates are taken from IRS publication A-123, which
  can be downloaded from irs.gov. The rates should be checked
  annually since they occasionally change. */
```

EXAMPLE 12-14

Commenting code is very important. It not only helps clarify what the programmer intended the code to do, it helps other programmers read and understand the flow of the logic. Comments can help reduce errors by forcing the programmer to give some thought to the code as they try to describe in normal language what it is supposed to do.

Comments are ignored by the computer when the program is being run, and so heavily commented code will run just as fast as code without comments. There's no downside for writing lots of comments in your programs.

Printing Out Values

Most programming languages include some type of statement that will print information on the screen or printer. In the Python programming language, for example, to print the value of a variable you'd simply write `print quizGrade` to print out the value of the variable `quizGrade`. JavaScript, however, was designed to run inside a browser, and so it doesn't have the concept of printing in the traditional sense. Instead, values can be displayed on the console, which is something like the program running your program. Most browsers offer a way to display the browser's console; in Safari the option is in the Developer menu (Show JavaScript Console).

To print a value on the console for inspection, the `console.log( )` statement is used. The value or values that you'd like to see are placed inside the parentheses. For example, to print the value of the variable `quizGrade`:

```
$ node
> let quizGrade = 98
undefined
> console.log(quizGrade)
98
undefined
>
```

EXAMPLE 12-15

We'll see two other methods of displaying information in the context of a web page in Chapter 13.

This kind of print statement can be written to print out more than one value. For example, if we wanted to be a little more informative about the number calculated, we could write:

```
let quizGrade = 98
console.log("Your quiz grade is", quizGrade)
```

EXAMPLE 12-16

The result would be `Your quiz grade is 98`. If you have more than two values to print, separate them with commas. It's fine to mix numeric and text values:

```
let quizGrade = 98
console.log("Your quiz grade is", quizGrade, "which is an A!")
```

EXAMPLE 12-17

About That "Undefined" Response

If you ran the example above on your own, you will have noticed that each time you entered a statement, Node responded with a statement of its own: `undefined`. This is expected; the JavaScript interpreter running inside Node is printing the returned value from each of the statements that you are typing in. None of the statements in the example return a value (as it might if you entered an expression such as `40+2`), and the interpreter dutifully prints out `undefined` since there was no defined value to print. If you find this annoying (and many do), there's a line of JavaScript that will turn this behavior off:

```
repl.repl.ignoreUndefined = true
```

EXAMPLE 12-18

The command sets the ignoreUndefined variable of the REPL (Read-Execute-Print Loop) interpreter to true, which turns off printing of undefined values. Here's an example of starting node, turning off printing of undefined values, and running the previous sample code—the result is much easier to read and much less annoying:

```
$ node
> repl.repl.ignoreUndefined = true
true
> let quizGrade = 98
> console.log(quizGrade)
98
>
```

EXAMPLE 12-19

Reading in Values

Another side effect of JavaScript having been designed to run entirely within a web browser is that there is no built-in way to read a value typed by the user on the console. That's not to say that reading typed-in values is not possible; it certainly is, but doing so requires several lines of JavaScript code. For the examples used in this chapter, values will be hard-coded into programs rather than read from the console. Chapter 13 will examine a few ways to read values from a web page (from a form, for example).

The Semicolon Controversy

There's one more bit of JavaScript history to discuss before we dive into the rest of the language. Until recently, JavaScript, like a large number of other languages, required each statement to end with a semicolon (formally called a delimiter). This was to help the JavaScript interpreter decide on where a statement ended. Our earlier example, with semicolons added to the appropriate spots, looks like this:

```
> repl.repl.ignoreUndefined = true;
true
> let quizGrade = 98;
> console.log(quizGrade);
98
>
```

EXAMPLE 12-20

It's pretty obvious where each line ends in the simple program, but as programs become more complex it often isn't immediately obvious. Recent versions of JavaScript have relaxed this requirement; while there are one or two special circumstances in which a semicolon is required, the vast majority of a program can now be written without them. This has led to a bit of a split between JavaScript traditionalists who demand a semicolon on every line and free-spirited programmers who feel that they've been released from the burden of reaching for the semicolon key every few seconds.

For our discussions of JavaScript we'll not worry about the semicolon. We won't run into those special circumstances where it is required, and the general trend seems to be to move away from using them.

Math Operators

Doing math in JavaScript is just the same as doing math on a calculator—the basic math functions are built into the language as well as a few that are tailored to a programming environment. Standard mathematical operators can be used in a JavaScript statement in the same way that you might write them on paper. Here's what the basic operators look like. Remember, statements are typed on the line with the Node prompt (>) and the result is printed on the following line:

```
>
> 10 + 32 //addition
42
> 58 - 16 //subtraction
42
> 2 * 21  //multiplication
42
> 126 / 3 //division
42
>
```

EXAMPLE 12-21 Basic mathematical operators

Programming languages define an order of precedence for mathematical operations, and JavaScript is no exception. The precedence of an operator such as + or * determines which will be executed first, then second, and so on. In JavaScript, multiplication and division will be calculated first, and then subtraction and addition. If several operators of the same type appear in a statement, they are evaluated from left to right. In Example 12-22, the result is calculated in this order: 6*4, then 4/2 (multiplication and division have higher precedence than addition and subtraction and proceed from left to right), which results in an intermediate state of 2 + 24 − 2 + 1. Addition and subtraction have the same precedence, and so each value is calculated from left to right, starting with 2 + 24 (26), then 26 − 2 (24), and finally 24 + 1 (25).

```
> 2 + 6 * 4 - 4 / 2 + 1
25
>
```

EXAMPLE 12-22 Order of operations in JavaScript

Precedence on its face is quite simple, but when mathematical statements start to get long it can be difficult to parse out which operation will happen before another. To help avoid confusion, we can use parentheses to group operations together—operations in parentheses are executed first, regardless of the precedence of the operation they contain. Here is the statement in Example 12-22 rewritten with parentheses:

```
> (2 + 6) * 4 - 4 / (2 + 1)
30.666666666666668

>
```

EXAMPLE 12-23 Overriding precedence with parentheses

Why is the result different from before? The parentheses force the statements inside of them to be executed first, and so the statement becomes 8 * 4 – 4 / 3. Once the statements inside the parenthese are taken care of, normal order of precedence is applied, with multiplication and division evaluated before addition and subtraction; this yields 32 – 1.333. Finally, the subtraction is carried out to determine the value 30.666666666666668.

Good programming practice is to use parentheses any time you are writing a mathematical statement, even if the order of precedence is obvious. Doing so prevents ambiguity and gives you, the programmer, a way to express your intent. It's important to keep in mind that the programs you write are not only read by the computer, but also by other programmers who might need to work on your code in the future (and sometimes that future programmer is you!). Removing ambiguity is a first step toward writing readable, maintainable code.

About Numerical Precision

Those with a sharp mathematical eye might have snorted in derision on reading the previous example. The result calculated by JavaScript, 30.666666666666668, is mathematically incorrect. In the second step of arriving at an answer (8 * 4 – 4 / 3), the expression 4/3 results in a value with an infinitely repeating decimal portion (1.33333 …) that has been rounded up. This isn't strictly a JavaScript problem; digital computers have a finite amount of space in memory to store numeric values and so must approximate those with infinite values.

In most applications this tiny bit of imprecision won't matter. If your program requires high-precision math (maybe you are calculating launch trajectories for a rendezvous with Mars), a third-party library can be included along with your program that will provide the necessary level of precision.

Other Math Operations

There are three additional mathematical operators built into the JavaScript interpreter:

Modulus – returns the remainder of a division (10 % 3 = 1; 10 divided by 3 is 3 with a remainder of 1)
Increment – adds one to a numeric variable (given aNumber = 5, aNumber++ = 6)
Decrement – subtracts one from a numeric variable (given aNumber = 5, aNumber-- = 4)

Any other math operation must be accessed through a *library* called Math. JavaScript comes with several special-purpose libraries; the Math library includes a large range of mathematical operators and functions. For example, if you need to find the square root of a number, that function, sqrt, is called from the library:

```
> Math.sqrt(16)
4
>
```

EXAMPLE 12-24

There are two elements of interest here. First is that the way to gain access to the sqrt function is with a dot (.) between the name of the library (Math) and the desired function (sqrt). Any function in the library may be accessed using this syntax—to find the cosine of a number, for example:

```
> Math.cos(1.123)
0.432980188431095
>
```

EXAMPLE 12-25

A good resource for learning about the Math library is the math page at W3Schools. com (https://www.w3schools.com/jsref/jsref_obj_math.asp).

JavaScript Libraries

Just as the Math library contains functions for various mathematical operations, around 60 standard libraries extend JavaScript in other areas. The following table lists several commonly used libraries; they are built into the language and can be used without any extra configuration.

Library Name	Provides	Example
Date	Time and date functions	Date.now( )
Map	Key/Value pairs	Map.set(2, "Perry")
Math	Math operations	Math.sqrt(4)
String	Operations on text	let c = "hello world" console.log(c.length)

In addition to the standard libraries, literally thousands of libraries have been written by third parties that provide an endless variety of features that can be included in your program. It is quite easy to write complex programs by combining functions from these libraries, removing the need to come up with complex code yourself.

Boolean Values and Conditional Statements

It is often the case that we need to know whether a statement is true or false. Usually this is so that a choice can be made as to what part of your program will run next. For example, your code might be calculating a user's age, and if the birth year that they entered is greater than the current year, there probably was a mistake, and you'd want to prompt the user to try again. Or, your program might be deciding whether to buy a certain stock, and will only do so if the current price is below a certain value.

These kinds of decisions are usually either-or, that is, one path or another will be taken through your code depending on the result of a comparison. In JavaScript, comparisons such as this return a value of either *true* or *false*. The comparisons themselves are less-than (<), greater-than (>), and equal-to (===). Note the use of three consecutive equal signs for the equal-to comparison. A common programming error is to use a single sign, as in a = b, which always returns true—the statement simply assigns the value in the variable b to the variable a. Here are a few examples:

```
> let large = 123
> let small = 5
>
> large > small
true
>
> small > large
false
>
> small === 6
false
> small === 5
true
>
```

EXAMPLE 12-26

By themselves, these kinds of comparisons are not all that useful. However, using them in a conditional statement is the bread and butter of programming. Conditionals, as they are called, are formed using the keyword *if*, just as you might in ordinary speech: "If the price is below five dollars I will buy the stock." Here's a short example:

```
> .editor
// Entering editor mode (^D to finish, ^C to cancel)
let stockPrice = 6.00
if (stockPrice < 5.00)
```

```
console.log("Buying stock")
if (stockPrice > 5.00)
console.log("Still too expensive!")
^d
Still too expensive!
>
```

EXAMPLE 12-27

In Example 12-27 we used Node's editor to enter several lines of a program, followed by typing Control-d to run the program. (Control-d is entered by holding down the Control key while typing the letter *d*). First, the variable stockPrice is set to 6.00 (to represent $6.00). Then two conditional statements follow; depending on the price, one of the two conditions will be true and the statement following the conditional will execute. In this case, 6.00 is greater than 5.00, and so the statement "Still too expensive!" is printed on the console.

Another important thing to note is that the conditional statement itself is enclosed in parentheses: if (stockPrice < 5.00). The parentheses are required—the program will not run without them, and an error will be displayed.

The Else Keyword

This kind of either-or test works just fine as written, but there's a handy shortcut used by JavaScript programmers: the else keyword. It is used in cases where you want to do one thing if a condition is true, otherwise a second thing is done. Here's the same decision-making program using the else keyword:

```
> .editor
// Entering editor mode (^D to finish, ^C to cancel)
let stockPrice = 6.00
if (stockPrice < 5.00)
   console.log("Buying stock")
else
   console.log("Still too expensive!")
^d
Still too expensive!
>
```

EXAMPLE 12-28

In this version, one of two messages will be printed, depending on the value of the variable stockPrice. The else keyword separates the two messages.

A Few Additional Comparisons

There are two additional aspects of conditional expressions that will help you refine your decisions. First, any of the operators we've seen so far can be modified with the *not* or *negation* operator, !, which "flips" the comparison. We can, for example, test whether two values are equal to each other (===) or not equal to each other (!==). We might expect the not-equal operator to be !===, which would be logical; however, it is simply !==.

We might also be interested in whether a value is less-than-or-equal (<=) or greater-than-or-equal (>=) to a value. These are shown in the Example 12-29:

```
> let aValue = 10
>
> aValue >= 10
true
>
> aValue !== 10
false
>
> aValue <= 5
false
>
```

EXAMPLE 12-29

Logical Operators

Another set of operators that we can use in comparisons are logical in nature. These allow us to make compound decisions; for example, we might want to buy a stock if its price is between two values, neither higher nor lower. Such a comparison in natural language would be, "If the stock is priced above this value AND below that value, buy it." In such a case *both* conditions must be true for the comparison to also be true.

We might, on the other hand, want to make a decision in which just one of several conditions is true. We might say, "If the stock is priced below this value OR the trade volume is greater than 100,000, buy the stock." Here *either* condition would satisfy the test.

In JavaScript, the AND conjunction is written as &&, and the OR conjunction is written as || (two "pipe" characters, also called vertical bars—on most keyboards this character is above the \ key).

Example 12-30 illustrates both:

```
> .editor
// Entering editor mode (^D to finish, ^C to cancel)
let stockPrice = 10.00
let volume = 150000
```

```
if (stockPrice > 5.00 && stockPrice < 15.00)
   console.log("Buying the stock.")

if (stockPrice < 10.00 || volume > 100000)
   console.log("Buying the stock.")



Buying the stock.
Buying the stock.
```

EXAMPLE 12-30

In the first part, both conditions are true, and the `&&` operator returns `true` for the comparison. In the second part, the first condition is not true; however, the second is, and the `||` operator again returns `true` for the comparison.

Loops

Many tasks carried out by programs are repetitive in nature. This makes sense, if you think about it; if we were interested in doing a task only once, there'd be little incentive to write a program to do it. In programming, repetition is accomplished using a loop, which repeats the same set of steps over and over until some condition is satisfied. You might, for example, be calculating annual compound interest on an investment over a 20-year period; the calculation is the same for each year though the initial value changes each time. A loop, running the calculation 20 times, would do the trick; it would look something like this:

Set the initial value of the investment
Calculate the interest on the balance
Add the interest to the balance
Repeat step 2 until enough periods have been calculated

Generally speaking there are two situations that we'll encounter when programming a loop:

The number of iterations (the number of times to execute the loop) is known in advance. The number of iterations is dependent on some external value or event.

JavaScript provides both kinds of loop, and they operate similarly, though the structure is slightly different between them.

For Loops

The *for* loop is used when the number of iterations needed is known ahead of time. Example 12-31 illustrates how this type of loop would be used to calculate the interest on an investment.

```
> .editor
// Entering editor mode (^D to finish, ^C to cancel)

//1. Set the initial value for the balance
let balance = 500

//2. Specify the number of times to run the loop; each time
through
//is one year's interest
let years = 8

//3. Set the interest rate for this investment
let interestRate = .04   //4% interest per year

//4. Calculate interest for each year, storing intermediate
values
//in the balance variable
for (let counter = 0; counter < years; counter = counter + 1)
{
    balance = balance + (balance * interestRate)
}

//5. Print out the final balance
console.log("Balance:",balance)
^D
Balance:  684.2845252026368
```

EXAMPLE 12-31   Calculating compound interest with a for loop

There are several parts of this syntax. In steps 1, 2, and 3, the variables for the balance, number of years to calculate, and the interest rate are defined and initialized. Step 4 implements a for loop that will run once for each year, totaling up the balance for each pass. The loop itself is enclosed between curly braces, { and }, which define the block of code to execute each time, also called the *body* of the loop. In this example there is only one line of code in the body; however, the body can include any number of lines. In this case, the line

```
balance = balance + (balance * interestRate)
```

EXAMPLE 12-32

is executed each time the loop is run. It calculates the interest on the current balance (`bal-ance * interestRate`), adds the interest to the current `balance balance + (balance * interestRate)` and stores that value back into the balance variable.

The structure of a for loop is explained in the following table.

for (	let counter = 0;	counter < years;	counter = counter + 1)
Begins the loop definition. It will be a for loop, and the opening parenthesis starts the conditions for the loop.	Defines and initializes a counter to keep track of the number of times the loop has executed. This portion is executed only once when the loop begins. Note that the keyword *let* is used here to define the variable before it is initialized with 0. The semicolon separates this part from the next element.	A test to see if the loop has run the specified number of times. The loop will continue as long as this test returns the Boolean value `true`. In this case, the variable `counter`, which starts at 0, will increase by one each time the loop is run; when the value of the counter is no longer less than the value of the variable years, the loop will end. This test is performed at the start of each loop pass.	An action to perform after the loop is run each time. Here, the counter is increased by one each time. The closing parenthesis ends the conditions for the loop.

There is nothing magical about the names of each variable. The variable `counter`, for example, might be named `count`, or `year`, or `Fred`. The name doesn't matter; it is used to hold the count of the number of times the loop has run, and counter makes sense in this case. Use variable names that are related to what they are holding to make your code easier to read and understand.

The test to see if the loop is finished, `counter < years` in this example, runs at the start of each loop pass, before the code in the body of the loop executes. This means that it is possible to set up conditions in which the loop body will never be executed. For example, if the number of years to calculate was initialized to 0 in step 2, the test `counter < years` would be the equivalent of $0 < 0$, which is false, and so the loop would exit before running the body.

The post-loop action, `counter = counter + 1`, can be any expression—in this example, adding a year to the counter makes sense for this problem, but it might be the case that reducing a variable or dividing it by some value would be more appropriate. The result of the post-loop action will be tested before the loop is run again. If you are simply incrementing or decrementing a variable by 1, a shortcut is to use the increment (++) or decrement (--) operator. For example, instead of `counter = counter + 1`, you could instead write `counter++`.

While Loops

In the second type of loop we can't specify ahead of time how many times the loop should run. Instead, an external event or value is used to test each time whether the loop should run again. You might, for example, write a loop that reads lines of text from a file; we probably don't know ahead of time how many lines there are, and so a while loop can be constructed that runs until the last line is read, which is the condition that we will test. In plain language we'd say, "Read a line of text from the file while there are still lines to read."

Let's apply this to our compounding interest calculation. This time, instead of calculating the value of our investment after a fixed number of years, we want to know how many years it will take, at a given interest rate, to reach a particular balance.

Here's our new program using a while loop:

```
> .editor
// Entering editor mode (^D to finish, ^C to cancel)

//1. Set the initial calue for the balance
let balance = 500

//2. Specify the desired end value; we want to double our money
let desiredValue = balance * 2

//3. Set the interest rate for this investment
let interestRate = .04   //4% interest per year

//4. Create a counter to keep track of the number of times the
loop
//has run; this will be the number of years it took to reach
the goal
let numberOfYears = 1  //start at year 1

//5. Calculate the new balance for each year, ending when it
meets
//or exceeds the desiredValue

while (balance <= desiredValue)
{
    balance = balance + (balance * interestRate)
    numberOfYears = numberOfYears + 1
}

//6. Print the number of years required to meet our goal
console.log("At", interestRate, "interest it will take", number-
OfYears, "years to double your investment.")
```

```
^d
At 0.04 interest it will take 19 years to double
your investment.
```

EXAMPLE 12-33

This program is very similar to the one that we wrote using a for loop, but we don't know in advance how many years (passes through the loop) it will take to meet the condition `balance <= desiredValue`. As with the for loop it is possible to specify initial conditions that cause the condition to be false immediately—setting `desiredBalance` equal to the balance would do it—since the test is executed before the loop is run. For this particular set of values, it will take 19 years to double our initial investment.

Strings

An important type of variable contains text. In JavaScript, as in many other languages, text is called a *string* because internally it is seen by the JavaScript interpreter as a string of individual characters. Strings are created by enclosing the text inside quotation marks. The string "Hello!" comprises six characters.

Creating a string variable is just the same as any other type of variable. Use the `let` or `const` keywords to set up a new variable, give it a descriptive name, and assign its value. For example,

```
let greeting = "Welcome to our lecture!"
```

EXAMPLE 12-34

JavaScript includes a large number of built-in features related to strings. Most text-processing operations can be accomplished in a single line of code, such as changing the case of a string, substituting characters or words, finding a string's length, or even reversing the order of the letters. These features are accessed by typing a period (.) after the name of a variable, then the operation that you'd like to do. For example, to determine the length of a string:

```
let greeting = "Welcome to our lecture!"
console.log("The length is", greeting.length)
The length is 23
```

EXAMPLE 12-35

Here's a way to convert a string to upper or lower case:

```
> let convertMe = "This String Is In Title Case"
> console.log(convertMe.toUpperCase())
THIS STRING IS IN TITLE CASE
> console.log(convertMe.toLowerCase())
this string is in title case
>
```

EXAMPLE 12-36

And here is a way to replace winter with summer:

```
> let weather = "Winter is coming!"
> console.log(weather.replace("Winter", "Spring"))
Spring is coming!
>
```

EXAMPLE 12-37

String Concatenation

A very useful property of strings is that they can be added to each other, an operation called concatenation, using the + symbol. We typically think of + in the context of addition, and this is extended to "adding" two strings together. For example:

```
let firstPart = "Hello "
let secondPart = "there!"
console.log(firstPart + secondPart)
Hello there!
```

EXAMPLE 12-38

The addition operator can also be used with numeric variables, which makes it easy to print statements using them:

```
    let theAnswer = 42
    console.log("The answer to life, universe, and everything is "
  + theAnswer)
    The answer to life, universe, and everything is 42
```

EXAMPLE 12-39

Behind the scenes, JavaScript notices that you are trying to "add" a number to a string and converts the numeric value to a string value in order to print it out. This kind of conversion, called *coercion*, can be both a benefit and a curse. JavaScript is a loosely typed language in which the type of a variable (string, number, date, etc.) is deduced from context. Strongly typed languages such as C++, on the other hand, require the programmer to explicitly state the type of a variable, and no behind-the-scenes conversions occur. In most cases coercion isn't a problem, but when working with JavaScript and web pages, especially forms, it can require extra attention, as you'll see in the next chapter.

The variable itself is not changed in type; it is just the value that is converted when concatenating it with a string. We can demonstrate this by using the `typeof` command, which returns the type of a given variable:

```
    let theAnswer = 42
    console.log("The answer to life, universe, and everything is "
  + theAnswer)
    console.log("Variable is a" + typeof theAnswer)
    The answer to life, universe, and everything is 42
    Variable is a number
```

EXAMPLE 12-40

Substrings

Many operations on strings require finding a substring, which is a portion of a string. For example, "hello" is a substring of "hello and welcome." JavaScript offers two ways to find or extract a substring: `substring( )` and `substr( )`. The two operate slightly differently from one another. In most cases the substring will be stored in its own variable for later use, or printed out in a message.

substring( )

The substring( ) function takes two arguments: the position of the starting character of the desired substring and the position of the last character plus one. Given the string

```
let aLongString = "This is a very long string"
```

EXAMPLE 12-41

we can extract the word "very" with

```
aLongString.substring(10, 14)
```

EXAMPLE 12-42

since the character 'v' is the 10th character, and 'y' is the 13th (adding one gives us 14).

substr( )

The confusingly similar `substr( )` function also returns a substring, but the way it finds that substring is slightly different from that used by a substring( ). It also takes two arguments, but this time we must specify the starting position and the number of characters desired (rather than the ending position). Given the string

```
let aLongString = "This is a very long string"
```

EXAMPLE 12-43

we can extract the word "very" with

```
aLongString.substr(10, 4)
```

EXAMPLE 12-44

since the character 'v' is the 10th character, and "very" has four letters in it.

Why 10?

Astute readers will note that in both of the examples above the first character in the word "very" is stipulated as being the 10th character in the string. Go back and count them.

Did you come up with 11? Ordinary folks do, but programmers know better! In the realm of computing, we start counting at 0 (zero) instead of 1, and so the 'T' at the start of the phrase is the zeroth character, not the first. The reasons for starting at 0 are both practical and historical. Our own department proudly states that it is "The Number 0 CS Program."

Other String Operations

In addition to properties such as length and functions, such as substring extraction and case switching, JavaScript offers about 20 additional operations, including ways to trim whitespace, determine if a string starts with a specific character, and split a string into several new strings based on a delimiting character. If there's something that you need to do to a string, there's a function for it.

Arrays

Another important type of variable is the array, which is an ordered collection of values. Arrays are accessed using square brackets; a few examples illustrate how they work:

```
> let courseArray = ["CS101", "CS111", "CS112"]
>
> console.log (courseArray[1])
CS111
>
```

EXAMPLE 12-45   A simple array

In Example 12-45, an array is created with three items, called elements, and then one of the elements is printed out. Elements of the array are separated by a comma. Note that, like strings and other data types in JavaScript, counting begins at zero, and so the second element of the array is selected using [1] and not [2].

Unlike other mainstream, strongly typed languages, JavaScript permits mixed data types in an array, so that we can store a string, an integer, and a floating-point number together in the same array:

```
> let mixedTypes = ["a string", 123.456, 42]
>
> console.log(mixedTypes[2], mixedTypes[0])
42 'a string'
>
```

EXAMPLE 12-46

Since variables represent values, we can store them in an array, and also store the result of an operation on variables:

```
> let oddNumber = 5
> let evenNumber = 6
> let numbers = [oddNumber, evenNumber, oddNumber *
evenNumber]
>
> console.log(numbers[2])
30
>
```

EXAMPLE 12-47

Arrays have properties similar to strings, and there are many built-in functions that provide ways to manipulate the data inside the array. For example, an array of strings can be easily sorted using the array's built-in sort( ) function:

```
> let dogs = ["Yellow Lab", "Black Lab", "Corgi"]
> console.log(dogs)
[ 'Yellow Lab', 'Black Lab', 'Corgi' ]
>
> console.log( dogs.sort() )
[ 'Black Lab', 'Corgi', 'Yellow Lab' ]
>
```

EXAMPLE 12-48

It is often useful to know how long an array is; this is a property that can be accessed with .length. In the code below, a loop is used to print only the even number from an array. Whether a number is odd or even is determined by using the modulo operator (%), which returns the remainder of a division. When dividing a number by 2, the remainder will be 0 for even numbers and 1 for odd numbers. For example, 42 % 2 results in 0, while 43 % 2 results in 1.

```
> .editor
// Entering editor mode (^D to finish, ^C to cancel)

let mixedNumbers = [3, 12, 11, 42, 66]
```

```
for (let index = 0; index < mixedNumbers.length; index++)  {
    if ( (mixedNumbers[index] % 2) === 0 ) {
        console.log(mixedNumbers[index] + ", at index " + index
+ ", is even")
    }
}
^d
12, at index 1, is even
42, at index 3, is even
66, at index 4, is even
>
```

EXAMPLE 12-49   Finding the even numbers in an array with a loop

Functions

The word *function* has been used several times in this chapter but not defined. A function in JavaScript is:

- A named sequence of steps that
- Accepts zero or more input values (called *parameters*) and
- Returns zero or one values as the result of its sequence of steps.

We use functions to consolidate similar steps in our program, and to provide building blocks that can be used to create new programs. It's important to note that functions in JavaScript are fundamental to the language, and the way that they are created and used ranges from the simple to the complex. In this chapter, just the basics are discussed.

The Parts of a Function
To illustrate the basic structure of a function, consider the following; it adds 5 to any number and returns the result.

```
function add5 (aNumber) {
    return aNumber + 5
}
```

EXAMPLE 12-50

The parts of this function are:

function	add 5	(aNumber)	{	return ...	}
The keyword function is used to let JavaScript know that we are defining a new function.	The name of this function; it must be unique within the program.	One or more optional variables that will hold any parameters that are input into the function. The variable names are enclosed in parentheses.	The body of the function (the steps that the function will perform) begins with a curly brace.	The return statement returns a value from the function. Here it returns the input value plus five.	The body of the function is ended with a curly brace.

Once a function has been defined, it can be used in your program as many times as necessary. Here, the add5 function is called twice.

```
> .editor
// Entering editor mode (^D to finish, ^C to cancel)
function add5 (aNumber) {
    return aNumber + 5
}
let result = 0              //initialize variable to hold results

result = add5(37)          //add5 will return 37 + 5
result = add5(result)      //add5 will return 42 + 5

console.log("Final value:", result)

Final value: 47
>
```

EXAMPLE 12-51   Using a function to add 5 to a value

The add5 function is very simple; its body has only one line of code. More typically, a function will incorporate dozens or even hundreds of lines of code.

Making Functions More Generic
One goal of using functions in programming is to reduce the number of lines of code that are written. An unwritten rule of coding is that the more lines are included in a program, the more likely it is that there will be errors. It also is more efficient to accomplish a task with fewer lines of code.

The `add5` function of Example 12-51 is very specific; it always adds the same number, 5, to the input value. Let's say, though, that our program required us to add 6 to a number several times, and also 42. One way to handle this would be to write two new functions, `add6` and `add42` that mimic `add5`, but already we are running into inefficiencies. If the requirement expanded such that we also needed to add 11, 9, 432, 116, and a random value calculated from the current time, the number of functions we'd need would grow proportionally.

A better solution is to look at `add5` and see if it can be modified so as to become more generic. What is `add5` really doing? It is simply adding two numbers together. Ignoring the fact that a simple + would do the trick, what we need is a function that accepts two input values and returns their sum. Example 12-52 accomplishes this:

```
> .editor
// Entering editor mode (^D to finish, ^C to cancel)
function sum (value1, value2) {
    return value1 + value2
}
let result = 0                   //initialize variable to hold
results

result = sum (32, 10)        //sum will return 42
result = sum (result, result)    //sum will return 42 + 42, or 84
console.log("Final value:", result)

^d
Final value: 84
>
```

EXAMPLE 12-52 A more generic addition function

A function can accept as many values as necessary to do its work. The `sum` function takes two values, and `add5` took just one. It is entirely possible to write a function that accepts zero values.

Zero-Parameter Functions

JavaScript was designed as a language for programs that run inside a web browser. Because of this history, there are several ways to provide input parameters to functions that don't involve passing them in as they were in `add5` and `sum`. A function might, for example, read the value that a user typed into a form on a web page.

For similar reasons, it isn't necessary to return a value from a JavaScript function. The function can write information directly onto the web page. We'll see how this is done in Chapter 13.

The code below shows both of these features. The function `writeDate` takes no parameters and does not return a result; instead it writes the current data on the console. Since it doesn't return any value, the return statement can be omitted; it is assumed that the program will continue to the next line of code once `writeDate` has done its work.

```
> .editor
// Entering editor mode (^D to finish, ^C to cancel)
function writeDate () {
    let currentDate = Date.now()
    console.log("The date is:", currentDate)
}

//Execute some code ...
writeDate()
//Execute some more code ...

^d
The date is: 1507482945212
>
```

EXAMPLE 12-53   A function that neither accepts nor returns a value

You might expect that `Date.now`, used in Example 12-53, would provide the date in a format such as "October 1st, 2017." Instead, it returns the number of milliseconds that have elapsed between January 1st, 1970, and "now". This is useful when you want to do calculations with dates; the start date in 1970 was chosen because it coincided with the release date of the UNIX operating system. The Date library provides several different functions for working with dates and times, including a few, such as `toDateString`, that will format the milliseconds value into a more readable format.

Bottom Line

Learning a programming language for the first time can seem intimidating. The key to success is to remember that you don't need to learn everything at once. JavaScript can be approached like any skill; learn the basics, then add complexity over time. Some very powerful programs can be written with just the simple elements offered in this chapter.

While JavaScript is becoming more and more popular as a general programming language, its niche is still providing interactive programs that run inside a web browser. Once you have mastered the material in this chapter you'll be ready to move your coding skills to the web, which we'll cover in Chapter 13 JavaScript and Web Pages.

Figure Credit

- **Fig. 12.1:** Copyright © by Node.js Foundation.

CHAPTER

13

JavaScript and HTML

JavaScript was originally intended to be a language that web developers could use to add interactivity to their web pages. When it was released in 1995, and for a few years after, there were competing languages that offered similar features. Toward the turn of the century, as JavaScript became standardized, it outpaced the competition to the point that it is extremely rare to see programs written to run in the browser in any other language.

During that same time frame we saw the applications written in JavaScript become more and more complex, and the introduction of Node.JavaScript in 2007, allowing JavaScript to run on the server, created an environment in which the language was not only dominant on the web, but also opened up a new way to write applications for mobile devices such as phones and tablets. All of the effects that you see on a web page—fancy menus, interactive images and text, automatically updating information such as stock quotes—are accomplished with just HTML, JavaScript, and maybe a little CSS.

This chapter focuses on the mechanism used to tie JavaScript and web pages together, and we'll just scratch the surface of what has become a complex development environment. That said, the techniques discussed here are a great springboard to developing more complex and richly interactive web pages.

Event-Driven Programming

Think about how you browse the web. Do you click the links or buttons on a page in a fixed order, spaced out so that each click or button press happens at precise times? I certainly don't, and neither, probably, do you. We react to the page we are viewing in different ways; sometimes we'll spend a lot of time reading one section, then get distracted by a puppy video and click on that, then come back to the page and fill in a form or click a menu item.

The way that we interact with the page isn't predictable. The programs running behind the page can't make any assumptions about what will happen next, or in what sequence things will happen, or how long it will be until the next. We say that our interaction is *asynchronous*—unpredictable. The JavaScript programs must also be asynchronous. To accomplish this the program must respond to events in the browser. Click on an image, and the program responds by enlarging the image. Mouse over a menu, and the program responds by sliding down a menu panel. Each thing that can happen on the page has a corresponding part of the program that will react to the event.

Listeners

Every element of a web page emits, or generates, an event each time it is interacted with. A button on the page, which is created with the HTML <button> tag, emits these events (among others):

This event ...	... is emitted when the user
onMouseOver	moves the cursor over the button
onMouseDown	presses a mouse button down
onMouseUp	releases the mouse button
onClick	clicks on the button (combines the previous two events)
onMouseOut	moves the cursor away from the button

Generally the response will be written as a JavaScript function, similar to those that we looked at in the previous chapter. For example, if we want a function named showJoeMessage to run when a button is clicked, we could write

```
<button onClick='showJoeMessage( )'>
```

EXAMPLE 13-1

Inside the HTML tag <button>, we specify first the event that we want to respond to (onClick) and the function to run when the event is emitted (showJoeMessage). Each time a user clicks the button, the showJoeMessage function runs.

Nearly every HTML tag, whether it be a paragraph, a list item, an image, or something else, emits these kinds of events. In addition to clicking, you can capture when a user moves the mouse across an element (called a *blur*), tries to drag something like an image, types in a form, arrives at or leaves the page, and so on. In each case, the specific action can be used to run a function.

Here's the showJoeMessage function set up to run when the user clicks a button:

```
<html>

<head>
    <script>
```

```
        function showJoeMessage() {
            alert("Eat at Joe's")
        }
    </script>
</head>

<body>
    <button onclick="showJoeMessage()">Show Me!</button>
</body>

</html>
```

EXAMPLE 13-2

Notice that the function is written in the `<head>` of the document and is enclosed by the `<script>` and `</script>` HTML tags. While the `<script>` tag typically is included in the head in this way, it is not a hard requirement, and in practice scripts can appear in the middle or at the end of an HTML document. The advantage of placing them in the head is that web browsers work on an HTML file from top to bottom; if the scripts are in the head of the document, they will be available to any portion of the document below them. If the scripts are placed at the bottom of the document, a portion of the main page that needs to run one of them might not see it until the page is completely loaded. For most documents, placing scripts in the head is the appropriate choice.

The function itself takes no parameters, and so it is defined as

```
    function showJoeMessage( )
```

EXAMPLE 13-3

without any parameters between the parentheses. We'll modify the function later to take a parameter so that the message displayed is not hard-coded.

The message is displayed by a second function, `alert( )`, that is built into the browser. Whenever `alert` is called a small pop-up window is displayed along with any text that has been passed to the function as a parameter.

Clicking the button results in a pop-up message, shown in Figure 13-1.

FIGURE 13-1 The function in action

Making a Function More Generic

In the previous example the message displayed in the alert box is hard-coded. What if we added a second button to our page and want an alert to appear that reads "Eat at Maggie's Instead!"? One approach would be to duplicate the code above and write a second function, perhaps called showMaggieMessage, that would display the new text:

```
<script>
        function showJoeMessage() {
            alert("Eat at Joe's")
        }
        function showMaggieMessage() {
            alert("Eat at Maggie's Instead!")
        }
</script>
```

EXAMPLE 13-4

For just two buttons and two messages this still works, but what if there were quite a few ways to display a message, and each text was different? It would be inefficient to write a new function for each of them. Instead we do something that is quite common in programming, which is to make a generic display function that accepts any message and displays it. In this way we only have to write and test one function, and the buttons or other elements on the page that want to display a message have only one function to call with their custom text.

The generic version looks like this:

```
<html>
```

```
<head>
    <script>
        function showMessage(message) {
            alert(message)
        }
    </script>
</head>

<body>
    <button onclick="showMessage('Eat at Joe\'s!')">Show Me!</
button>
    <button onclick="showMessage('Eat at Maggie\'s!')">Maggie's
FTW</button>
</body>

</html>
```

EXAMPLE 13-5

The text passed to show-Message from each button contains an escaped apostrophe (\'). The backslash is used to let HTML know that the following apostrophe is a literal character that should be displayed as text and not the end of a quoted string. Figure 13-2 shows the result of pressing the Maggie's FTW button.

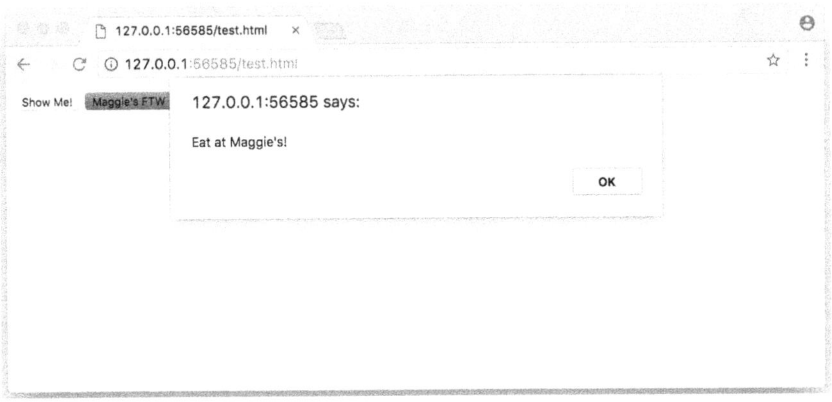

FIGURE 13-2 The result of using a more generic function

With this new generic version of the function we can create as many buttons and messages as we need, relying on the showMessage to display whatever we pass to it. In this version

```
function showMessage(message) {
        alert(message)
    }
```

EXAMPLE 13-6

the variable `message` is used to hold the string passed from the button. This function simply uses the message as it was passed from the button, but as you know from our previous discussion of strings, they can be easily modified. For example, you could add a reminder to each alert box like this:

```
function showMessage(message) {
        alert('Remember: ' + message)
    }
```

EXAMPLE 13-7

When this function is called, the alert that is displayed will read "Remember: Eat at Maggie's!" or "Remember: Eat at Joe's!"

The functions that you write can be very simple, like this one, or very complex, depending on what work it will do.

The Document Object Model (DOM)

Displaying information in alert boxes is one way of interacting with users, but after a few of them they can be quite annoying. Usually what we want to accomplish is to make changes to the web page when a function runs; highlighting links, expanding images, dropping down menus, and the like. JavaScript has the capability to do this through the Document Object Model (DOM) provided by the web browser.

The DOM is a data structure that organizes each element of the page. For every HTML tag there is a corresponding data element in the DOM, along with several elements that we don't see on the page itself. In JavaScript we can treat these elements as variables, both accessing their values and changing them.

Structurally, the DOM is set up as an inverted tree with the page (which the DOM calls the document) at the top (Figure 13-3). The DOM begins, as does an HTML document, with the `<html>` tag, followed by the `<head>` and `<body>` tags. In this DOM, the first thing in the body of the page is an `<h1>` tag and its text.

FIGURE 13-3 A portion of JavaScript's Document Object Model

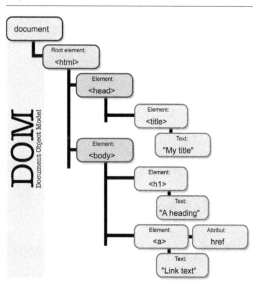

Identifying Elements with the ID Attribute

Since the DOM is structurally similar to its web page it is possible to locate each element by "walking" the DOM from the top. In Figure 13-3 we could find the text of the `<h1>` tag by following the DOM, stating at the top level document, down the tree. We use a "dot" notation for this, placing a period between each element. So, to get that text, we'd start at the top and write `document.html.body.h1.text`, which would yield the value "A heading."

This technique works well, but as pages become more complex, with dozens of headers and hundreds of paragraphs and other elements, it becomes a little more difficult to find a specific item, especially when the DOM labels each element the same (`.h1` in the previous example). Finding one `<p>` out of a hundred can be a challenge.

Fortunately, HTML provides a simple way to give an element a unique identifier which can then be quickly found through JavaScript on the page. The attribute is `id`, and it may be included in any HTML tag. It should be unique in the document; if it is not, JavaScript will find the first instance of a tag with the `id` and ignore the rest.

The format for an id (shown here with a <h1> tag) is:

```
<h1 id="identifier">
```

EXAMPLE 13-8

The identifier is a simple string of characters and may contain letters, numbers, and punctuation, including spaces. You can choose any value that you like, but it is a good practice to use values that are descriptive, so that someone reading your code can quickly understand what the identifier is associated with.

Finding Elements with getElementById

Once a tag has an identifier, it can be quickly accessed from JavaScript by using the built-in function `getElementById`, which returns a reference to the element that can either be used directly or stored in a variable. Example 13-9 shows how to create a variable to hold a reference to the HTML `<h1>` tag; the function is executed when the user presses the Change Text button through the button's `onClick` event.

```
<html>

<head>
    <script>
        function changeOpener() {
            var openingH1 =
                document.getElementById('openingHeader')
            openingH1.textContent = "Let's eat!"
        }
    </script>
</head>

<body>
```

```
        <h1 id="openingHeader">Maggie the Dog Says</h1>
        <button onclick="changeOpener()">Change the Text</button>
</body>

</html>
```

EXAMPLE 13-9   Getting a reference to an HTML element with getElementById

In the example, the statement `var openingH1 = document.getElementById ('openingHeader')` finds the element with the id `openingHeader` and stores a reference to it in the variable `openingH1`.

Changing the Text Value of an HTML Element

Once an element has been located on the page using `getElementById`, several things about it can be changed, including the font, its size and color, its position on the page, and the text that is displayed. Each has a corresponding property associated with the tag. For example,

```
        document.getElementById('openingHeader').textValue = "Time
to eat!"
```

EXAMPLE 13-10

will find the tag with an id of `openingHeader` and replace the text it is holding with the string `Time to eat!` Note that in this instance we are finding the element and changing its text all in one line of code.

In Example 13-9 the `<h1>` tag was found and a reference to it stored in the variable openingHeader. The variable can be used to change the header's text:

```
        openingHeader.textValue = "Time to eat!"
```

EXAMPLE 13-11

Similarly, the text itself can be found and stored in a variable:

```
        var theText = document.getElementById('openingHeader').textValue
```

EXAMPLE 13-12

Figure 13-4 shows the result of clicking the Change the Text button from Example 13-9. As expected, the text displayed in the <h1> tag is changed.

FIGURE 13-4 Clicking the button changes the text of the <h1> tag

Changing the Color of an Element

To further illustrate the idea that we have complete control from JavaScript over the contents of a web page, Example 13-13 expands on Example 13-9 by changing not only the text displayed but also its color and font, from plain black to red and italicized. Note that this is done in four steps; first the element is found by its id and a reference stored to it, then the reference is used to change the text and the font color and variant.

The color and font style are style changes to the text; each is accessed through the element's style variable. For example, openingH1.style provides access to all of the element's style attributes (size, color, font, and more), and openingH1.style.color is used to set the font's color.

```
<html>

<head>
    <script>
        function changeOpener() {
            //1. Get a reference to the appropriate element
            var openingH1 = document.
                    getElementById('openingHeader')

            //2. Change the text displayed
            openingH1.textContent = "Let's eat!"

            //3. Change the color to red (this is a
    style change)
            openingH1.style.color = "red"

            //4. Change the font to italic (this is a
    style change)
            openingH1.style.fontStyle = "italic"
        }
    </script>
</head>

<body>
    <h1 id="openingHeader">Maggie the Dog Says</h1>
```

```
<button onclick="changeOpener()">Change the Text</button>

</body>

</html>
```

· ·

EXAMPLE 13-13 *Changing the color, style, and text from JavaScript*

In this example a single line of text is changed by clicking the Change the Text button on the page, but any element on the page can receive similar treatment. Example 13-14 changes the font and color of a paragraph, and adds a sentence to the end of it when the button is clicked. A key concept here is in step 2, which on the right-hand side of the assignment operator (=) takes the contents of the paragraph and adds additional text to it. The new value is then stored back into the paragraph. This is a common way to update a value without having to first store it in a new variable.

· ·

```html
<html>

<head>
    <script>
        function changeOpener() {
            //1. Get a reference to the appropriate element
            var paragraph1 = document.getElementById('paragraph1')

            //2. Add a sentence to the displayed text
            paragraph1.textContent =
                paragraph1.textContent +
              "Oh, for more food in the bowl!"

            //3. Change the color to red (this is a
style change)
            paragraph1.style.color = "red"

            //4. Change the font to italic (this is a
style change)
            paragraph1.style.fontStyle = "italic"
        }
    </script>
</head>

<body>
    <h1 id="openingHeader">Maggie the Dog Says</h1>
```

```
            <p id="paragraph1">It was the best of times,
              it was the worst of times.
                The food bowl was full, and then it was empty.</p>

            <button onclick="changeOpener()">Change the Text</button>
        </body>

    </html>
```

EXAMPLE 13-14 Rewriting and reformatting the text in a paragraph

One final note about modifying the text in a paragraph or head or other element. The attribute textValue modifies only text; if you try to place an HTML tag into the new text, it will be displayed on the screen literally. To include HTML tags in the modified element, use the innerHTML attribute instead. For example, if we wanted the word **"more"** in step 2 of Example 13-14 to be bolded,

```
        paragraph1.innerHTML =
        paragraph1.innerHTML + "Oh, for <b>more</b> food in the bowl!"
```

EXAMPLE 13-15

would do the trick.

Input Boxes

It is often the case that we need to read some value that a user has typed into a box on the web page. In HTML these boxes are called *inputs*, and are created with the `<input>` tag. There are several different kinds of inputs, and each is handled slightly differently. The `<input>` tag accepts an attribute named type that specifies which of the various inputs will be displayed. Types include:

- checkbox
- hidden (not displayed on the page)
- text
- password (displays *s as the user types)
- radio (only one selection allowed)

The complete list runs to 22 different input types; some are not supported by all web browsers. To specify the type, include the attribute in the <input> tag. For example,

```
<input type="text">
```

EXAMPLE 13-16

creates a box that accepts text.

Adjusting the Height and Width of an Input

The <input> tag accepts several modifiers that allow you to adjust its size, position, color, and more. A common task is to create one or more input boxes that are a specific width and are centered on the page. Width and height are typically expressed in pixels (px), a unit of measurement that uses the tiny dots on the screen. A monitor that is 1024 × 768, for example, has 768 rows that each contain 1,024 pixels. To create an input box that is roughly 1/10th of the screen wide, a value of 100px would suffice. Other common units are inches, points, picas, percent of the screen width, and so on. The best way to get a feel for these units is to try them out on your own so that you can see how they change the size of the input box. Here's a text input box that is 100px wide and centered:

```
<input type="text" width="100px" align="center">
```

EXAMPLE 13-17

As you can see, the <input> tag can accept more than one attribute; simply separate them with a space.

Reading the Value of an Input Box in JavaScript

Typing a value into a box isn't all that exciting. What we really want to do is to read the value in the box and take some action with it in a JavaScript function. To do this we need one more attribute: The id that we used earlier. By providing each <input> with a unique identifier, we can read and write the values in them from our functions. Example 13-18 illustrates a page that displays two input boxes; clicking on the Add button adds the two together and displays the result in a third input box. You would think that an <input> tag would be used only for inputting values, but since we can both read *and* write values in JavaScript, they also are a handy way to display a result.

```
<html>

<head>
    <script>
        function addTwoNumbers () {
            //1. Read the values in the first two input boxes
            var number1 = document.getElementById('box1').value
            var number2 = document.getElementById('box2').value

            //2. Add the two together
            var sum = number1 + number2

            //3. Place the sum in the results box
            document.getElementById('resultBox').value = sum
        }
    </script>
</head>

<body>

    <h1>Adding two numbers together</h1>
    <input type="text" id="box1"> <br/>
    <input type="text" id="box2"> <br/>
    <button onclick="addTwoNumbers()">Add</button><br/>
    <input type="text" id="resultBox"> <br/>
    </body>

</html>
```

EXAMPLE 13-18 Adding two numbers together: Attempt 1

Here is the result of running Example 13-18. Not quite what we expected!

When Is a Number Not a Number?

Remember the old joke, "When is a door not a door? When it is ajar."? Even though we've typed the numbers 30 and 12 into the boxes on the page, the boxes were created with the HTML tag <input type="text">. When JavaScript reads the values from those boxes, they are treated as text strings, not numbers. Recall that text strings can be concatenated (added together) by using the + operator. What has happened is that

FIGURE 13-5 What happened? It appears that the two input values, 30 and 12, were not treated like numbers at all

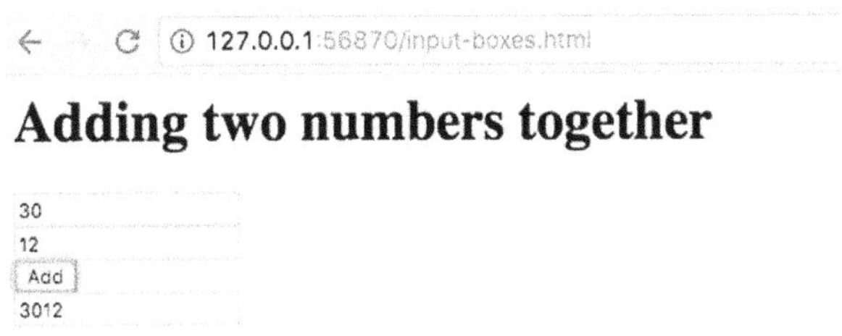

← C ⓘ 127.0.0.1:56870/input-boxes.html

Adding two numbers together

30
12
Add
3012

JavaScript sees "30" + "42" and does what it is supposed to do; it concatenates the two to get "3042".

Even though we specified in steps 1 and 3 of Example 13-18 that we wanted the value of the text box (using the .value property), it isn't enough. What's a programmer to do?

In order to convert the string values that JavaScript reads from the input boxes into proper numbers, we can take advantage of a built-in function, Number(), that will do the conversion for us. Number() takes as a parameter a string to try to convert into an actual number. The conversion returns either the number or JavaScript's Not a Number value (NaN). For example, to convert the value "123.456" into a number, we use:

```
Number("123.456")
```

EXAMPLE 13-19

This is one of those times that JavaScript, which normally does conversions such as this behind the scenes, simply doesn't. Example 13-20 shows how we can use the Number() function to solve our problem. Note that two methods are shown in step 1: the first stores the input value in a variable which is then passed to Number() to convert; the second uses Number() to convert the input value directly. Either is appropriate; the former benefits from clarity, though most JavaScript programmers will do the latter. The variable sum will hold a number type since it is storing the result of adding two numbers together.

```
<html>

<head>
    <script>
        function addTwoNumbers () {
            //1. Read the values in the first two input boxes; use
            //Number() to convert the text values to numbers
            var number1 = document.getElementById('box1').value
            var number2 =
                Number(document.getElementById('box2').value)

            //2. Add the two together
            var sum = Number(number1) + number2

            //3. Place the sum in the results box
            document.getElementById('resultBox').value = sum
        }
    </script>
```

```
    </head>

    <body>

        <h1>Adding two numbers together</h1>
        <input type="text" id="box1"> <br/>
        <input type="text" id="box2"> <br/>
        <button onclick="addTwoNumbers()">Add</button><br/>
        <input type="text" id="resultBox"> <br/>
    </body>

</html>
```

EXAMPLE 13-20   Adding two numbers together, a better version

.Value, .TextContent, and .InnerHTML

We've seen three different ways to manipulate what is displayed on the web page from JavaScript. Use this table as a guide as to which to use when:

Use	when you need to
.value	read or write text from an input box
.textContent	manipulate just the text of an element without any HTML tags
.innerHTML	include HTML tags when working with an element

Bottom Line

The combination of JavaScript and HTML, connected through the DOM, gives us a powerful tool to do just about anything that can be imagined on a web page. JavaScript is truly the programming language of the web; nearly every effect you see on the web sites that you visit are created through JavaScript functions.

This chapter is the briefest introduction to programming for the web. It is intended to give you a taste of what is possible, but by no means is what we've discussed here all that can be accomplished. If this kind of work interests you, the web is full of tutorials and introductory texts that will help you take the next steps toward more complex web pages. There really is no substitute for trying things on your own to see what happens; this is the basis of learning a skill such as JavaScript programming.

Figure Credit

CHAPTER
14

JavaScript Objects

rogramming is the art of solving problems with code. That's not to say that every problem has to be big or important; sometimes the problem is that we are simply bored. Some of the problems we are confronted with are esoteric and theoretical, but the vast majority relate directly to the world that we live in: How many potholders do I need to sell this month to pay the rent? What's the optimum number of hours to study for each of my courses?

For problems like these we try to write computer programs that represent real-world actions and items in a way that allows us to treat them computationally. While there are many approaches we could take, in JavaScript (and many other programming languages) the primary way of modeling real-world things in code is with a construct called an *object*. Using objects to solve problems is called *object-oriented programming*.

Styles of Programming

When analyzing programming styles it's useful to place a given program into one of three broad categories:

- Even-based, functional programming
- Procedural programming
- Object-oriented programming

The three style use the same syntax, libraries, and other language features but differ in how problems are solved. In many cases the problem itself will dictate the style that we will choose when writing our programs.

Event-Based Programming
In event-based programming, the program responds to events when they happen. This is the kind of programming that we used to connect JavaScript to the HTML of a web page; when a user pressed a button on the web page, a function would execute. This style

of programming is sometimes called asynchronous, since we can't predict ahead of time what events will happen or the order that they might occur. Typically there is a one-to-one correspondence between an event and a function. We say that the function *handles* the event, and these functions are often called *event handlers*.

We use event-based programming quite a bit when building interactivity into web pages, but it's an appropriate choice any time the program needs to respond to asynchronous events. A self-driving car would need this kind of programming to handle events coming from sensors like radar or its cameras.

Procedural Programming

A procedural program starts at the top and executes its lines of code in order until the bottom is reached. We might call functions to do work in the program, but generally execution is in a straight line. Cooking recipes are like this—we start at the top, add ingredients in a specific order, and cook the item according to the instructions after the preceding steps are done. Any time a problem looks like a series of steps, a procedural approach is a good choice.

Object-Oriented Programming

Object-oriented programming sees problems as the interactions of more-or-less independent pieces of code called objects, which are written to model how a similar object in the real world might behave. For example, if we were trying to figure out the best way to pack several different items into a box in order to get the maximum number of items packed, we might model the box and all of the items—each would have height, width, depth, weight, and so on—and then write a small amount of code to manipulate the items in various ways, looking for the best fit.

Parts of an Object

To this point in our discussion of JavaScript, we've used simple variables that store one thing; a number or a string, or some other simple piece of data. To store the number 42 in a variable, we might use:

```
let theAnswer = 42
```

EXAMPLE 14-1

While it's possible to write complex and useful programs that rely on this level of simplicity, it's often the case that we need to model something more complex, especially real-world things such as a train or a rocket or a planetary system. For this kind of work, we use variables that store more than one value, and that also can contain functions. These are called *objects*.

The combination of variables and functions allows us to create a new, complex data type that not only can store values but can respond to request for information about those values, and that can do work for us. In object-oriented terms, the variables are *attributes* and the functions are *behaviors*, also called *methods*.

Attributes

An attribute of an object is simply a piece of information, or data, held in a variable. Objects can hold more than one attribute, which is common when modeling real-world things. We'll use an egg as an example. What are all of the data points that might describe an egg? A quick first cut at a list might result in:

- Color
- Weight
- Size (medium, large, and so on)
- Days since the egg was laid
- Breed

These would be modeled in an Egg object with variables, as show in Example 14-2. We could come up with dozens more ways to describe an egg; in programming we often simplify the models that we use when solving problems, so the porosity of the shell (definitely an attribute of an egg) might not be important for the problem at hand, and we can choose not to include it in our object.

```
let anEgg = {
    color: 'white',
    weight: 2.0,  //ounces
    size: 'medium',
dateLaid: '10 March 2019',
breed: 'Rhode Island Red'
}
console.log(anEgg.breed)
```

EXAMPLE 14-2 Printing an attribute from a simple object

Running the code in Example 14-2 will print "Rhode Island Red" on the console. Note the use of the . (dot) character in the statement `anEgg.breed`; it tells JavaScript to access the breed attribute that belongs to the object `anEgg`. You can think of the . operator as the "belongs-to" operator. Similarly, if we wanted to print or otherwise work with the `color` attribute of `anEgg`, we would use `anEgg.color`.

The curly braces { and } identify which lines of code belong to the object. You can think of this as defining the body of the object, which is, in this example, called `anEgg`.

When writing an object body in this way, a variable name followed by a colon (as in `size:`) is the name to use when working with the attribute; it is often called a key. The actual value assigned to the variable follows the colon. A comma is used at the end of each statement defining an attribute in order to separate the attributes.

Behaviors

A collection of variables and their values is pretty useful, and sometimes it is all you need to solve a problem. A more sophisticated technique is to define several functions, called *behaviors*, which can interact with other parts of your program. One very common addition to an object is to provide a set of behaviors that either set or retrieve the value of a particular attribute. These are called *setters* and *getters*, and they are so common that many JavaScript programming editors have a handy "Generate Setters and Getters" button that automates the process.

Example 14-3 shows a setter and a getter for the color attribute of our egg object. They are part of the object, and so we can use the belongs-to operator (.) to access either of the methods.

```javascript
let anEgg = {
    color: 'white',
    weight: 2.0,   //ounces
    size: 'medium',
    dateLaid: '10 March 2019',
    breed: 'Rhode Island Red',
    setColor: function (newColor) {
        color = newColor
    },
    getColor: function () {
        return color
    }
}


anEgg.setColor('blue')
console.log(anEgg.getColor())   //prints blue
```

EXAMPLE 14-3   Using a setter and getter on an object

The setter for the color attribute takes a new color to apply. This is called an *argument,* or *input parameter* to the method. The value passed in to the method will be stored in the temporary variable `newColor`, and then the object's `color` attribute is then set to the value that was passed in.

The getter for the `color` attribute simply returns the current value of color to the line of code that requested it.

Behaviors aren't limited to simply setting or returning the value of an attribute. In fact, adding more complex behaviors to an object is where we start to give our programs intelligence and the ability to more realistically model real-world things. Let's say we were interested in knowing whether an egg was fresh or not. Eggs have a relatively long shelf life, and it isn't uncommon in US markets to see an egg being sold two weeks after it has been laid, and it will be fresh for another two to three weeks past the purchase date.

One way to determine the freshness of our egg is to retrieve the `dateLaid` attribute and then do a calculation on the value, like:

```
let laid = new Date(anEgg.dateLaid)
let today = new Date(Date.now())
let daysSinceLaid = (today - laid) / (24*60*60*1000)
if (daysSinceLaid < 30) {
    console.log('Egg is fresh')
} else {
    console.log('Egg is not fresh')
}
```

EXAMPLE 14-4

You should recall from our discussion of time and dates in an earlier chapter that JavaScript (and most computers) record time as the number of millisecods that have transpired since January 1st, 1970, and so we use the formula `(today - laid) / (24*60*60*1000)` to convert milliseconds into days (since there are 24 hours per day, 60 minutes per hour, 60 seconds per minute, and 1000 milliseconds per second). The result, 18 at the moment this was written, is small enough that the egg is considered fresh, and that fact is written to the console.

This isn't a terrible approach, but it means that if we are working with several egg objects, we'll need to ask each egg its date laid and do the calculation and decision each time.

A more efficient way to solve this problem is to move the calculation into the egg object, and just ask the egg itself whether or not it is fresh. This approach is shown in Example 14-5 (the setters and getters have been removed to reduce clutter).

```
let anEgg = {
    color: 'white',
    weight: 2.0,   //ounces
    size: 'medium',
    dateLaid: '15 March 2018',
    breed: 'Rhode Island Red',
    isFresh: function () {
        let laid = new Date(anEgg.dateLaid)
        let today = new Date(Date.now())
        let daysSinceLaid = (today - laid) / (24*60*60*1000)
        if (daysSinceLaid < 30) {
            return 'fresh'
        } else {
            return 'not fresh'
        }
```

```
        }
    }
    console.log('This egg is', anEgg.isFresh())
```

EXAMPLE 14-5   The egg can now indicate its freshness

Since this was written just a few weeks after the egg's `dateLaid`, the result on the console is the statement "This egg is fresh."

Another decision we need to make is whether the egg should return "fresh" or "not fresh" or a Boolean value (true or false). The two are equivalent, but returning a Boolean value rather than a string is a way to simplify both the method inside `anEgg` and the code that uses it. This approach is illustrated in Example 14-6, and while it is a little more complex than the scope of our discussion, it shows how programmers think: We try to come up with a solution that is both correct and that is flexible. When returning "fresh" or "not fresh," we are assuming that those precise words are being used; however, it might be the case that we are counting the number of fresh eggs in a carton versus those that are not fresh, and returning a string from the function makes us take a few extra steps.

For the curious, the simplifications made in Example 14-6 are that, since `daysSince-Laid < 30` is either true or false, we can simply return that result and dispense with the `if...else` statements. For the print statement we use the ? conditional operator, which executes the statement to the left of the colon if the condition is true, and the statement to the right if it is false. The condition being tested is `anEgg.isFresh()`.

```
    let anEgg = {
        color: 'white',
        weight: 2.0,   //ounces
        size: 'medium',
        dateLaid: '15 March 2018',
        breed: 'Rhode Island Red',
        isFresh: function () {
            let laid = new Date(anEgg.dateLaid)
            let today = new Date(Date.now())
            let daysSinceLaid = (today - laid) / (24*60*60*1000)
            return (daysSinceLaid < 30)
        }
    }
    console.log('This egg is', anEgg.isFresh() ? 'fresh' :
'not fresh')
```

EXAMPLE 14-6   Simplifying the freshness test

Object Constructors

In the examples we've seen so far, there is just one egg, `anEgg`. Usually, when we are working with objects we'll want more than one of a particular type of object. We could rewrite the code for each new egg, giving it a color, weight, and so on that is unique to that egg, but this would quickly become tedious if we needed more than just a handful of the objects.

Luckily, JavaScript offers a way to write a template for an object that can be used to create any number of new objects of that type. You can think of the template as like a cookie cutter in the shape of an egg—we can use the template to cut as many eggs as we need, and they will all have the same shape. In our case, the shape includes things like the color, weight, and size of the egg. Such a template is called a *constructor* because we use it to construct, or build, new objects.

Constructors look similar to an object, but rather than being a named variable (anEgg), they are functions. We typically provide each of the attributes of the object with default values in the constructor, and also setters and getters for the attributes so that we can change them if the defaults aren't appropriate to our problem.

Example 14-7 shows a simple egg object constructor with just one attribute, its weight, which is set to a default value of 0.0. The constructor also provides a setter and getter for the weight attribute.

You'll notice the use of the keyword *this*, used several times in the constructor. We're going to create several eggs, and once an egg is built, when we interact with it in our program, we need a way to specify that we are working with this egg and not some other egg that exists. That's what the *this* keyword does for us: `this.weight` is the weight of the egg we are currently working with, and not some other.

```
//Egg constructor
//
function Egg(weight = 0.0) {
    this.weight = weight
    this.getWeight = function () {
        return this.weight
    }
    this.setWeight = function (newWeight) {
        this.weight = newWeight
    }
}
```

EXAMPLE 14-7   An egg constructor

The constructor also is slightly different from the earlier single-egg object in that it uses the = operator rather than the : operator to set up attributes and methods. For example,

```
this.weight = weight
```

EXAMPLE 14-8

rather than

```
weight: weight
```

EXAMPLE 14-9

Creating Object from Constructors

The egg object from Example 14-2 is hard-coded—the values of its attributes are assigned directly in the object. That's fine for a single-use object, but we're now interested in creating multiple copies of our egg object. For this we can use the new operator—it builds a new object based on the constructor and lets us assign a variable to hold the newly created object.

Since the egg constructor in Example 14-7 provides a way to pass in a value for the egg's weight, we can specify a weight at the time the egg is created. For an egg with a weight of 2.2:

```
let egg1 = new Egg(2.2)
```

EXAMPLE 14-10

We now can set or get the weight value of the new egg:

```
let theWeight = egg1.getWeight( )
```

EXAMPLE 14-11

We also can change its weight:

```
egg1.setWeight(3.3)
```

EXAMPLE 14-12

To create a second egg with a different weight:

```
let egg2 = new Egg(4.2)
```

EXAMPLE 14-13

The two eggs, `egg1` and `egg2`, are completely independent of one another, though they are identical in structure since they were created from the same constructor.

Solving a Problem with Objects

Now that we know how to set up an object and a constructor, we can use objects to work on a problem that relates to the real world.

Imagine that you work at an egg farm. Each day, eggs (from very happy hens) are loaded onto a truck and sent out for delivery to several local stores. There's just one small problem: The truck must cross a bridge over the stream near the farm, and the bridge is quite old and rickety, such that it will fall into the stream if too much weight is placed on it.

We'd like to maximize our profit on each run, and so you have been asked to design a program that will allow the truck to be loaded with cartons of eggs such that the total weight of all the cartons doesn't exceed the maximum weight the bridge can bear. Since all of the eggs have slightly different weights we'll need to keep track of how many eggs have been loaded and how much they all weigh.

This is a common problem—maybe not eggs, specifically—in which we need to optimize a value given a set of constraints.

We already have a pretty good egg object from Example 14-7. We now need a carton to put the eggs into. Each carton will hold exactly 12 eggs, and we'll create each egg with a slightly different weight, then place it into the carton, repeating until the carton is full.

An Egg Carton

For our carton we can use a simple array. Recall that an array is a data structure that holds items in a numbered order; in our case we'll create a carton with 12 slots for eggs, as shown in Example 14-14. The carton uses the push method of an array, which takes a value and adds it to the front of the array. The function `addEgg` is responsible for this; it takes an egg object as an argument and pushes it to the carton's array. The array itself is referenced by the variable `slots`, which has an initial value of [ ], an empty array.

```
//Carton constructor
//
function Carton() {
    this.slots = []
    this.addEgg = function (anEgg) {
```

```
            this.slots.push(anEgg)
        }
    }
```

··

EXAMPLE 14-14   A constructor for the egg carton

Placing Eggs into the Carton

We want each carton to hold 12 eggs, and the eggs should have slightly different weights to make it interesting. We can use a loop for this; since we know in advance how many times the loop must run (12), we'll use a for loop rather than a while loop.

Once 12 eggs are in the carton we can calculate the overall weight of the carton. Unfortunately, our intern neglected to weigh the eggs as they went in, so we'll need to take each egg out of the carton, weigh it, add that weight to the running total, then place the egg back in the carton. Once again, we know how many times this must be done (12) and so a for loop is the appropriate way to work with each egg.

Example 14-15 shows the program to do all of this. First we create a new, empty carton, then create 12 eggs with random weights, place them in the carton, then pull them back out to weigh them.

A refinement might be to add a method to the carton that returns the carton's total weight. As an egg is placed into the carton (via Carton.addEgg), we could record the egg's weight and add it to the carton's total weight. This would simplify things later when we need to see what each carton weighs. This kind of thinking is how programmers view their designs: Which object—egg or carton—is responsible for keeping track of the carton's weight? We try to build objects that closely resemble how they might be used in the real world; having the carton report its weight might make sense in that light. For our example program, we manage weight per egg, mainly to get some practice using loops and arrays.

··

```
//Carton constructor
//
function Carton() {
    this.slots = []
    this.addEgg = function (anEgg) {
        this.slots.push(anEgg)
    }
}


//Egg constructor
//
function Egg(weight = 0.0) {
    this.weight = weight
    this.getWeight = function () {
        return this.weight
```

```
        }
        this.setWeight = function (newWeight) {
            this.weight = newWeight
        }
    }
    //Set up a new, empty carton
    //
    let carton = new Carton()

    //Add 12 eggs to the carton with random weights; a medium
    //egg is roughly 2 ounces, so add a random fractional value
    //between .000 and .999 to 2 to get each egg's weight
    //
    for (let count = 0; count < 12; count++) {
        egg = new Egg(2 + Math.random())
        carton.addEgg(egg)
    }


    //Calculate the weight in the carton; unfortunately we forgot
    //to tell the packer to weigh the eggs as they were being
    //packed, and so we have to pull each one out and weigh it
    //
    //Create a variable to hold the running total of the weight
    let totalWeight = 0

    //Pull each egg out and weigh it; add the weight to the total
    //
    for (let count = 0; count < 12; count++) {
        totalWeight = totalWeight + carton.slots[count].weight
    }
    console.log(totalWeight.toFixed(2) + " ounces in this carton")
```

EXAMPLE 14-15   Loading a carton with a dozen eggs

Since the eggs each weigh slightly differently, multiple runs of the program will yield slightly different results. Here are the results from three consecutive runs:

```
28.71 ounces in this carton
29.21 ounces in this carton
30.91 ounces in this carton
```

EXAMPLE 14-16

Loading the Truck: Simplified Version

We are close to having enough code to pack the truck optimally. Example 14-15 provides a way to pack and weigh a single carton, and so we just need a second loop that will load freshly packed cartons onto the truck, taking care not to exceed the maximum allowed weight.

This second loop depends on a condition—the current weight of all of the cartons— which means that we don't know in advance how many times the loop will run. This calls for a *while* loop, which runs until a condition is met.

For this simplified version of our program, shown in Example 14-17, we will set the maximum allowed weight to 400 pounds, which will be the maximum weigh of the eggs. We're ignoring several constraints here, and making some assumptions, such as that the cartons are weightless.

```
//Set up initial values for total weight and number of cartons
//
let totalWeight = 0
let maxWeight = 2000 * 16 //in ounces
let totalNumberOfCartons = 0


//Carton constructor
//
function Carton() {
    this.slots = []
    this.addEgg = function (anEgg) {
        this.slots.push(anEgg)
    }
}


//Egg constructor
//
function Egg(weight = 0.0) {
    this.weight = weight
    this.getWeight = function () {
        return this.weight
    }
    this.setWeight = function (newWeight) {
        this.weight = newWeight
    }
}



//Outer loop: run this until total weight is more than

// the truck can handle
```

```
    //
    while (totalWeight < maxWeight) {
        //Create an empty carton and add 12 eggs
        //
        let carton = new Carton()
        let cartonWeight = 0
        for (let count = 0; count < 12; count++) {
            egg = new Egg(2 + Math.random())
            carton.addEgg(egg)
        }
        //Weigh the eggs
        //
        for (let count = 0; count < 12; count++) {
            cartonWeight = cartonWeight + carton.slots[count].weight
        }
        //Convert the weight in ounces to weight in pounds, and add
        //one to the number of cartons loaded so far
        //
        totalWeight = totalWeight + cartonWeight
        totalNumberOfCartons = totalNumberOfCartons + 1
    }
    //Convert ounces to pounds
    //
    let weightInPounds = totalWeight / 16

    console.log('Total cartons loaded:', totalNumberOfCartons)
    console.log("Total weight in all cartons: " + weightInPounds.
toFixed(2), "pounds")
    console.log("An average carton weighs " + (weightInPounds /
totalNumberOfCartons).toFixed(2), "pounds")
```

EXAMPLE 14-17   Loading cartons onto a truck (simplified version)

A sample run of the program in Example 14-17 yields:

```
    Total cartons loaded: 1067
    Total weight in all cartons: 2000.61 pounds
    An average carton weighs 1.87 pounds
```

EXAMPLE 14-18

In the program it is important to note the first few lines, which set up the initial conditions in three variables. Two of the variables, `totalWeight` and `totalNumberOfCartons`, are set to start at 0 and accumulate the results of our calculations during each pass through the loop. The third variable, `maxWeight`, is used as the stopping point for the while loop.

Loading the Truck: More Complex Version

We made quite a few simplifications in the program in Example 14-17 and let a few things slide. For example, it's possible (even likely) that the total weight of the load will be just slightly more than the bridge can handle, since the while loop checks the total weight of the load *after* it creates and loads a new carton.

The responsibility for recording the weight of the carton is moved to the carton; as each egg is placed in the carton, the egg's weight is added to the total. This is the equivalent of printing the weight on the side of each carton. The carton itself also weighs a bit, and that's added to the total packed carton weight.

We can improve our analysis a bit by checking the total load after the while loop exits, to be sure that the weight doesn't exceed the crossing weight of the bridge. If it does, the program advises us to remove a carton.

This new version also creates eggs with weights that spread over a larger scale in order to amplify the impact of a single carton.

Finally, note the use of the *const* keyword in the first few lines of the program. If a variable will not change during the running of a program, we mark it as a constant value with *const*. Examples are `truckEmptyWeight` and `maxLoadWeight`. Variables that will change are created with the *let* keyword, such as `totalLoadWeightInPounds`.

```
//Set up initial values
//
const truckEmptyWeight = 1500 //pounds
const maxBridgeCrossingWeight = 4000 //[pounds
let totalLoadWeightInPounds = 0
const maxLoadWeight = (maxBridgeCrossingWeight - truckEmpty-
Weight) //pounds
let totalNumberOfCartons = 0
const emptyCartonWeight = 1.0 //ounces

//Carton constructor
//
function Carton() {
    this.slots = []
    this.cartonWeight = emptyCartonWeight

    this.addEgg = function (anEgg) {
        this.slots.push(anEgg)
        this.cartonWeight += anEgg.getWeight()
```

```
        }
        this.getWeight = function () {
            return this.cartonWeight
        }
    }
}


    //Egg constructor
    //
    function Egg() {
        this.weight = 0
        //we'll only worry about weight
        this.setWeight = function (min, max) {
                this.weight =  Math.random() * (max - min) + min;
        }
        this.getWeight = function () {
            return this.weight
        }
    }



    //Outer loop: run this until total weight is more than

    // the truck can handle

    //
    while (totalLoadWeightInPounds < maxLoadWeight) {
        //Create a new, empty carton
        //
        let carton = new Carton()
        let cartonWeight = 0
        const maxNumberOfEggsPerCarton = 6

        //Make eggs of varying weight and place them in the carton
        //
        for (let count = 0; count < maxNumberOfEggsPerCarton;
count++) {
            egg = new Egg()
            egg.setWeight(2,8) //set the weight to between min, max
ounces
            carton.addEgg(egg)
            // console.log("Egg weight:", egg.getWeight().toFixed(6),
"oz")
        }
```

```
    //The carton knows its weight, add it to the total load
    //
    totalLoadWeightInPounds = totalLoadWeightInPounds +
( carton.getWeight() / 16) //16 ounces in a pound
    totalNumberOfCartons = totalNumberOfCartons + 1
  }


  //Reporting
  //
  console.log("Total number of cartons loaded:",
totalNumberOfCartons)
  console.log("Total weight in all cartons: " +
totalLoadWeightInPounds.toFixed(2) + " lbs")
  let averageCartonWeightInPounds = (totalLoadWeightInPounds /
totalNumberOfCartons).toFixed(2)
  console.log("An average carton weighs",
averageCartonWeightInPounds, "pounds")


  //Make sure we haven't exceeded the max crossing weight
  //
  if (totalLoadWeightInPounds > maxLoadWeight) {
      let cartonsToRemove = 0
      while (totalLoadWeightInPounds > maxLoadWeight) {
          totalLoadWeightInPounds -= averageCartonWeightInPounds
          cartonsToRemove++
      }
      console.log("Please remove",cartonsToRemove, "carton(s)
before departing the dock.")
  }
  console.log("Total crossing weight:", (truckEmptyWeight +
totalLoadWeightInPounds).toFixed(2), "pounds")
```

EXAMPLE 14-19 Loading cartons onto a truck (more complex example)

A sample run from the updated program is shown below.

```
Total number of cartons loaded: 1294
Total weight in all cartons: 2501.58 lbs
An average carton weighs 1.93 pounds
Please remove 1 carton(s) before departing the dock.
Total crossing weight: 3999.65 pounds
```

EXAMPLE 14-20

Although the new program is a little closer to real-world conditions, there are still refinements that could be made to get a more accurate carton count. Practically speaking, we'd run this program several thousand times to get a distribution graph of weights, and then use that information to establish a fixed number of cartons that we can load on the truck each day rather than measuring the weight of every single egg. Still, it would be worth weighing the truck after all of the cartons have been loaded just in case a goose or two slip into the flock.

Bottom Line

Object-oriented programming (OOP) lets us use code to model real-world things and events. While some programming languages, such as C++ or Java, are heavily object-oriented, OOP really is a design approach rather than a feature of any particular language, and JavaScript, which isn't at all an object-oriented language, is perfectly suitable for applying OOP principles.

Thinking about programming in terms of modeling real-world effects takes some of the mystery out of writing programs; we code in a way that reflects our world, and in turn we use our programs to understand and predict the world around us. Even more exciting, we can envision and model in code things that don't exist at all in our world yet, or that obey different natural laws.

CHAPTER 15

Security and Privacy on the Internet

I n the 1600s the Great Migration was a mass of humanity flowing from Europe to the New World. In the 2000s, the great migration is to a new world that is entirely online. It happened quite quickly; we've gone from the disco balls and massive, expensive desktop computers of the 1980s to computers so small, so fast, and so part of our culture that we think nothing about strapping one to our wrist. You probably have three or four computers on you right now. Along with the spread of inexpensive lightweight computing devices is coming a need to push information to a place where all of those devices can access it, something we call the cloud.

Today's environment was the dream of computer scientists for decades. Especially when we started to see small, inexpensive personal computers move into the consumer market, the idea of ubiquitous computing, the notion that at some point in the future we would interact on a minute-to-minute basis with intelligent devices that would have access to all of the information we could possibly need, was the vision. The reality is pretty close to that vision. Think about how you interact with computers on a day-to-day basis. When we need a weather report, or to work on a document for school, or to talk to a friend, we pull out our phone, our laptop, or sit down at the desktop machine, or, more recently, simply speak into the air—there's probably a computer listening to you right now that can answer any question that you have, or connect you with anyone you like.

Ubiquitous computing is still in its infancy, but even now we're sometimes not sure where our information is stored or where it is coming from. Let's say that you've stored some of your photos on "the cloud." Do you know where those files reside physically? More to the point, when you store documents on a cloud server such as Google Drive, Dropbox, or Microsoft Azure, do you know whether or not someone else is looking at them? Is some third party snooping on your files as they are being transmitted from your computer to the cloud server?

In most cases, the answer to this question is, "I don't know."

Sometimes, the answer is, "I don't care."

On the Internet, Security Is Not Job One

There are two issues at play here. The first is *security*. When we talk about security in an online context, most often we are thinking about whether or not a hacker can break into a device and either steal or in some other way compromise our information. The other issue is that of *privacy*. When we think of privacy, we are concerned with whether or not a third party can eavesdrop on our communications, read our e-mails or instant messages in transit, or collect information about us that might be used either commercially or for some criminal activity.

When the Internet protocols were being designed 50 years ago, there wasn't much concern given to the ideas of either privacy or security. This was well before the World Wide Web came about, even before e-mail, and the principal goal was to connect computers together in such a way that they could exchange data. TCP, IP, and the application layer protocols just weren't designed with security or privacy in mind. This was a very naive time in computing history; no one had ever seen a computer virus, there were no hackers, and the number of machines being connected was relatively small.

Unfortunately or not, the introduction of the World Wide Web in the late 1990s fueled a massive expansion of both the number of individuals coming online and in the number of machines networked together on the Internet. Expansion was so rapid that there just wasn't time to go back and reengineer the protocols with security in mind. The underlying structure of the Internet hasn't really changed much in the past 50 years; it's gotten faster, and more convenient, but the original designs are still the same.

One of the goals of early network engineers was simplicity. Think about all of the layers of the network stack, and the way that packet switching breaks up messages and sends them in all sorts of directions on the network; this happens billions of times a day on the modern Internet, and if any of those protocols in the stack were complex, they would simply stop working. Each layer is incredibly simple, and even the interaction of the layers in the stack is quite simple from an engineering standpoint. Adding security and privacy to any of these protocols would result in more complexity, which would be prone to failure more often.

There was also a measure of trust in those early designs. No one really expected that hackers would descend upon the networks to steal valuable information; remember that in the early days networking was mostly between university and military campuses and was used to share research, information about projects, research, and news. The idea that somebody would deliberately break into a computer and steal information about your project was pretty remote. We now are at a point in the growth of the Internet where so many machines have been deployed, so many individuals are online, and so many documents are being stored, that it's just not possible to go back and retrofit those early protocols to add security and trust.

Overcoming Inertia

We see this kind of technical inertia in many areas of our lives. Credit and debit cards are great examples. In the United States, account information is embedded in a magnetic stripe on the back of credit and other cards. Everything that a criminal needs to know about your account is right there on the card; if they want to copy the information, it's relatively trivial to accomplish. Small devices called *skimmers*, capable of reading the stripe and recording its information, are so small that they can be hidden in ATM machines, point-of-sale devices, gas station pumps, and anywhere else that you might use your card. Once the information is recorded, it's simple to "play back" that data, recording it onto a new card. That new card is identical to the original, and it isn't until you see spurious transactions in your account that you even know that your information has been stolen.

Several technologies exist right now that would completely eliminate this kind of theft. Chip and PIN cards, common in Europe, has only recently been introduced in the United States, and they are much more secure than this simple magnetic stripe card. Even the chip and PIN card, though, has security drawbacks. United States banks have decided that PIN numbers are too difficult for the average American to remember, and so in many cases the PIN is done away with in favor of a signature. Even *that* apparently is too complicated for most people, and most establishments only require the signature if the purchase is above a certain dollar amount, say $50. Below that amount, you simply insert your card into the reader, and then pull it out. There's no PIN, there's no signature, no check at all to see if you were actually the owner of the card. Granted, chip and PIN cards are much more difficult to copy, and so a thief would need access to the physical card before they could make purchases.

Cryptographic techniques such as Apple's Apple Pay completely eliminate these issues, using strong encryption and secure protocols in order to protect each transaction. However, it requires that merchants install special point-of-sale equipment to accept such payments, and no one wants to spend the money. The result is that we are stuck with inferior technologies for the short term, technologies that weaken our privacy and are susceptible to hacking and theft.

Is There Really Any Privacy?

We have to assume that everything we do and say online, including the sites that we visit, the people we communicate with, the documents we create, the photos we upload, basically everything, is being examined by third parties. All your online actions, including your cell phone conversations, are being recorded, stored, and analyzed. Their are two main entities engaging in this: commercial concerns and the government.

Let's look at commercial concerns first. The saying goes, *If you are not paying for something online, you are the product.* There is no such thing as "free." Online, businesses have to monetize the traffic to their site. So-called free services are monetized by gathering information about their users. This includes services like Google Search, Google Docs, Microsoft Azure, and free tiers of popular cloud services such as Box.net and Dropbox.

What drives this model? Many online services make money by selling information about their users, primarily to advertisers. Sometimes they'll sell ad space as well. Everything you do online is collected and aggregated into a profile. The profile is very valuable to advertisers, because it indicates things that you're interested in, plans you might have, maybe for travel, or a purchase, and other information about yourself such as how old you are, who your friends are, where you live, and so on. This allows advertisers to display very specifically targeted information to you, which increases the chance of a sale. Google, for example, knows more about you than most of your friends do. They sell information

FIGURE 15-1   Google revenue sources

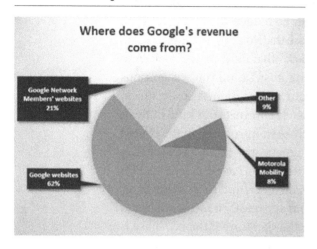

about you to advertisers; in fact, the majority of their revenue comes from this practice (Figure 15-1, Google Websites). The free services that they offer, such as search, document storage, and e-mail, all are designed to collect that information from you.

For example, if you sign up for Google Docs online, you would probably click on the terms and conditions of service without reading them. We all do this, those contracts are dozens of pages long, and are often written in legal terms that are difficult to understand, especially for casual users. If you bother to read Google's terms of service, however, you discover that when you use Gmail, or store documents in Google Docs, you are giving Google blanket authorization to scan through your e-mails, or documents, republish them, share them with third parties, and basically do anything that they want with them even after you terminate the service. Storing a document on Google Docs means that you have given that file unconditionally to Google.

Here's the relevant section of the agreement that you clicked OK on:

> *When you upload, submit, store, send or receive content to or through our Services, you give Google (and those we work with) a worldwide license to use, host, store, reproduce, modify, create derivative works (such as those resulting from translations, adaptations or other changes we make so that your content works better with our Services), communicate, publish, publicly perform, publicly display and distribute such content. The rights you grant in this license are for the limited purpose of operating, promoting, and improving our Services, and to develop new ones. This license continues even if you stop using our Services (for example, for a business listing you have added to Google Maps)*
>
> *Our automated systems analyze your content (including emails) to provide you personally relevant product features, such as customized search results, tailored advertising, and spam and malware detection. This analysis occurs as the content is sent, received, and when it is stored.*

In 2017 Google announced that they had deployed technology that would tie your credit card purchases back to your Google profile, increasing the value of those profiles to advertisers. Even if you're not specifically using Google, most sites use analytics provided by Google to track site activity. This consists of a small piece of JavaScript code on each page of the site that is executed when you load the page. It collects information about you, and what you're doing on the site, and relays that information back to Google. This is easy to test; visit a few pages on the web shopping for shoes, or do a Google search for shoes, and for the next month or so all of the ads on all of the sites you visit will be displaying ads for shoes.

Another "feature" of Google search that most people don't understand is that Google records every search that you make on their site. *Every search.* If you're logged into your

Google account, and do a search on Google's search page, that search is recorded and stored indefinitely. You can see these at https://myactivity.google.com. Fortunately, there's a way to opt out, in the settings pane of your Google account. Of course, we don't really know if turning off this feature really turns it off, or just hides it from our view.

Voice assistants such as Siri and Alexa are another popular technology that many of us use multiple times a day. When you ask Siri a question on your Apple device, for example, it seems as if your phone is responding instantly. That's not the case, however. When you speak your question into your phone, your speech is digitized and sent to Apple's servers over the network. There, the speech is analyzed, a response is formulated, and sent back to your phone. Apple has stated that they store Siri queries for "up to two years."

What about private browsing mode, sometimes called incognito mode? Most browsers have this feature, and when you turn it on the browser changes its appearance in a dramatic way, and makes it seems that everything you do in private browsing mode is very secret. In fact, the *only* thing private browsing mode accomplishes is that it does not store a history of the sites that you visit. That's it. Everything else is just as if you were in normal browsing mode; your ISP can see the sites you visit, anything you send to that site is visible to the site itself, and generally it is no more secure than regular browsing mode.

Speaking of ISPs, or Internet service providers, they have the most visibility of all into your activities online. Because they are the first connection you make to gain access to the Internet, they see every bit of traffic coming from your e-mail client, your browser, your Skype calls, your music streaming, and so on. In 2016 reports were published detailing how some ISPs were intercepting network traffic coming from web servers back to your browser and inserting advertisement into them. Recent changes to privacy laws made by the Trump administration have made it even easier for service providers to collect as much information as they want about you and share that information with third parties without your consent.

Government Entities

We know from our discussion of the Internet protocols that every time you make a connection on the Internet, your data is sent through a series of routers, perhaps dozens of them, as it moves across the network to its destination. Figure 15-2, a document leaked by National Security Agency (NSA) contractor Edward Snowden, shows points in the Internet where the US government taps in and copies network traffic. Each circle represents an intercept point on the Internet. This information, representing millions of conversations each day, is stored, indexed, and analyzed by our government.

FIGURE 15-2 NSA collection points on the Internet

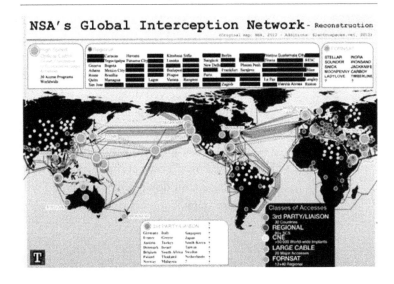

FIGURE 15-3   A connection to eff.org rerouted to London for collection

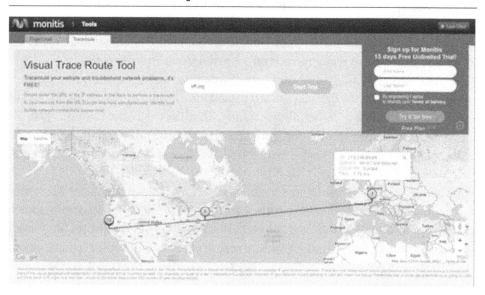

Of course, the NSA by law is not allowed to collect information on US citizens. To keep to the letter of the law, some traffic originating in the United States is intentionally rerouted (the government term is "shaped") to routers in countries that have an intelligence-sharing agreement with the United States Figure 15-3 shows the result of a network trace originating in California to the web site of the Electronic Frontier Foundation at eff.org. EFF advocates freedom and privacy online and openly opposes many of the policies of the US government. The connection in this example starts in California, is routed to London, and then back to Washington where EFF maintains their servers.

Much of the intelligence gathering done by the US government is authorized by the so-called Patriot Act, signed into law just 25 working days after the terrorist attacks that occurred on September 11th, 2001. The legislation ran to 363 pages, and little of it was read by Congress prior to the vote. Among other things it creates a process for government agencies such as the FBI to obtain search warrants that allow them to collect any data from a specific site that the government feels might help in their investigations. These warrants are issued by a secret court, set up by the Foreign Intelligence Surveillance Act, in which there is no representation. Warrants are approved 99% of the time and come with gag orders attached so that the target of the warrant is prevented from disclosing that they have received one.

This means that if the government wanted to know what was in the documents you were storing on Dropbox, a FISA warrant would be issued to Dropbox, who would be compelled to comply and would be prevented from telling you that your documents had been turned over. Some companies that were founded to protect individual privacy, like Lavabit, have shut down when presented with a FISA warrant rather than disclose their customers' data.

Attacks on Privacy and Freedom

It isn't just your Internet activity that provides fodder for those who are interested in gathering information about your activities. Improvement in computing, image processing, and networking have provided fertile ground for the development of new ways to monitor what you're doing in your daily life. In some cases these are commercial entities who are interested in selling you something, sometimes it's your government keeping track of what you're doing, who you're talking to, and where you're going, and sometimes it is a hacker who wants to steal your information and either sell it or use it for some criminal activity. Let's take a look at some of the ways that our privacy and security can be compromised.

Cell Phones

Your cell phone is a two-way radio. Anytime that it is turned on, it is communicating with radios located on cellular towers. You probably have seen these towers; in metropolitan areas they are quite close together, and even in rural areas you'll see one every mile or so, especially along major highways. When somebody places a call to you, the cellular network needs to figure out where your phone is in relation to nearby cell towers so that it can properly route the call. Your phone periodically checks in with these towers, every few seconds, to let them know where you are physically located. Even though you might be in range of three or four individual towers, one of them is going to be closer to you and have a stronger signal, and that's the one your telephone will communicate with.

Think about this for a minute. You carry around what essentially is a beacon with you all of the time. It is constantly checking in with the cell tower network around you, reporting where your phone is located. Let's say that you were trying to have a secret meeting. If everyone in the meeting has their cell phone turned on, all of those phones will be checking in with local towers, and it's easy for law enforcement to see that all of those phones were in the same place at the same time. Likewise, if you say you were in one place, and your phone says that you weren't, which will a court believe? This kind of information is called *metadata*, and it includes information about where you are, who you're with, who you are calling, the duration of that conversation, and other information that is broadcast by your phone.

A surveillance device used by law enforcement called a *stingray* takes us one step further. A stingray (Figure 15-4) is essentially a portable cell tower. It's about the size of a suitcase, and law-enforcement officers can set it up anywhere that they want to collect information about cellular conversations. Maybe they suspect that a particular café is being used as a meeting point for criminals; they can set up the stingray around the corner, and the cell phones in use in the café will see the stingray as the strongest signal of all of the cell towers in the area. Since it's the strongest signal, cell phones at the café will connect to it, and law enforcement can not only record metadata being emitted by the phones, but in some cases they can decrypt the digital signals coming from the phones and record the actual conversations. Stingrays have

FIGURE 15-4 A stingray cell interception device

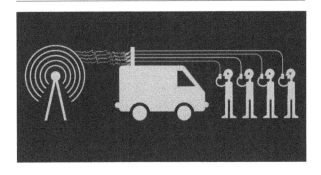

been around for a couple of years now, and agencies such as the United States Federal Bureau of investigation (FBI) have gone to great pains to conceal both their existence and their operation, in some cases even abandoning prosecution of cases when it became clear that the use of a stingray would be revealed in open court.

In operation, once a stingray intercepts a cell phone signal, it records as much of the information as possible, and then forwards the call to the real telephone network. This kind of interception is called a *man in the middle attack*, and is particularly insidious because the individual being attacked usually doesn't know that the attack is happening.

Documents released by Edward Snowden revealed that the United States National Security Agency was engaging in the mass collection of cell phone metadata, not only that of foreign nationals, but also of US citizens. As a result of these disclosures, Congress acted to limit the authority of the NSA in such collections, and the agency stated that it had ended this sort of collection against US citizens. It instead requires telecommunication companies to record and store this information, and hand it over to the NSA in response to secret court-ordered search warrants.

License Plate Readers

You might be familiar with so-called red light cameras, which are placed at intersections by local law enforcement to automatically capture an image of any car that runs a red light. In some municipalities, this process is completely automated, and when the cameras spot a car running a red light the image is processed, stored in a central database, and a ticket is automatically issued to the owner of the car. These cameras have been used for several years now, quite successfully in many cases. One defense against such a ticket, of course, is that is difficult to prove who was actually driving the car. It might not necessarily be the owner of the car.

Advances in image processing technology over the past few years has led to a different kind of camera, similar to stoplight cameras but more sophisticated. The idea is the same: images are taken of a license plate and fed back to a central computer, which processes the image, records the license plate number, along with metadata such as the time of day and other information. Known as Automated License Plate Readers (ALPRs), the devices provide real-time information about the vehicle and its owner to law enforcement agencies (Figure 15-5).

These cameras aren't necessarily in fixed locations. At our school, for example, such cameras are mounted on trucks that are owned by the parking department. These trucks drive up and down the parking lots, recording the license plate of each car, and comparing them against a database of individuals who have permits to park in those lots. It's a simple matter to identify a car that shouldn't be there, and either ticket it or tow it.

In some cases additional information is recorded. In Washington, DC, for example, there are more

FIGURE 15-5   An ALPR fitted to a squad car

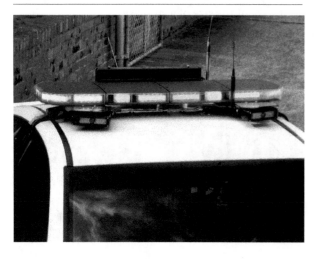

than 250 cameras installed covering nearly every block in the district. These cameras record 1,800 images per minute in total and feed the information into a central database. These cameras, though, don't just record the license plate; they also record images of the occupants of the vehicle. According to documents obtained by the ACLU, these readers can store 10 images per vehicle including up to four occupant photos. US courts have upheld the notion that driving is a public activity, and therefore there is no expectation of privacy in cases when you're in your car. In Washington, DC, law enforcement agencies know where you are driving, when you are driving, and who you are driving with. There are so many cameras in the district that a continuous trace of individuals, whether they are driving the car or just a passenger, can be made.

Sometimes this kind of technology can be used for benign purposes. At many large airports across the country, upon returning from a trip, you can pay for parking your car in the airport garage at an automated kiosk. In many of these systems, when you insert your ticket, the location of your car is printed on the receipt for you in case you have forgotten where you parked. How does this work? The answer is a combination of technologies that we've already discussed. When you arrive at the garage, you must stop and take a ticket from an automated machine. While your car is stopped, license plate readers record your license plate number. You drive in, park your car, and haul your luggage into the airport.

While you are gone, license plate readers mounted on trucks drive through the garage, recording the location, including the floor and parking spot number, of each parked car. When you return from your trip weeks later and insert your ticket into the automated pay kiosk, that information is matched with your ticket number, and your car's location is printed on the receipt.

This seems like a real convenience to travelers, with a very large caveat. Consider all of the pieces of data that the system collects about you. It knows when you arrive at the airport, and it knows when you return. It can match your credit card number to you, since most people will pay by credit card at the kiosk. If a link is made to the state motor vehicle database, the data can be cross-referenced with your driving record, which is in most states publicly available. That's quite a bit of information that you are giving away just for the convenience of not having to remember where your car is parked!

Facial Recognition
Law enforcement organizations are increasingly deploying facial-recognition technology in order to scan crowds for persons of interest. Once again, our courts have ruled that if you're in public, you do not have an expectation of privacy, and so if you are attending an event, a rally, a parade, or just hanging out in the park, it's perfectly legal for the government to take your picture and cross-reference that with any databases that they have. Combining this kind of facial-recognition technology with the sort of cameras that record images of vehicle occupants, as are deployed in Washington, DC, can make for a very rich data set about who was in a car, who they were there with, where they're going, when they got there, and so on.

Most recently, the Department of Homeland Security has deployed facial-recognition technology at airports and other ports of entry at the border and are photographing and analyzing every passenger arriving on international flights.

Social Media

Much of our lives is lived online. Some people are prone to publishing their every thought on Facebook, Twitter, and other social media platforms. These platforms are rich fishing grounds for agencies looking for information on potential threats, or who want to build a profile of a particular individual. In November 2016, Twitter announced that it authorized the FBI access to what Twitter calls its *firehose*, which is the raw feed of tweets going across their platform, essentially every tweet that appears on Twitter servers, transmitted in real time. The FBI is interested in keywords that could lead to potential threats; however, local law enforcement also are using this feed and combining it with geo-fencing, which means that they can do searches along the lines of, "show me all of the tweets that mention drugs in this particular neighborhood in the city." In some cases they are able to identify the IP address of the sender, which often can be correlated with the physical address. What could possibly go wrong?

Eavesdropping

As we learned earlier in this chapter, the networking protocols that we use every day, TCP, IP, and Ethernet, are not really designed with security in mind. Certainly, we can bolt on security measures to these protocols, but in most cases they don't exist. This makes it possible for individuals to eavesdrop on network conversations that are happening around them, especially on wireless connections. Let's say you're at your Starbucks having a double grande caramel latte macchiato, and you want to check on your bank account. You open up your laptop, connect to the WiFi at the café, and happily hit the web to visit your bank's website.

What you haven't noticed is the individual sitting in the corner of the café with his own laptop open, and a little smile on his face. What's happening is that this person has set up software on their laptop to capture all of the wireless data being transmitted in the café, and it's easy to read any of the information that is being sent back and forth. This can include things like your user names, your passwords, the text of instant messages you are sending, the text of e-mails, and so on. Keep in mind that anytime you're using public WiFi, there's always the possibility of an eavesdropper.

Phishing and Spearphishing

Phishing and Spearphishing are e-mail attacks, and they typically are more directed than some of the other techniques that we've looked at so far. An individual launching a phishing attack will create an e-mail that looks legitimate. The e-mail is crafted so that while the message is general in nature, the e-mail headers, the From address, and other features look legitimate. This might involve sending the e-mail from the domain that is being registered that is close to a legitimate domain; for example, an attacker might register FIDEL1TY.com, which in some fonts looks very similar to fidelity.com. A casual glance might not tell the difference.

Phishing attacks like this typically include a link with an urgent message. Perhaps the e-mail states that a breach has occurred at your bank and asks you to click a link to reset your password immediately. When you click the link, you sometimes are taken to a site that looks similar to the real site, but in fact is fake, and information about you is being collected at that time. Sometimes the link just takes you to a site that delivers malware to you. These kinds of attacks work because if the attacker sends out 100,000 emails stating that a breach has occurred, even if all the recipients don't have accounts at that bank, some will, and some small percentage of those will click through. A good way to protect against this kind of attack is to hover your mouse over any link in an e-mail; most e-mail clients will display the actual URL in the link, and most of the time it's easy to tell that the link is fraudulent.

Spearphishing on the other hand is a much more difficult attack to prevent. In Spearphishing, personal information about the target has been collected and used to craft e-mail that looks like it's coming from the target's friend, associate, or boss, someone that the target feels that they will need to respond to. A sophisticated Spearphishing attack consists of several e-mails and exchanges, each collecting slightly more information than the last. These e-mails are so carefully crafted that it's very difficult to tell them from the real thing. Once again, however, hovering the mouse over any link in an e-mail will at least show you whether a link was genuine or not.

Phishing attacks are relatively common on the Internet, and fortunately they are typically very badly done, with misspellings in the text, graphics that are missing or out of place, and generally they just don't look right. Spearphishing attacks on the other hand are extremely difficult to detect; if you are the target of a Spearphishing attack, you probably have bigger things to worry about.

What Can You Do?

If you are the target of an investigation by a government agency, there is very little that you can do to successfully evade surveillance. However, there are a few things that you can do to help protect yourself against leaking private information onto the Internet. We'll look at:

- Strong passwords
- Encryption / HTTPS
- VPNs

Strong Passwords

We've been taught for years that passwords should be complex to make it more difficult for hackers to crack them. For example, one technique is to replace letters with numbers, so that **mypassword** might instead be **myp4ssw0rd**. The thought is that it's much harder to guess a password that combines letters and numbers.

Unfortunately, hackers don't guess, they use computer programs to crack passwords, and the program simply sees a collection of characters—it doesn't care if they spell a real word or not; **mypassword** and **myp4ssw0rd** are equivalent to such a program. If your password is 10 characters long and includes numbers, there are 62 possibilities for each character, and 10^{62} combinations in total for the password. 10^{62} is 10 followed by 62 zeros, which seems like a very large number. However, computers can perform billions of calculations each second, and though it might take a few days, with enough computing power this kind of password can be cracked.

Worse, many people reuse passwords—they might have a small number of passwords for all of their accounts, and once a password has been compromised on one web site, it's trivial to try that password on other sites.

The longer a password is, the more difficult it is to crack. Security experts have long promoted the use of pass phrases rather than passwords, primarily due to their length, and also because they are easier to remember than random strings of characters. For example, you might use the password **this-is-my-really-long-passphrase** which has 33 characters and would be nearly impossible to crack using current technology, but is at the same time really easy to remember.

Also, consider using a password manager such as 1Password; these tools generate long passwords for you for each site that you use and store them in an encrypted database secured by a long pass phrase. Password managers automatically fill in your passwords when you log on to a site, so that you don't have to remember any of them save for the master pass phrase.

Encryption

Encrypting information with a secret key makes it impossible to read without the corresponding key. Most of us don't use encryption on its own, but you can select applications and web sites that incorporate strong encryption into their products and pages. For instant messaging, for example, both Signal and Whatsapp use end-to-end encryption to render every text unreadable by a third party, and Signal goes further by not storing any information about the conversation on their servers. If Signal were served with a secret FISA warrant, there would be nothing for them to turn over to the government. For this reason, many repressive regimes around the world ban the use of text messaging apps that use this kind of technology.

Another place that we are seeing encryption take hold is on the web. You might have noticed that many web sites are switching their address from http:mysite.com to https://mysite.com. The https part of that address indicates that the site is using an encrypted network connection between your browser and their server. Most browsers will show this as a small green lock or other symbol next to the site's address. Without the https, your connection is unencrypted and vulnerable to a third party intercepting and reading your data as it crosses the network.

VPNs

There's one glaring caveat to using https to connect to your favorite web sites, which is that your Internet service provider (ISP) can still see the connection itself, even if they can't read the content. The metadata about the connection is extremely valuable; it pinpoints the sites you visit, when you visit them, potentially what you are looking at (based on the URL), and more. Since the ISP is providing your connection to the Internet it is trivial to associate this traffic with you personally. Congress in 2017 cleared the way for ISPs to collect this information about you and sell it to third parties without your consent, and there is no requirement that they notify you of their activity.

How, then, can you prevent your daily traffic from being recorded by your ISP? For some the answer is a *virtual private network* (VPN). A VPN (Figure 15-6) is an encrypted network tunnel that is set up between your computer and a remote server. All network traffic from your computer is encrypted and sent to the server, where it is decrypted and passed on to the Internet as a regular connection.

The advantage is that your ISP only sees a single encrypted connection to a remote server; it is unable to decrypt the contents of the connection, or even to see any metadata such as the address of web sites that you are visiting. However, you really are just pushing your trust from your local ISP out to the VPN provider, who *does* decrypt the network data and can potentially record any information that they like. Trust is an important issue, and with all of the news stories circulating about privacy a large number of companies have sprung up to provide VPN service. Take the time to research the VPN providers that you are interested in to see. A good resource to compare VPN providers is thatoneprivacysite.net; another excellent resource is the Electronic Frontier Foundation at eff.org.

FIGURE 15-6   A VPN is an encrypted network tunnel

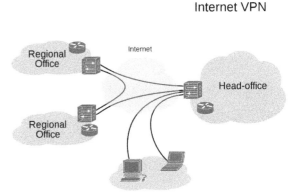

Bottom Line

Privacy and security are polarizing issues. On the one hand we want to feel safe from criminals and terrorists that mean us harm; on the other we recognize that these are being used as excuses by government to erode our personal privacy. Commercial interests make the issue even muddier as they try to extract as much money as possible from our online activities.

It isn't possible to be completely secure online. However, it is important to understand the threats that we face and at least be aware of the risks as we browse, chat, and use the network. It is also important to stand up for your right to privacy whenever possible; if we don't, there is no barrier to further assaults on our individual rights.

Figure Credits

CHAPTER 16

Making Money on the Internet

Everybody wants to get rich on the Internet. It was only about an hour after the invention of the World Wide Web that ads started appearing for various products and services, scams, Nigerian princes begging for cash, and commercial sites. Although the World Wide Web is only 20 years old, in these two decades we've seen a massive shift of retail activity from brick-and-mortar stores into the online world. Entire segments of the marketplace have disappeared: physical bookstores, record stores, even food, all have either moved online or have been replaced by online offerings. The attraction of the Internet, and the World Wide Web especially, is that transactions are nearly frictionless; it takes little effort to set up a shop on the web, and not much more effort to accept payments and ship products, especially if that product is something in digital format.

In addition to this shift of retail operations to the online world, consumers have also shifted their perceptions of how safe it is to buy something online. In its infancy, online commerce was restricted primarily to large companies that consumers were already familiar with. Web pages allowed customers to browse catalogs, make choices, and have products shipped to their home, but it wasn't until the past 10 years or so that we have started to see widespread acceptance at the consumer level of shopping online.

Today, even traditional large-scale retailers such as Sears, JCPenney, Sports Authority, and others are seeing their sales at physical stores erode as more and more customers turn to online resources, and we've also seen the rise of small-scale operations, sometimes selling just a single product, emerge and gain acceptance in a variety of market segments.

We can separate online sales into five categories:

- Selling bits
- Selling atoms
- Selling services,
- Selling space or eyeballs
- Selling access

All of these are similar in that they seek to capture an online audience and monetize visits to a website, and each has its unique challenges and rewards. Some categories are easier than others to set up; in this chapter will take a look at the opportunities presented by each of these categories, and provide a few pointers on how you can start making money online.

Selling Bits

A market segment that barely existed before the introduction of the World Wide Web is selling bits. By this I mean selling products that are in digital format: music, video, e-books, and images. The rapid rise of this category has a lot to do with the low bar to getting started. In addition, digital products can be purchased and delivered with almost no effort from either the buyer or the seller. And while early entries into the space relied on a straight sales model, we are now seeing a model emerge that provides rentals or leases for digital products, whether the product be books, or software, or services. Subscription services like Spotify or Ancestry provide the retailer a steady stream of revenue that is fairly predictable, which makes business planning significantly easier than if a physical product was being sold.

Much of the overhead costs of providing a physical product are avoided. For example, you do not need to store anything, and so don't need a warehouse. You're not shipping anything, and so you don't need boxes, paper invoices, postage, or delays in the time between when a customer purchases your product and receives it. Things don't get damaged in shipping, and if there is a problem with the digital product it is easily replaced almost instantly online.

Another advantage that some people don't think about is that because you're not tied to a physical product, you can be based anywhere in the world. Successful digital entrepreneurs can pretty much pick where they want to live.

What to Sell

There are nearly no limits to the digital products you can sell. Popular categories like books and music are crowded with retailers, but even niche products can be sold online. One strategy along these lines is described by Seth Godin in his book *Purple Cow* as "building your tribe." The idea is that you use an online presence; for example, a Twitter feed, or a Facebook page, to build an audience who is interested in what you have to say. As your audience grows and interactions with them increase, the audience will begin to tell you what they want. For example, you might host a Facebook page or website that discusses wild mushrooms in New England, which is a pretty narrow topic. As you guide these discussions in your feed or on your site and your audience grows, you might see a trend in the conversation along the lines of, "It'd be really great to have a reference on mushroom foraging in Massachusetts," or "I wish I had some kind of reminder to tell me which mushroom is fruiting at this time of the year."

These hints allow you to formulate a strategy to develop products that your audience, or tribe, is already interested in. Essentially what you're doing is market research without doing obvious market research. Once you develop the product or service that your audience is interested in, you get further instant feedback on it from that audience, which helps to plan the next product. If that feedback indicates that there is an issue with your product, because it's a digital product it is a simple matter to fix the issue and replace the digital files so that the very next customer who purchases your item gets the updated version.

E-Books

One category with an extremely low bar to entry is e-books. Just about everybody has something to say, and publishing an e-book on a particular topic is a quick and easy way to both generate revenue and grow your audience. Many people are intimidated by the thought of writing a book, but in fact you don't need to write a thousand-page novel in order to be successful in this space. Are you a poet? A small offering of 10 of your best poems, sold for a few dollars, is plenty to get you started. Interested in politics? Write a 20-page essay on how you think the political system could be improved, and offer it up for 99 cents. The point is that it isn't necessary to spend years writing the Great American Novel in order to get started in this space.

The vast majority of e-books are written for and sold on Amazon's Kindle family of e-book readers, of course, but there are other players in this field, including Barnes & Noble with their Nook line, and online sites that offer PDFs. An advantage of going with a large player like Amazon is that they have an established process for uploading content of your e-book, pricing it, taking payments from customers, and sending your royalties back to you. This level of service comes with a price, however, and online sellers such as Amazon will typically take 20 to 30% of the sales price of your book as their fee. For that fee though, you get access to a large and growing worldwide audience, and services such as simple authoring tools to make it easy to create your e-book. Unless your book is highly dependent on format, you can use familiar tools for writing and laying out your book such as Microsoft Word or Apple Pages, both of which can export files that Amazon and other e-book sellers will convert for you into the appropriate format for their readers. Amazon will even take a standard Microsoft Word document and create an e-book for you, a process that takes just a few minutes.

E-books are a wonderful way to get started in online sales due to their low overhead, and are also a great way to build interest in your audience for additional products and services. It is even possible to publish material that you have not written on your own; a small segment of this market is made up of individuals who take out of copyrighted material, typically older novels and references, and then convert them into e-books for sale in the various outlets. Project Gutenberg, for example, is an online repository of books in electronic format that are no longer under copyright protection, and it's a simple matter to choose one, drop the text into a Word or Pages document, clean it up a bit, and then publish the material as an e-book on Amazon.

Selling Atoms

By "atoms," I mean that you are selling a physical product. This is the more traditional sales model, involving manufacturing, warehousing, and shipping, and the only online component is sales and marketing. Generally speaking this is a more difficult endeavor to get into and sustain, than, say, selling bits.

Many entrepreneurs in this space start small selling someone else's product and only online. One significant change in this space that the Internet has brought to us is the shrinking of the supply chain. It used to be that if you wanted to sell a physical product, maybe a fancy phone case, you'd have to arrange for its manufacture, probably in a country such as China, and manage all of the details of the supply chain from ordering product, to shipping and customs, to boxing, to quality assurance, to marketing, and finally, getting your product into your customers, hands. In fact, just finding a manufacturer was a large barrier, and an entire industry was built to help new retailers broker deals.

Now however, sites such as China's AliBaba provide direct access to manufacturing, cutting out several steps in the process and at the same time cutting out all of the middlemen in the wholesale purchasing process. Whereas before the retailer might purchase products at wholesale from a distributor who in turn had purchased products from the manufacturer, now individuals can purchase products in any quantity directly from those manufacturers and have them shipped at low cost to their place of business.

This elimination of the distributor step in the process and its associated fees means that retailers can offer products at lower prices than the traditional markets supported, and because there's really no physical presence such as a store, margins can be higher since overall costs are much lower. Another advantage is that the retailer can purchase small quantities, reducing the requirement for warehousing and associated issues with spoilage, overstocking, and other problems. You literally can buy one or two of an item, and although it takes a significant amount of time to ship those items from overseas, if you model your sales properly you can keep small quantities arriving just in time for your customers to purchase them.

A great example of the kind of disruption that online sales and distribution has brought is the book industry. In the traditional publishing model, once a book was ready to be printed, wholesalers would purchase large quantities of the book from a publisher, who would order a print run to satisfy all of the those orders plus additional stock to cover incidental sales. Publishers might end up with a warehouse full of books. The wholesaler sells books to a distributor, who has relationships with brick-and-mortar bookstores. Those bookstores purchase books from the distributor, typically on a 90-day-to-pay invoice, and place the books in their stores so that customers can find and buy them. Any books that are unsold after a period of time (usually just under 90 days) are typically taken off the shelf and sent back to the publisher for credit. These books end up back in the publisher's warehouse if they are in salable condition.

Each of these steps requires payment of some sort. The printer expects to be paid for their printing effort, the distributor and wholesaler take a cut, the retailer expects to make a profit on a book and so buys the book from the distributor at a discount, and so on. It isn't uncommon for a book that sells for $25 to yield a dollar or even less in royalties for the author. Compare that with the nearly frictionless world of on-demand printing. In this model, an author contracts with an on-demand print service, such as CreateSpace or LightningSource, and uploads digital files to that service. Books are advertised online on sites such as Amazon, Barnes & Noble, and others, and when a purchase is made a single copy of the book is printed by the print-on-demand service. This eliminates the distributor and wholesaler and the physical inventory that the publisher might keep.

This model can be made even simpler by drop-shipping books directly from the printer to the customer. When a sale is made, say, on Amazon, an electronic message is sent to the print vendor with the name and address of the customer, and a single copy is printed, placed in an envelope, and shipped directly to that customer. In this kind of system, the publisher or author never has to touch that purchased copy. One would think that this would have led to lower prices for books, but that hasn't been the case. Readers are already used to paying a certain price for a certain size book, and there is no incentive to reduce that price if the consumer is willing to pay it.

Selling Services

Many people sell services online. Maybe you are an editor, or a designer, or someone who paints houses; it's a simple matter to create a website that highlights your skills and services and acts as an advertisement to attract customers. In this case the Internet really is being used as an advertising medium, connecting consumers with providers of services.

Even students can benefit from this kind of economic model. You might be good at editing term papers, or perhaps you have some extra time to run errands for someone, or you might want to provide tutoring in the subject that you're particularly strong at. Some sites offer the service of creating a page to advertise *your* service, acting as a hub for consumers to find one of a large number of providers.

There's not a lot of effort involved in setting up this kind of business, apart from the time it takes for you to actually perform the service. As in most businesses, marketing and advertising are the key to generating a steady revenue stream.

Selling Space

On the Internet, content is king.

Most people spend a significant portion of their day browsing the web. Some read news, some read blogs, or participate in forums, and sites that generate the most traffic are the ones with the most compelling content. That content can be leveraged to monetize the website. There are several approaches to this, but a common one is to sell advertising. There are basically two models in this space:

Pay-per-click
Pay-per-view

Each has its upsides and downsides, but both require a site to generate compelling content to attract readers to the page.

Pay-per-Click

The pay-per-click advertising model rewards content creators who have placed ads on their site for each time a user clicks through a specific advertisement. The advantage to the advertiser is that this is essentially a *qualified* lead; the user has taken a positive action in clicking on an ad to find out more information about the advertised product or service. This kind of lead is more valuable than someone who just sees an ad and doesn't take any action, since it really isn't known whether that user has any interest at all in the product. For this reason pay-per-click ads typically pay a higher rate than do other kinds of advertising.

The downside for the content generator, or site operator, is that the advertisement distracts the user. If you're on a web page and notice an ad that strikes your interest, and click on it, very often you were taken off the original site and to the advertiser site to learn more about the product. Your interest has been diverted from the content on the original site, and it's not possible to predict whether you will go back to that site or be led off in some other direction. So, for the site operator, the risk is that traffic will be moved off of their site onto someone else's site.

Pay-per-View

The second kind of advertising common on the World Wide Web is pay-per-view. Here, payment is made to a site owner each time an ad is displayed on a webpage. It isn't necessary for a user to click on the ad to generate revenue, it just has to be seen. These are *unqualified* leads, and the rate paid for this kind of advertisement is an order of magnitude of more or less than that paid for pay-per click.

This kind of advertisement is measured in thousands of views, and an advertiser might be willing to pay a dollar for 1000, or 10,000, or 100,000 views on a web page. Because the rates are so low, pay-per-view advertising really makes sense only for sites that generate a large amount of traffic. Again, that traffic has to be created by first offering compelling content—if you write it, they will come.

Both the pay-per-click and pay-per-view models work better when the advertisements are aligned with the content on a particular web page. It doesn't make sense to advertise party balloons on a site dedicated to automobile racing, for example. Google, which most people associate with their search engine, is by far the largest supplier of advertisements on the World Wide Web. The Google ad networks allow advertisers to leverage Google's deep scanning of websites, which in turn allows Google to select ads that have a high affinity for the content on a particular page.

For popular keywords, there might be 100 different advertisers interested in placing an ad on the page that has only one spot for an ad. This is handled through an online auction that occurs the moment you begin to load the page. As the page is loading, the JavaScript code used to create a space for an ad is executed, and a message is sent to Google that an ad is required. At that moment an auction takes place among all of the advertisers interested in placing an ad in that spot. The auction takes only a few milliseconds to finish. Each advertiser has specified a range of payment that they are willing to offer to a website owner for that ad placement. As the auction progresses, the winner is the advertiser with the closest affinity to the page's content and the best offer. The ad itself is then downloaded to the web page.

In most cases, this auction happens so quickly that we don't even notice that something other than the page's content is being loaded. This kind of auction works for both pay-per-click and pay-per-view, and ad networks such as Google take a percentage of the revenue generated as their placement fee. In fact, almost two-thirds of Google's annual revenue is generated through placement of ads and the sale of user profile information back to the advertisers. We talk about this more in our discussion of security and privacy, but essentially Google is tracking everything you do on the web, compiling your actions into a profile, and then selling that profile to advertisers. The upside for the advertiser is that they can more closely target ads to you; if you've just spent a few hours online searching the best price for a trip Europe, expect to start to see advertisements for luggage and language instruction on the websites that you visit for the next two weeks.

While the pay-per-click model generates better revenue per ad placement, from the advertiser's standpoint it doesn't make sense to sell just a few ads on a site with low traffic, and so these ads are often available only for sites that see a large number of users per day. The key to generating that large number of users is, of course, content. Compelling content will drive traffic to your site, and make it more attractive for this kind of advertising. Pay-per-view ads are the digital equivalent of taking a bunch of flyers and throwing them onto the ground, hoping someone will pick one up. Low-traffic sites are good candidates for pay-per-view, especially if the metric used is thousands of views; on low-traffic sites, it may be difficult for the site owner to reach the threshold for any payment whatsoever from the advertiser. The advertiser basically is getting free advertisements.

Selling Access

Another content-is-king approach is to sell access to your content. Traditionally this has been a subscription model—sites publish information that readers place value on, and access is sold on a recurring basis, such as for a monthly or yearly fee.

The subscription model works reasonably well, but it is an attempt to fit an existing model to a new medium. More appropriate for many sites is a pay-for-view model that requires users to pay for each individual item read or accessed. This rewards compelling content and encourages content providers to pay attention to what their audience wants to read. The downside is that this model quickly becomes an annoyance for both publishers and consumers who are faced with managing micro-payments, possibly just a few cents or fractions of a cent.

Micro-Payments
The idea behind micro-payment is that users who might balk at a flat subscription fee might welcome a system in which they pay a very small amount for each item that they read. For example, instead of paying $20 per month for access to an entire site, each article costs 5¢.

In practice this is problematic. Most payment processors such as Visa and MasterCard aren't set up for such tiny transactions; in fact, they impose a processing fee of 3% to 5% for every transaction that moves through their network. A swarm of tiny payments would quickly both overwhelm the payment network and make it more difficult for publishers to turn a profit.

One promising solution is to use digital-only currencies such as Bitcoin and Ethereum. Most transactions in Bitcoin are already for small fractions, and since the currency itself is digital it is well suited for real-time transactions at any volume. Unfortunately the mere mention of cryptocurrencies makes many users panic; it's a new financial instrument and hasn't built up the level of trust and comfort that traditional currencies hold. We'll occasionally see a large site experiment with micro-payment and cryptocurrency (Bernie Sanders, for example, accepted campaign contributions in Bitcoin during the 2016 presidential election cycle), but for now we seem stuck with systems designed for pre-web business.

Bottom Line

The web is an ideal platform for businesses of all sizes. It has broken down traditional models of commerce by shortening the supply chain and reducing the friction in transactions. The barrier to entry is so low that anyone can try their hand at selling online, and if the first attempt isn't successful, there's very little lost and valuable lessons to gain.

While most think immediately of selling atoms when considering a business, there are so many other ways to generate revenue, including selling digital products, advertising space, and access to content. Each of these has its own set of rewards and risks, but overall risk is exceptionally low.

Remember that commercial giants such as Amazon started with a small online presence, selling one thing!

CHAPTER 17

Operating Systems

When we talk about a computer running Windows, or OS/X, or Linux, what we're really talking about is what *operating system* the computer uses. An operating system is nothing more than a program running on your computer, just like your web browser, word processor, and calendar. Of course, it does have special powers; you can think of it as being first among equals.

The problem that the operating system is trying to solve is this: There are literally hundreds of programs running on your computer, but the physical resources—the hardware—are limited. There's only so much memory in the computer, and only one or two ports for a network connection. There are probably one or two disk devices in the box. The operating system's job is to manage these limited resources and access to fairly provide access to them for all of the programs that want to use them.

The operating system also hides most of the details of the hardware from running programs. A program doesn't have to know which specific model of a hard drive it is reading files from and what special codes it needs to operate. Instead, the program asks the operating system to read the file on its behalf, and the operating system takes care of the details.

This kind of layering of responsibility, in which one layer hides the complexity of an underlying layer, is quite common in computer science, and it offers tremendous benefits. In the case of a program requesting a file from disk, since the operating system handles the request on the program's behalf, the program doesn't know what kind of disk is being used. This means that we can replace the disk with something completely different—a solid-state disk instead of a traditional hard drive, for example—and the program doesn't even know that this has happened.

We use the term abstraction to describe this kind of relationship. It means that a simplified view of something more complex is offered to a layer above or below. The operating system provides a simplified view of reading or writing files to disk to the programs that need them.

The operating system, then, sits between running programs and the hardware (Figure 17-1).

FIGURE 17-1   High-level view of an operating system

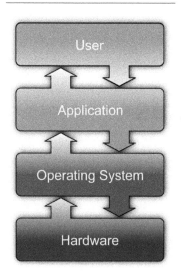

FIGURE 17-1   High-level view of an operating system

What It Isn't

Usually we can glance at a computer screen and tell immediately which operating system is in use. Windows, Mac OS/X, and even Linux all have a look-and-feel that is recognizable. The windows, menu bars, and even the color and shape of buttons on the screen are giveaways.

However, what we see on the screen is not the operating system, but instead is just another program, called a *window manager*, running on the computer (Figure 17-2). It is quite possible to run a different window manager with a different look and feel. The Linux operating system, for instance, offers several popular window managers such as Gnome and KDE, which can be themed to mimic Apple OS/X or Microsoft Windows, or use their own unique style.

Window Managers

The window manager is what users see every time they start up their computer, and so companies like Microsoft, Apple, and Google spend a

FIGURE 17-2   The Gnome window manager running on the Linux operating system

great deal of time and money on its design. When was the last time you heard someone say, "I stopped using that operating system because I didn't like the way the scheduler was choosing processes to run."? Instead we talk about how we don't like the shape of the buttons, or that the menu is in an awkward place. These companies understand that most users equate the quality of the operating system with what they see on the screen.

The window manager is responsible for the position, size, and functionality of common graphical user interface elements such as buttons and menus. It handles interaction with a mouse or trackpad, and allows users to reposition and resize windows on the screen. Behind the scenes it is responsible for managing each program's use of graphical resources.

Since the operating system and window manager are not the same, it is entirely possible (and in some companies the default) to run an operating system without a graphical interface. Figure 17-3 shows a screenshot of a Linux terminal. In situations where computers are being used as servers or are otherwise unattended, it doesn't make sense to provide a graphical interface.

A Brief History of the Operating System

The concept of what an operating system is has evolved greatly over the past 50 to 60 years. Early computers such as ENIAC ran only one program at a time, and switching to another program was not an easy thing to do; often it meant inputting a program by hand using switches, or even moving physical wires around. A program might take several hours

FIGURE 17-3   A Linux computer running in console mode

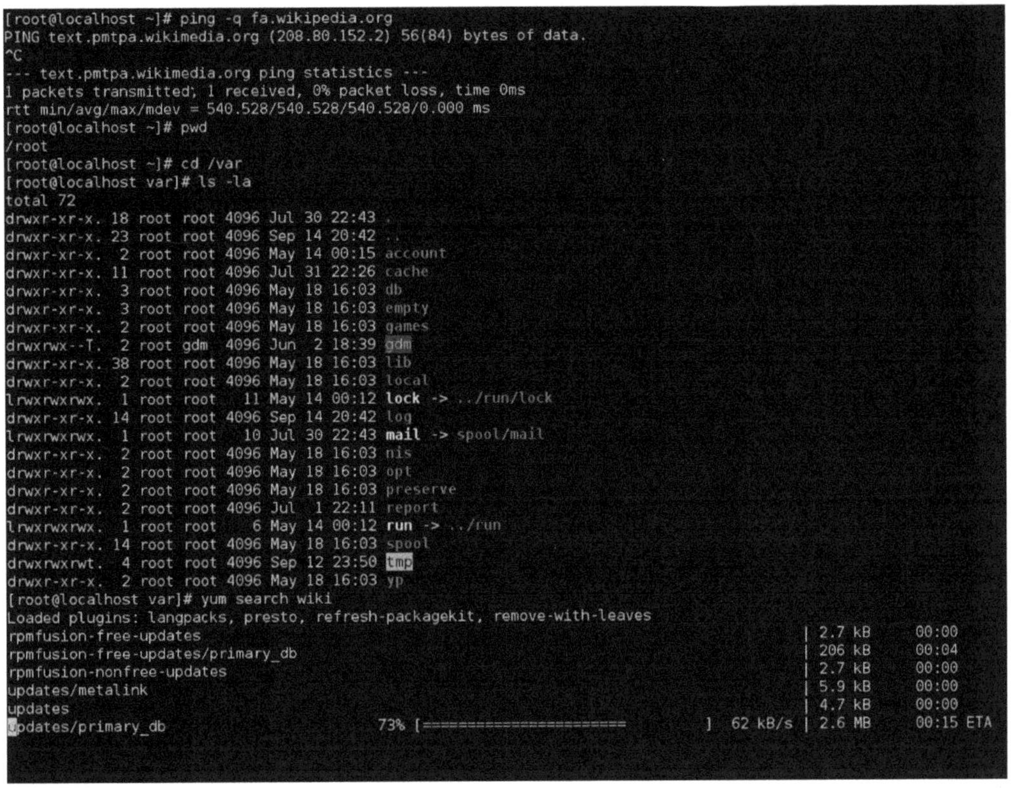

```
[root@localhost ~]# ping -q fa.wikipedia.org
PING text.pmtpa.wikimedia.org (208.80.152.2) 56(84) bytes of data.
^C
--- text.pmtpa.wikimedia.org ping statistics ---
1 packets transmitted, 1 received, 0% packet loss, time 0ms
rtt min/avg/max/mdev = 540.528/540.528/540.528/0.000 ms
[root@localhost ~]# pwd
/root
[root@localhost ~]# cd /var
[root@localhost var]# ls -la
total 72
drwxr-xr-x. 18 root root 4096 Jul 30 22:43 .
drwxr-xr-x. 23 root root 4096 Sep 14 20:42 ..
drwxr-xr-x.  2 root root 4096 May 14 00:15 account
drwxr-xr-x. 11 root root 4096 Jul 31 22:26 cache
drwxr-xr-x.  3 root root 4096 May 18 16:03 db
drwxr-xr-x.  3 root root 4096 May 18 16:03 empty
drwxr-xr-x.  2 root root 4096 May 18 16:03 games
drwxrwx--T.  2 root gdm  4096 Jun  2 18:39 gdm
drwxr-xr-x. 38 root root 4096 May 18 16:03 lib
drwxr-xr-x.  2 root root 4096 May 18 16:03 local
lrwxrwxrwx.  1 root root   11 May 14 00:12 lock -> ../run/lock
drwxr-xr-x. 14 root root 4096 Sep 14 20:42 log
lrwxrwxrwx.  1 root root   10 Jul 30 22:43 mail -> spool/mail
drwxr-xr-x.  2 root root 4096 May 18 16:03 nis
drwxr-xr-x.  2 root root 4096 May 18 16:03 opt
drwxr-xr-x.  2 root root 4096 May 18 16:03 preserve
drwxr-xr-x.  2 root root 4096 Jul  1 22:11 report
lrwxrwxrwx.  1 root root    6 May 14 00:12 run -> ../run
drwxr-xr-x. 14 root root 4096 May 18 16:03 spool
drwxrwxrwt.  4 root root 4096 Sep 12 23:50 tmp
drwxr-xr-x.  2 root root 4096 May 18 16:03 yp
[root@localhost var]# yum search wiki
Loaded plugins: langpacks, presto, refresh-packagekit, remove-with-leaves
rpmfusion-free-updates                                            | 2.7 kB    00:00
rpmfusion-free-updates/primary_db                                 | 206 kB    00:04
rpmfusion-nonfree-updates                                         | 2.7 kB    00:00
updates/metalink                                                  | 5.9 kB    00:00
updates                                                           | 4.7 kB    00:00
updates/primary_db                    73% [====================    ] 62 kB/s | 2.6 MB   00:15 ETA
```

or even days to run, so it wasn't the case that programmers were rushing around madly trying to get the machine to switch to a different program every few minutes, but it still was a lot of work.

Fairly early in the development of these machines someone came up with the idea of loading two programs at once, and then switching between the two as needed. As with most simple ideas in computing, this introduced new problems. What should be done with the data from one program when switching to another? Should it be completely removed, or was it allowable to leave it in the machine? What if the first program wasn't quite finished running, was there a way to suspend it and pick up later where it had left off? How much time should be provided to each program?

The motivation for switching programs quickly was in part financial. These early machines were very expensive to build and operate, and in order to recoup their cost there was a strong desire to keep the machine busy. If the computer was just sitting there doing nothing, it was wasting money. The time required to switch programs manually was non-productive—the computer wasn't doing any work during that time—and any method that reduced the time required was beneficial.

Solutions to this problem were simple at first, but quickly became more complicated. If it was good to switch between two programs, why not three? Or ten? Or a hundred? With each new advance came new problems to solve, and it wasn't too long before the simple switching program had become more complex than many of the programs it was switching among.

FIGURE 17-4 Borland's Sidekick TSR

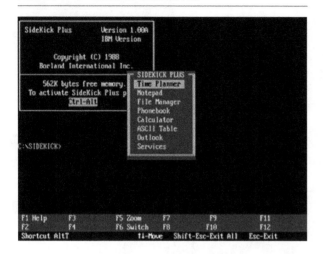

FIGURE 17-5 Apple's Macintosh desktop in 1984

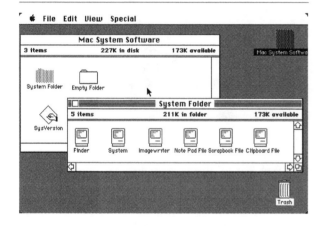

Early versions of Microsoft's operating system, MS-DOS, which ran on IBM's new Personal Computer (IBM PC), was relatively simple and could run just one program at a time. Loading a program meant reading it into the computer via cassette tape, which stored the program as bits encoded with audio tones. To run a different program, you would insert and read a new cassette, and the original program would be overwritten.

A glimmer of what was to come was revealed by a new kind of program, called Terminate and Stay Resident (TSR). TSRs had the ability to remain in the computer's memory even when a new program was loaded, and a keystroke sequence could switch between a running program and the TSR. Because the TSR was in memory, it could share data with the co-resident program. The most popular of the TSRs for MS-DOS was Borland's Sidekick (Figure 17-4) which included a contact list, calendar, calculator, and other conveniences.

The year 1984 saw the first commercial use of what we would consider a graphical user interface running on top of an operating system. Employees of Apple Computer, including Steve Jobs, had been invited to Xerox's Palo Alto Research Center (PARC) for a demonstration of the experimental Xerox Alto, which introduced several new concepts, such as the idea of a "desktop," the mouse, and icons representing files and programs. In return for the visit, Xerox was allowed to buy shares in Apple. The Apple team refined the ideas they saw at Xerox and introduced the new windowing environment along with the Macintosh computer in 1984 (Figure 17-5). Microsoft responded with its own version, called Windows, in 1985.

We are so used to this kind of graphical interface that we take it completely for granted. At the time of its introduction it was truly revolutionary; no one had ever seen anything like it. Software manuals of the time typically included an entire chapter on how to use a mouse, and courses were designed to train employees on how to move icons around the desktop. The basic metaphors used in those early versions are still with us today, to the point that even small children intuitively understand how to use the interface.

With all of that said, though, don't forget that the windowing system and graphical interface are just programs running on the computer—they are not the operating system!

What the Operating System Does

The modern operating system provides four major services:

- Scheduling
- Hardware abstraction
- Memory management
- Files and directories

The specifics of how each operating system implements these services is what makes each operating system unique.

Scheduling

In the operating system, a special program called the *scheduler* decides which programs get to run and in what order. Before we can talk about scheduling, it's necessary to dispel a common misconception. If someone were to ask you how many programs the CPU in your computer could run simultaneously, what would you say? Some people think about all of the programs that they use during the day and guess a dozen. Others, with a little more computer knowledge under their belt, realize that there are programs we don't necessarily see on the screen; they might answer with a number closer to one hundred.

Here's the thing: The CPU in your computer can do only *one thing at a time*. There are exceptions, of course, and we'll get to those in a moment, but all of the programs that you use on a daily basis—e-mail, word processing, web browsers, streaming music or video— are executed by the CPU one at a time. The trick is that each is executed for only a very short time, and then another program gets to run, and then another, and then another. The switch between running programs is done so quickly that it creates the illusion that the programs are all running simultaneously.

This trick, switching back and forth rapidly, is the same one that is used in motion pictures (Figure 17-6). If you look closely at a length of movie film, you'll see that it is made up of many individual still images, called frames. When shown in the theatre, the film travels through the projector at a rate of 24 frames per second; our eyes can't process the individual frames that quickly, and so are tricked into thinking that the motion is continuous.

FIGURE 17-6   Individual frames of a motion picture

Multitasking

This rapid switching-in-and-out of programs is called *multitasking*. As computer users, we want to be able to seamlessly drag an image from our photo app into an e-mail and send it on its way, but behind the curtain the photo app runs for a tiny amount of time, then the app providing windows and menus, then the e-mail app, then back to the photo app, and so on.

Early computers also did multitasking, but the process of switching among running programs was manual. Borland's TSR program, Sidekick, described earlier, required a special sequence of keys to switch from a foreground task to Sidekick and back again. Even though switching among programs was manual, Sidekick was an important step in the push toward modern multitasking, and it showed users the power of having several programs running more or less at the same time. We got used to writing a letter in a word processor and being able to quickly pop up a calendar to check on a date for a meeting.

The next step in the evolution of multitasking was to let the computer handle the switching process. This makes sense in retrospect. Since the operating system controls every aspect of a running program, shouldn't it also manage which programs are running, and when they run?

The Quantum

Once the step was made to automate switching, an important question arose. Given that the computer is rapidly leaping from one program to another, how long should any program run? A second? An hour? Something more or less?

Think again about motion picture film. The still images need to be displayed rapidly enough that our eye no longer sees them as individual pictures; a rate of one frame per second, for example, would result in annoying flickering and probably a headache as our eyes struggled to adjust to each individual image. If we display the frames too fast, though, the reel of film would get larger and larger. If, for example, we increased the frame rate to 48 frames per second, which is double the normal rate, the strip of film would end up being twice as long.

It's the same with programs. We want a smooth, continuous flow of programs running, but if we switch them too quickly the computer would spend a significant amount of time simply handling the switching itself. Operating systems define a unit of time, called the *quantum*, that specifies how long a program can run before it is switched out and another program starts up. The length of time varies among operating systems but is generally a value between 10 milliseconds and 100 milliseconds.

It doesn't feel as though 10 milliseconds is enough time for a program to do anything meaningful. Just as it has finished its coffee and settles in to start working, the program is suddenly yanked out of the CPU and another program has to rush in. Modern computers, though, are astonishingly fast; even an inexpensive home computer can complete around 30 million program instructions *per second*, which is quite an impressive number. In 10 milliseconds such a CPU would execute 300,000 instructions. That's plenty of time to finish a cup of coffee.

Blocking

The quantum is the maximum time that a program is allowed to execute instructions in the CPU before it must step aside and allow another program to run. But what should happen if a program begins to run, and then immediately executes an instruction that will take a relatively long time to finish? We don't want to waste the CPU's time, doing no work while the instruction runs, but we also want to be fair to the program. In most operating systems the solution is to remove the program from the CPU and let another program run. This is called *blocking* and happens quite frequently.

A common reason for a program to block is when it requests that data be read or written to a hard disk. The disk is, in many cases, a mechanical device and it might take

several hundred milliseconds to process the request and return the data
to the program. *Blocking I/O* (input /
output) such as this causes the scheduler to step in and remove the program
from the CPU, and the program is
placed into a sleep state, ready to run
as soon as the information is retrieved.
Another program is granted the CPU
by the scheduler.

FIGURE 17-7 An ISR responds to a key press

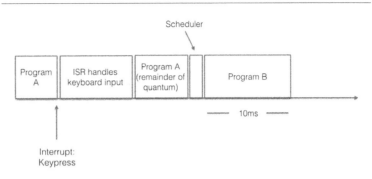

How long does the blocked program sleep? Until its alarm goes off! But the alarm isn't
the sort that we use to get up in the morning ("Wake me up at 6:30 a.m."), it's an event-
based alarm ("Wake me up if something interesting happens."). In the case of a read or
write to disk, the interesting event is that the read or write operation has completed.

Other events that the operating system has to manage might be that the mouse has
moved, or a key is pressed on the keyboard, or a byte of data is received on the network
interface. We can't predict when these events will occur, but we can detect when they do.
These events are called *interrupts*. An interrupt is something that needs to be taken care
of right away, and the program currently running in the CPU is replaced by an *interrupt
service routine*, a small program that deals with the event and then steps out of the way so
that the interrupted program can use the remainder of its quantum (Figure 17-7).

Scheduling Algorithms

The scheduler in any operating system is one of the most frequently run programs on the
computer. Since it runs so often, its programming code must be extremely efficient, and
it is typically very small and highly optimized. The scheduler isn't really doing any useful
work, compared to the other programs that are running, and so we want to minimize the
amount of CPU time that it consumes.

Another consideration is that there are potentially several hundred programs that
need to run, and the method used to choose which program runs next must be fair to
the others that are waiting. The scheduler uses one of several algorithms, or methods, to
make its decision.

Common scheduling algorithms include:

> **Round-Robin**: Programs run sequentially in the order that they appear in line,
> and when a program is finished running it goes to the end of the line. Programs
> A, B, and C would run in the order A-B-C-A-B-C. Round-robin is a very simple
> algorithm, but it does give each program an equal chance of running.

> **Priority Lists**: Priority-based algorithms assign different priorities to programs
> that are ready to run based on what they have done before. For example, a program
> that has been sleeping after requesting data from the disk drive might be given
> a high priority and move to the front of the line since it has the data needed to
> keep running. Likewise, a program that has been waiting a long time might have

its priority periodically increased so that it moves up more quickly the longer it has waited.

Real-Time: Most computers run programs that must be executed the moment that they are ready. Sometimes these programs are part of the operating system itself, but often they are regular programs that shouldn't wait. If you had a program that monitored the cooling system temperature on a nuclear reactor, you probably wouldn't want it to have to wait in line behind the program that managed e-mails on the computer!

Schedulers typically combine Priority and Real-Time approaches so that all programs get to run, and the most important ones run first. An important consideration of this method is to avoid *starvation*, which means that an unlucky program might constantly find itself ready to run but behind some other program that has a higher priority.

The most important program of all is the scheduler itself, and it is executed at the end of every quantum period. A hardware-based clock on the computer's motherboard ticks the milliseconds away and interrupts the running program when quantum expires; the interrupt service routine for this clock is the scheduler. A special hardware bit is set to prevent the scheduler itself from being interrupted.

Hardware Abstraction

Another job of the operating system is to provide programs access to the computer's hardware. There are two reasons for this. The first is that while there might be hundreds of programs running on the computer, there is only one network connection, one set of memory, one video monitor, and just a few disk drives. There must be some organized way to provide access to these limited resources.

When a program wants to write data to a disk drive, for example, it doesn't do so directly. Instead the program asks the operating system to write the data on its behalf. If several programs have requested disk access, the operating system decides which will be honored first, second, and so on. The disk request will block the program, which will sleep until the request is complete.

FIGURE 17-8 Hardware abstraction layer

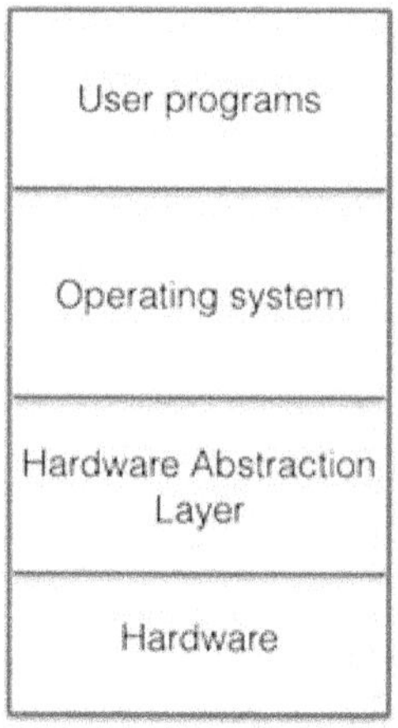

This offers several advantages. Poorly written or malicious programs do not have direct access to the computer's hardware. The operating system can be optimized for a specific set of hardware. Finally, programmers do not need to know what kind of hardware a given computer has; instead they are able to write their programs to use generic services offered by the operating system.

This notion of making the computer appear generic on the programming side and specific on the hardware side is known as *abstraction*, and it is a concept that we see over and over in computing. Think about the last time you were in an electronics store; there were dozens of different brands and models of computers: some were laptops, some were tablets, and others were desktops. They had very different specifications and hardware. All of them, though, ran Microsoft Windows. Is there a different version of Windows for each brand and hardware configuration? Not at all—Windows provides an abstraction layer that sits between the hardware and the running programs. Figure 17-8 shows this arrangement.

| User programs |
| Operating system |
| Hardware Abstraction Layer |
| Hardware |

The abstraction layer operates as a translator, taking generic requests and restating them as the specific command that a piece of hardware needs. This often takes the form of a driver, a small program that works with the operating system to do the translations. If you install a new video card in your computer, for example it will come with an installation disk that includes the driver. The operating system receives a request from a program to display something on the screen, then passes the request to the driver to do the specific work required.

The abstraction layer pushes responsibility for figuring out how to work with a specific piece of hardware to the lowest level possible. Above the abstraction layer, programs and the operating system work in generalities; save this file, send this data on the network. It is the Hardware Abstraction Layer that turns those generic requests into specific commands. Abstraction is such a powerful concept that we see it in almost every area of computing: networking; program design; web sites; databases; and so many more.

Memory Services

A computer's memory is one of its most limited resources. How can this be? We might have 8, or 16, or even 32 gigabytes of memory in our computer—that's a lot! Recall that there might be hundreds of programs running at any given time. Each of those programs needs access to the computer's memory—in order to execute a program, it must be in physical memory. More importantly, each of the programs runs with the assumption that it has 4 gigabytes of memory all its own.

Let's do some math. Assume that 100 programs are running, each of which thinks it has 4 gigabytes of memory to use; 4 gigabytes * 100 = 400 gigabytes. Clearly there is more memory committed than we have available. And yet, this is exactly how it works.

Virtual Memory

The solution is a technique called *virtual memory*. All of the programs running on the computer are allocated 4 gigabytes of virtual memory, not physical memory. The operating system takes care of translating virtual memory requests for reads and writes into physical memory, as shown in Figure 17-9. In this diagram, a process is equivalent to a running program. This is another example of an abstraction; the program sees a generic view of memory, and the operating system handles mapping the generic requests into an operation involving a physical memory chip.

It is possible in most cases to satisfy all of the memory requirements of a program, because it is unusual for a program to require all 4GB of its allocation; in fact the requirement is usually much smaller than this. In a computer with enough physical memory most programs will remain resident in memory during their life cycle. Since the operating

FIGURE 17-9 Arrangement of virtual memory in physical memory

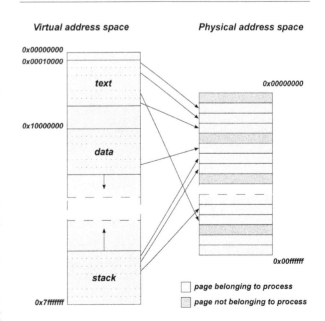

system gets involved in translating requests to read and write to memory, it can perform additional steps, such as checking to see if a read or write request is valid. When a program crashes, it's often the result of a request to access a memory location that doesn't belong to it.

Paging and Swapping

With so many programs needing memory, and with physical memory being such a limited resource, sometimes there just isn't enough memory to go around. If a program requests memory and the operating system can't accommodate the request because there isn't enough physical memory left, a portion of the memory being used by a non-running program will be moved to a file on a hard disk called the *page file* in an operation called *paging*. It's perfectly normal for paging to happen; when a program needs to access memory that has been paged, the operating system steps in and retrieves that information from the page file, loading it into physical memory.

When space gets extremely tight, the operating system has another tool available: the *swap file*. While the page file is used to store small pieces of a non-running program's memory, the swap file stores all of a program's allocation of physical memory. This is a fairly severe thing to do, since it will take a significant amount of time to load all of this information back into physical memory when it is the program's time to run, but sometimes it's all that can be done.

While paging is normal and expected, if a system is swapping a lot it can be a sign that there is insufficient physical memory installed. In extreme conditions a program will be ready to run but swapped, and there is not enough physical memory available to swap the program in, causing another program to swap, over and over, a condition called *thrashing*. When a computer is thrashing, it is spending nearly all of its time swapping programs in and out of disk, and very little else gets done.

Files and Directories

When we use our computers for day-to-day work, we work on files and store those files in folders and directories. As you might have guessed, this is, in reality, just another abstraction provided by the operating system. The reality is much messier.

Files are stored on disk in small units called *blocks*. A typical block size is 4,096 bytes (4 kilobytes). An MP3 file of your favorite song might be 10 million bytes. Obviously we can't stuff 10 million bytes into a container that can only hold 4,096 bytes. The answer is that, on disk, the file is spread out and stored one block at a time. Normally these blocks aren't right next to each other on the disk platter but scattered all around it. Each block contains the location on the next block in the file, so that when the operating system wants to read the file, it only needs the location of the very first block—the rest of the blocks are found, one by one, as each points to the next block in the chain.

Directories and folders operate along the same lines, storing the locations of the first blocks of each file in a directory or folder. The directory is just a file containing a list of other files.

This level of detail isn't something that regular programs should have to worry about, and so the operating system provides the abstraction of a file for them to work with. Once again the operating system is hiding the complexity of the hardware from the programs that it provides services to.

Which Operating System?

It wasn't that long ago that there was a sharp divide among users who opted for one of the three major operating systems: Windows, MacOS, and Linux. Windows was seen as a platform for businesses (remember the "I'm a Mac, I'm a PC advertisements?) and for serious gamers. Often it was the default choice, since Microsoft commands 80–90% of the PC market, and most new computers that you might find at your local electronics store come pre-installed with it. MacOS was seen as a tool for "creatives" with a focus on graphics, design, music, and other art forms. For quite a long time it was rare to see a Macintosh computer in a corporate environment; Apple itself pushed this view in its marketing campaigns. The introduction of the iPhone and iPad changed this. Employees began to rely on their Apple devices and demanded to be allowed to bring them to work and have them supported on the corporate network. While still relatively rare, MacOS is making inroads in this environment. Finally, Linux was (and still is) seen as an operating system for geeks and power users who aren't afraid of opening up the hood and tinkering with what is inside. Only a fraction of the home-use market is held by Linux computers; however, in the data center the opposite is true; since Linux is ideal for use as a server, its use is widespread in that area. Over 85% of the web servers deployed today run some form of Linux. It doesn't hurt that Linux is free!

A newcomer to the operating system party is network-based offerings such as Google's ChromeOS. This new operating system is designed to be very lightweight so that it can run on less complex and less expensive hardware, and it relies on much of the heavy lifting associated with traditional operating systems to be done on a remote server. ChromeOS devices are similar to "smart" terminals in that they have limited memory and local storage.

Bottom Line

The operating system manages access by programs to limited physical resources such as memory, disk, and the CPU itself. Through the scheduler it is responsible for running multitasked programs in a fair manner. Finally, it provides useful abstractions such as files and directories to users of the computer. All of these details are hidden from users by abstracting them into high-level functions, such as saving a file or opening a program.

We don't often choose which operating system we will run on a given computer. Really, the choice is becoming less interesting as the major operating systems converge on a similar look and feel. Most users aren't looking to "run" an operating system, they simply want to get something done, and will choose whatever machine and operating system run the programs that they need to get those things accomplished.

Figure Credits

18 Computer Components

W alk in to just about any store that sells computers, and you'll find row after row of nearly identical boxes, sometimes a little smaller, sometimes a little bigger, but almost all of them some shade of gray or black, and almost all of them shaped as some kind of a rectangle. Prices on these look-alike boxes can range from just a few hundred dollars to several thousand dollars, however. What is it that is inside these nearly identical boxes that justifies such a large price differential? In this chapter we'll take a look at what's inside of a computer, especially one that you might buy from the store, not from some theoretical architectural standpoint, but rather an examination of what's important to look for when you're buying your own computer.

General-Purpose Computers

You might recall from our earlier discussion of computer history a description of the Von Neumann architecture, developed in the mid-1940s and which, in the 1950s, was the predominant model of a general-purpose computer (see Figure 18-1). Prior to that time, most computers were purpose-built, often for just a single program. In the late 1970s and into the 1980s, however, general-purpose computers became more popular and less expensive, and this is the time that we saw the rise of the personal computer. These machines had to do lots of different tasks, and do all of them well, or least reasonably well. The Von Neumann architecture offered a blueprint for this kind of machine. Even now, the components of that architecture are the most important things that we will look for when we are purchasing our own machines.

One of the problems that we face when we're buying computers is that those machines really *do* look alike, and the descriptions on the marketing material in the store is full of numbers and terms and abbreviations that you might not be familiar with. Which ones actually make a difference? Ten or 15 years ago the components inside of these computers were highly configurable, and it wasn't unusual to buy a bare-bones machine, with not much inside the box, and add our own components, such as video cards, modems, networking cards, and so on. Now, however, it's more common to find computers with everything built

FIGURE 18-1   Von Neumann computer architecture

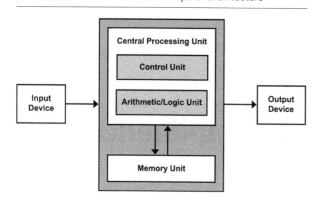

into a single board, meaning that the things that we can configure makes a very short list. Hobbyists will still buy bare-bones machines and configure them to their liking, especially gamers who are always looking for that extra small percentage of performance, but for most of us we are just buying something off the shelf.

One quick bit of terminology that we'll use in this chapter: The computer's *motherboard* is a large circuit board on which most of the computer's components, such as the CPU and memory, are mounted. A typical motherboard is shown in Figure 18-2.

Three Things to Look For

There are four components that we are most interested in when we are comparing computers, and they align nicely with the Von Neumann architecture. We will look at each of these in turn:

- CPU
- Storage
- Memory

FIGURE 18-2   A computer motherboard, showing its features

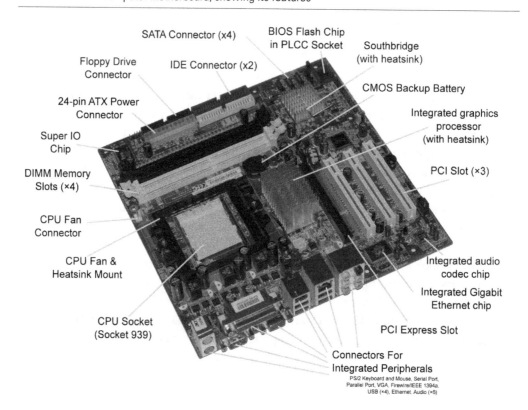

It is the performance of all of these taken together that determines how well a given computer will perform, but it is possible to optimize just one of these, depending on the application that you're interested in running on your computer. If you're on a budget, some of these are less expensive to upgrade than the others; we will examine the pricing differences in our discussion.

CPU

The Central Processing Unit (CPU) is the brain of the computer. It is responsible for executing instructions of your programs, including those of the operating system. There are two major manufacturers of CPUs currently: Intel and AMD. For the most part, the CPU chips made by these two manufacturers are compatible in terms of the programs that they will run, that is, most of the programs that you purchase or the games that you want to play will run on either; however, electrically and physically the chips themselves are different, and so an AMD chip will not fit onto a motherboard designed for an Intel chip and vice versa. Figure 18-3 shows the front and back of an Intel i7 chip, which is approximately 4 inches on each side.

Fortunately, the two companies compete for market share with each other, which keeps the overall price of CPUs at a lower level than it might be if one of the companies were to dominate. That said, Intel holds the lion's share of the market for general-purpose computer CPUs, and we tend to think of AMD as developing CPUs that are more geared toward a gamer market.

Clock Speed

The most visible metric that we can discuss about a CPU chip is its clock speed, and that's the number that you typically will see at the top of the list of marketing materials and signage at the store. The numbers range from 1.5GHz to 3GHz, and sometimes into the 4GHz range. In casual conversation we might say that a CPU is "a four gig i7." What does that mean? What is a gigahertz, and why do we care?

FIGURE 18-3   An Intel Core i7 CPU chip, front (l) and back (r)

Each computer literally has a clock built into it. The clock ticks very rapidly, and at each tick of the clock some action is performed by the computer. For example, on one clock tick the CPU might issue an instruction to fetch a piece of data from memory; on the next clock tick that information will be retrieved and presented to the CPU; on the next clock tick the CPU will execute an instruction based on the data that it just retrieved; and on the next clock tick it might store a piece of data back into memory. The clock is what regulates the execution of programs and the movement of data inside the computer.

The clock ticks quite rapidly. One gigahertz (1GHz) is equal to 1,000,000,000 cycles per second, or, in our case, 1 billion *ticks* per second. So, if the CPU is advertised at having a 2.5GHz clock speed, that means that the internal clock is running at 2.5 billion ticks each second. You'll be correct in assuming that for the most part, a faster clock speed means a faster computer, with all other things being equal. If one computer has a clock running twice as fast as another, it is not a bad assumption that the first computer will be twice as fast, or least nearly so. There also are several ways to effectively multiply that clock speed, which we'll look at below.

Multiplier: Cache

The first speed multiplier that we will examine is called *cache*, which is a very small piece of memory that is physically located on the CPU chip. It might seem odd to think about, but it takes a significant amount of time for an electrical signal to get from one side of a computer's motherboard to the other. Remember, electrons are limited by the speed of light, which is roughly 300,000 m/s in a vacuum, and since the electrical signal is not traveling in a vacuum, but rather copper and aluminum circuitry, the speed is reduced to some large fraction, on the order of 60% to 70% of the speed of light. That's still incredibly fast, but it really does take a measurable time for a signal to get from one side of the board of the other.

Another problem is that most of the chips on the computer's motherboard, such as the memory chips, operate much more slowly than it CPU itself. What ends up happening is that the CPU makes a request to memory for a piece of data, and then it has to wait several clock cycles to receive the data back. Remember, the CPU is operating with a clock that ticks 3 billion times per second, or 3GHz, and any delay in receiving data back for memory means that the CPU essentially can't do anything for all of those clock ticks while it's waiting. This gets even worse if the CPU requests a piece of data, waits for it, and then right away has to request another piece that was nearby the first piece in physical memory.

To avoid this problem of waiting, the CPU has a very small piece of very fast memory, called cache, that is built into the CPU chip itself. Because it is colocated with the internal mechanisms of the CPU, the signals don't have to travel all the way across the motherboard when reading or writing memory, which saves a significant amount of time. Also, this memory operates in such a way that if the CPU requests a piece of data from memory, values stored nearby in memory are also returned and stored in the cache, the idea being that if the CPU needs data from memory location 1000, there's a very high probability that it will next need the memory from memory location 1001. This idea of pre-fetching more data than is needed in the hope that you're going to use it is based on a technique called *locality of reference*.

It turns out that by carefully tuning the algorithm used to fetch data and manage the cache, cache hits, that is, when a piece of needed data is found in cache, avoiding a request to slower memory, can approach the mid-90% mark: that is to say, more than 90% of the time, when you need something from memory it's already sitting in cache, and the CPU doesn't have to wait at all.

There's literally one small problem with cache memory. The problem is that the CPU chip itself is physically small, not much bigger than your thumbnail, and its components, its execution unit, video circuitry to drive a monitor, arithmetic units, clock conditioners, and so on vie for space with cache memory. We say that the "real estate" on the CPU chip is limited. Because of this, we just can't physically fit all that much cache memory onto the CPU chip. Further, this kind of really fast memory is expensive and difficult to build, which further limits its size. If you are comparing CPUs, and one chip has 4 megabytes (4MB), of on-chip cache, and another has 8MB, at the same clock speed the chip with a larger cache will generally perform slightly better.

This concept of caching data is common across many parts of computer science. The general problem that it solves is that we have some resource that takes a lot of time to look up, so that if we are ever in a situation where we need the data more than once, it makes sense to keep the data in memory rather than in storage, say, on a disk drive, because memory is much faster than a mechanical hard drive. For example, if you visit a website that displays current news, the news items themselves are stored in a database, usually on a hard disk. Because thousands of website visitors need to see the same story, the information is read once from the database, placed into memory, and then subsequently served up from the memory location.

Caching of course raises other issues, such as the situation where the information in the database changes; how can we determine whether the copy of the data that we have in memory is the most current version? We won't dig into that here, but caching is a major topic in computer science, and touches just about all of its areas.

Cores

The second specification that can affect the performance of the CPU is the number of *cores* it includes. Until relatively recently, if you were to pop the lid off of a CPU chip, you'd find just a single CPU. In the past several years, however, manufacturers have started to include what essentially are multiple CPUs on a single chip; these are known as CPU cores, and each operates as a mini CPU. In most cases the more cores a CPU chip has, the more expensive that chip will be, and manufacturers such as Intel and AMD market their CPU families in a price range that factors in the number of cores. For example, the Intel i5 chip can be purchased with two or four cores, with a corresponding difference in price. Figure 18-4 shows an AMD quad-core CPU.

So what does a core actually do? It is essentially a mini CPU and is capable of executing instructions, managing cache, and doing everything that a normal CPU would do. The big win here is that in a single-CPU chip, the CPU really can only do one thing at a time. Even though when we are multitasking on our computers it seems like we're doing several things at once—reading e-mail, following our Twitter feed, cutting and pasting items from a spreadsheet into a document, and so on—really the CPU chip is executing

FIGURE 18-4 An AMD Phenom CPU die showing four processing cores

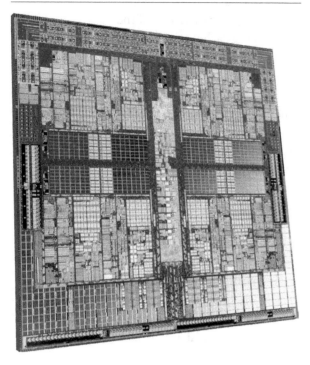

only a single instruction at a time. It does this very quickly, so that we have an illusion of many things happening at once. By adding cores, we add parallel threads of execution; two cores, for example, do roughly two instructions simultaneously; four cores can do four instructions at once; and so on. This is not strictly true, as some time is taken up communicating among the cores, managing resources on the CPU chip, general housekeeping, and such, but a rough rule-of-thumb is that the number of cores multiplies the number of things that the CPU chip can do by that amount.

There's a big caveat here. Not all programs are designed in such a way that they can take advantage of multiple cores. Some games are, as is some high-end graphic and video-editing software, but for the most part you can't expect any random program to fully utilize all of the cores on the CPU. This isn't really a bad thing, because the operating system will step in and manage how programs access those cores, so rather than having a single program run across all four cores, the operating system might direct four programs to run on one core each, which still gives us a performance gain.

Similar to cache, the more cores the CPU has the faster it will be at the same clock speed, compared to one with fewer cores, and the price will go up stepwise to reflect the number of cores on the chip. Some very high-end CPU chips, especially those in the Intel Xeon class, have 8 or even 16 cores or more (Intel's Xeon E7-8894 sports 24 cores and 60MB of cache!), but once we get into this range we're really talking about specialized hardware designed to be run in a server environment, or some extremely intense graphics or video-editing applications, and you are unlikely to see that kind of machine at your local computer store. That Xeon E7, for example, runs $9,000 just for the CPU chip!

Storage

The next variable that will affect both the performance and price of a computer is the type and size of any storage that it includes. Note that here we are talking about either a hard drive or a solid-state drive; many people mistakenly use the term "memory" when what they really are talking about is a hard drive. For example, you might hear someone say, "I'm running out of memory!" which would lead us to believe that they need to throw a couple of extra sticks of memory in the computer, but in fact what they really mean is that they're running out of storage on their hard drive.

The kind of storage that we're interested in here is called *nonvolatile storage*; that is, when you turn the power off, the information stored on the device persists. When you turn the power back on, your information is still there. There are two kinds of persistent storage available in consumer computers: hard drives and solid-state drives.

Mechanical Hard Drives

First, let's consider a mechanical hard drive. Until just a few years ago, if you had a "drive" in your computer, it was one of these. Mechanical hard drivers rely on magnetism to read and write data. If you open the rectangular box that houses a hard drive, you'll find inside two major components: a set of platters, or disks, and a small armature that contains a tiny read/write head. Figure 18-5 is an illustration of the major components of such a drive.

FIGURE 18-5   Internal workings of a hard disk drive

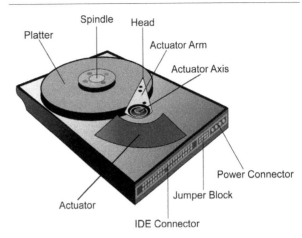

Platters inside the hard drive are made of aluminum coated with a magnetic material. When the drive is powered up, the platters spin at a high rate of speed; 5400 rpm (revolutions per minute) for consumer-grade devices, and 7200 rpm for higher-end models. The read/write head, attached to the actuator arm, flies just above the surface of the platter; its height is just a fraction of the diameter of a human hair. The distance between the head and the platter is so small that a particle of smoke looks like a boulder in comparison! The actuator arm moves across the disk from the outside to the inside and back again, and as it moves the read/write head is either magnetizing tiny spots on the platter, or reading those magnetized spots. Data is stored on the hard drive in units called *blocks*, typically 512 bytes, one kilobyte (1KB), or 4KB, depending on the operating system and the specifications of the drive itself.

Mechanical devices like this are relatively old technology; the first commercially available disk drives came to market in the late 1950s and were roughly the size of a washing machine. The platters weighed several pounds each, and the spin rate was relatively low compared to today's devices. Still, the technology is the same.

Hard disk drives like the ones we see in today's personal computers are quite slow compared to the rest of the computer. Recall that the CPU clock is ticking at the rate of up to 3 billion times per second, but to read or write data from the disk drive it is necessary to move the actuator arm to the correct track, wait until the correct spot spins under the read/write head, read the data, get it into a temporary storage location on the hard drive, and then send it to the CPU. This takes an enormous amount of time from the CPU's perspective. Many disk drives come with an internal cache memory, which is all electronic, and try to anticipate what data is going to be requested next, keeping it in cache, so that when the request does come it can be served immediately from the disk drive's cache memory without having to wait on the mechanical device to find the data. Likewise, for write operations, the write is done to memory located on the disk drive itself, and in the business of getting the data onto the mechanical platter is done asynchronously, saving quite a bit of time.

The storage capacity of mechanical hard drives and their prices have followed a curve similar to Moore's Law and processing power versus price; about every six to eight months storage capacity doubles and the price either drops or remains the same. Today you can expect to find devices that range from 500MB of storage all the way up to 2 to 4TB of storage (one terabyte is 1 trillion bytes, or 1,000GB). Prices range at the low end from $50 up to $150-$200 for the larger devices. When you are buying or comparing hard drives, capacity and speed are the two metrics to look for; once you have devices that are roughly comparable in those two areas, you can compare price. Note that some hard drives available off the shelf are designed specifically for servers, and those drives are engineered so that they can be in continuous operation for years at a time. This kind of disk drive is slightly more expensive than normal consumer-grade disk drives, but they do tend to be more reliable.

Solid-State Drives

Solid-state drives (SSDs) have no moving parts; they are all electronic and operate very similarly to computer memory. The difference between a solid-state drive and computer memory is that a solid-state drive is *persistent* storage; that is, when the power is turned off, the data stored on the SSD remains, whereas in computer memory the data vanishes without power. SSDs have been on the market for about 10 years, and when they were first introduced they were fantastically expensive! Like most electronic devices, though, prices have fallen while performance and capacity have increased, to the point where if you are purchasing a new computer it almost doesn't make sense to get a mechanical hard drive for it, because a solid-state drive of similar capacity will be roughly the same price. A typical SSD is shown in Figure 18-6.

SSDs are not just a little bit faster than a hard drive, they are an order of magnitude faster, and replacing an old hard drive with a new SSD in an older computer is one of the most dramatic upgrades that you can do. Because there are no moving parts, data can be read and written from and to an SSD very rapidly, and SSDs with built-in cache also exist that speed up operations even more. New technologies are pushing the speed even further; however; for a typical desktop machine it isn't necessary to get the cutting-edge (and expensive) version of an SSD, as you possibly won't notice a difference in the overall speed of your computer. These newer SSDs tend to be about 20% more expensive than traditional drives, though we can anticipate that in a few years time the price point will drop to roughly the current price of a standard SSD.

The only real disadvantage with an SSD is capacity. While it is very common to see a 2TB hard drive in a computer off the shelf, a 2TB SSD is still quite expensive. More typical sizes are 250GB to 500GB, with prices running from under $50 to $250 for the larger sizes. A good strategy is to have two storage devices in your computer; an SSD to hold files that you access frequently, such as the operating system, applications, and so on, and a second, mechanical, hard drive with a larger capacity that you use for storing data that isn't frequently accessed. So, you might have a 250GB SSD and a 1TB hard drive.

This two-drive configuration isn't common for consumer-grade computers. The strategy for those on a budget would be to buy a computer with a hard drive preinstalled and add an SSD to it yourself.

FIGURE 18-6 A typical solid-state storage device (SSD)

Memory

The last component to talk about in our computer is its memory. When we use the term *memory*, we are talking about *volatile* storage, not about hard drives or SSDs, which are nonvolatile. Any instruction that the CPU is going to execute, and any data that the CPU is going to operate on, has to be in memory before it can be fetched into the CPU. That means that if you are opening a file from an SSD, the data is moved from the SSD into memory and then from memory into the CPU for processing.

Computer memory is very easily upgradable by the consumer, and the price difference between buying a computer off the shelf with a certain amount of memory and buying a computer with a smaller amount of memory and then upgrading it later is quite significant; you can save literally hundreds of dollars by doing the upgrade yourself. For example, two recent Dell desktop machines differ only in that one has 8GB of memory while the other has 16GB; the price difference is around $150; 8GB of memory purchased separately and installed yourself is around $60. It only takes a few minutes to install memory, and it is very difficult to do it wrong.

So, how much memory should you buy? Most off-the-shelf computers at your local computer store come with 2, 4, or 8GB of memory already installed. For most applications, 8GB is plenty, but if you are a gamer, or doing video editing, or audio mixing, or something else that is data intensive, up to 16 or even 32GB of memory might be more appropriate. One thing to watch out for is that some computers do not have upgradable memory. This is especially true of laptops, and some all-in-one computers, where the memory is soldered down to the motherboard and can't be removed without destroying the motherboard. Most computers, however, have two or four slots available to place memory sticks into. The sticks, shown in Figure 18-7, come in various sizes, typically 2, 4, 8, or 16GB. As of this writing, 16GB of memory will cost around $120 and will likely be sold as two 8GB sticks.

Most manufacturers will triple or quadruple this price when the memory is installed in an off-the-shelf computer, so that if you're looking at one machine that has 8GB of memory and another with 16 GB of memory, and both are using essentially the same CPU, disk drive, and so on, the price differential can be $300 to $400. The more economical choice is to buy the computer with the smaller amount of memory, buy the extra memory yourself, and put it in. For most applications 16GB is going to be plenty, and it doesn't make sense to install much more than that unless you have specialized computing needs.

Do-It-Yourself

An alternative to buying a complete computer is to build one yourself. This might sound like a technically challenging task, but in fact it's quite easy, and most folks can build a machine in just a few

FIGURE 18-7 A 4GB memory stick

hours once they have assembled all of the parts. In addition to the components that we discussed in this chapter, you'll need a few more items, such as a case to house your computer, a motherboard to plug your components into, and a power supply.

In the past, many hobbyists built their own computers to save significant amounts of money, but this is becoming more difficult, especially on the low end of the commercial computer price range. It's possible to buy a quite capable computer with lower specs for just a few hundred dollars off the shelf, and building the equivalent computer would likely cost you at least a hundred dollars more than that. However, on the higher end of the computing spectrum, such as gaming machines, computers with high-end CPUs, more memory, and the like, significant savings can be achieved by building rather than buying. There are many guides on the web that will help you assemble the parts, put them in the case, plug everything together, and install your operating system of choice, whether it be Windows, Linux, or even a Mac OS.

Assembling the components is quite simple, as there are just a few cables involved, and they are designed in such a way that they will only fit in one direction. It is extremely difficult to get it wrong. Components such as the CPU and memory are also designed so that they only fit one way onto the computer motherboard, eliminating the possibility that you can get something in backwards.

It's even possible to build a Mac computer, something called a "Hackintosh," although care must be taken to assemble components that are known to work with the Mac OS. An excellent website, tonymacx86.com, can lead you through all of the steps, and includes lists of parts that you can purchase to build various-size Mac computers.

Apart from the price advantage, especially at the high end, you get the satisfaction of having built a working computer, and if something goes wrong, since you are the builder, it's much more likely that you'll be able to fix it. There's also a very large online community of hobbyists who enjoy building machines that can help you if you get stuck.

When building your own computer you will need to decide whether or not to purchase a graphics card. Most mid- and high-level CPU chips include built-in graphics capabilities; for example; the Intel i5 and i7 Core family of chips includes Intel's Iris graphics, which are more than capable of driving even high-end monitors. This means that when you're shopping for a computer or components to build one, you don't necessarily need to have a separate graphics card—the video signal coming off of the motherboard, which is coming from the CPU chip itself, is typically just fine. Gamers and those who are doing heavy video editing might benefit from a discrete graphics card, but those are pretty specialized applications.

Bottom Line

Choosing a computer from the store can be difficult, because they all look very similar, and the specifications that are listed on the marketing labels are filled with numbers and abbreviations and acronyms that most people just are not familiar with. By focusing on the three areas that we discussed in this chapter, and understanding the numbers associated with each of them, you can make a much more informed decision when purchasing a computer, and when comparing two similar computers.

In terms of which of the four areas is more important, CPU speed will only get you so far, and the difference in performance between a 2.5GHz clock speed and a 3.5GHz clock speed might be negligible, especially if the faster computer has a slow hard drive in it and the slower computer has a fast SSD in it. In fact, in that situation, the computer with the slower clock speed might "feel" faster because of the speed gain of the SSD. Unless you are a gamer or a video editor, you can get away with a computer with a slower clock speed; however, do pay attention to storage and be sure that the computer that you are buying has an SSD rather than a mechanical hard drive. It's worth the extra hundred dollars or so to get the SSD; you'll notice significant speed improvement over the mechanical hard drive.

Memory is a little trickier; the sweet spot here is around 8GB of memory, with the understanding that you can save a few hundred dollars by buying a computer with less memory, and then upgrade it yourself. Just be sure that the computer actually is upgradable, as some have the memory soldered to the motherboard, or use nonstandard parts.

As for storage, it's pretty unusual to see an off-the-shelf computer that has both an SSD and a mechanical hard drive, and computers with an SSD are likely to be priced significantly higher than the equivalent machine with a mechanical hard drive. Consider buying a computer with, say, a 1 or 2TB hard drive for storing photos, music, and other files, and then adding a 250GB or larger SSD yourself later on. Just like memory, adding an SSD to a computer is very simple, and the two cables required are keyed in such a way that you can't get them in backwards. It's a five-minute job and you will save a significant amount of money by installing the SSD yourself.

Figure Credits